UNDERSTANDING
IMMIGRATION

UNDERSTANDING IMMIGRATION

Issues and Challenges in an Era of Mass Population Movement

MARILYN HOSKIN

SUNY PRESS

Published by State University of New York Press, Albany

For information, contact State University of New York Press, Albany, NY
www.sunypress.edu

Production, Ryan Morris
Marketing, Kate R. Seburyamo

Library of Congress Cataloging-in-Publication Data

Names: Hoskin, Marilyn B., 1945– author.
Title: Understanding immigration in an era of mass population movement / Marilyn Hoskin.
Description: Albany : State University of New York Press, [2017] | Includes bibliographical
   references and index.
Identifiers: LCCN 2016053170 (print) | LCCN 2017022141 (ebook) | ISBN 9781438466897 (ebook)
   | ISBN 9781438466873 (hardcover : alk. paper) | ISBN 9781438466880 (pbk. : alk. paper)
Subjects: LCSH: Emigration and immigration—Government policy—Case studies. | United States—
   Emigration and immigration—Government policy. | Great Britain—Emigration and
   immigration—Government policy. | Germany—Emigration and immigration—Government
   policy. | France—Emigration and immigration—Government policy.
Classification: LCC JV6271 (ebook) | LCC JV6271 .H67 2017 (print) | DDC 325/.1—dc23
LC record available at https://lccn.loc.gov/2016053170

10 9 8 7 6 5 4 3 2 1

Contents

Illustrations

Figures

Tables

Preface and Acknowledgments

Immigration has become one of, if not the top, hot-button issues of the twenty-first century. However urgent questions of border violations, overcrowded urban ghettos, or cultural differences appeared to be in earlier times, the combination of terrorist attacks and seemingly uncontrolled flow of refugees into the United States and Europe since 2001 have made immigration the epicenter of a host of new challenges: strident national election campaigns, increasing instances of hate crimes, paralyzed and unresponsive legislatures. More generally, population movements have highlighted the permanent consequences of globalization, fractured societies, human and natural disasters. If immigration has always tested the resilience of governments and citizens, its emergence as a global force surpassing all previous levels presents a challenge of historic proportions.

While no part of the 2016 world has been exempt from this challenge, it is especially poignant in the United States and Europe as highly sought destinations for millions of actual and potential immigrants. The nations included in this study were selected to represent that status, but also to provide essential variations in their experience with immigration. The United States is an obvious choice for a long history with migration and a national definition based on the diversity of its population. The three European states offer markedly different histories, which nonetheless led to common needs for labor, for government policies to legitimize immigrants chosen for admission, and for widespread adaptation to pluralist societies. Studied together, they provide assessment of a broad range of factors, which should assist in explaining both the evolution of immigration in the past century and the options nations have in dealing with it as an ongoing challenge.

My history with the study of immigration began with undergraduate and graduate work in Germany in 1966 and 1971, when the first migrants were working as temporary labor there. They lived mostly in crowded quarters in urban centers, socialized in the central railroad stations, and only rarely had families in residence, but sheer numbers and obvious need for their labor invited further study. A 1980–81 Fulbright leave in Mannheim provided that opportunity, and led to publication of a series of articles and, ten years later, a book comparing public opinion toward immigrants in Germany and three other nations (Britain, Canada, and the United States). Years of teaching about immigration brought two conclusions. First, students had little knowledge of the rich and varied immigration experiences so important to understanding their own nation's contemporary challenges, and second, real understanding would require that they systematically compare critical components of immigration in their own and other nations. Since immigration is a classic example of a topic crossing academic disciplines, that would mean exposing them to geographic, historical, economic, and political analyses. This book is a first step in facilitating such understanding.

Including four distinctive nations, and framing the immigration challenge in terms of four important components, allows the reader to step back from immediate situations to evaluate them in the context of multiple forces, which define this critical issue across very different settings. It also, however, runs the inevitable risk of emphasizing breadth over depth in any of the areas considered. For those new to the topic, however, this approach has the advantage of introducing key elements that cause variation or similarity in nations confronting the challenge of twenty-first-century immigration—some for the first time, some as a new chapter in a longer history. If it does not produce definitive answers to current issues (it certainly does not), it points students to areas where they can pursue further exploration, in disciplines they might have otherwise avoided. If this kind of introduction leads to expanding knowledge of the many dimensions of immigration, it will have served its primary purpose.

The book has relied on a host of sources and careful studies undertaken by others, including scholars, university and other nonprofit institutes dedicated to providing data and analysis of important issues, and, of course, data collected by national governments and international organizations and made available for scholarly and general analysis. Government departments in all four nations collect and make publicly available vast databases, quarterly and annual reports, and volumes of organized data displays—the Office of National Statistics (ONS) in Britain, the National Institute for Statistics and Economic Studies (INSEE) in France, the Federal Office for Migration and Refugees in Germany, the Census Bureau and Department of Homeland Security in the United States. In addition, several regional and international organizations collect and distribute data on a regular basis; the United Nations Office of the High Commission on Refugees (UNHCR) and the Organization for Economic Cooperation and Development (OECD) have been especially useful for this project. To optimize reliability of high quality survey data, I have limited use of public opinion surveys to those produced by established survey research and polling organizations that utilize national samples and standard or carefully tested question formats. Most make their data and overall results available through the Inter-University Consortium for Political and Social Research, whose collection includes national election studies in the U.S., Britain, and Germany, the more general social surveys conducted by the National Opinion Research Center, the Eurobarometer series sponsored by the European Union, the German Omnibus (Allbus) surveys. Polling divisions of national news services have added multiple perspectives on public views, over time, and this wide collection provides best evidence of the state of opinion in the nations studied here. The Pew Research Center has a large and diverse array of survey data, again available to scholars for secondary analysis and reproduction. Important studies published by scholars of American and European immigration have been listed as sources of further information in each of the chapters as well.

As is always the case, this work has benefited from the counsel and contributions of many who have concerned themselves with, or experienced, immigration. Colleagues on the dozens of panels I have participated in or attended over the years invariably opened eyes and doors to questions needing further attention. Several joined my classes as co-teachers or to offer expertise in specific areas. Fellow faculty and researchers at the University in Mannheim as well as the University at Buffalo, University of New Hampshire, and City College of New York provided valuable feedback and ideas for dealing with comparative data. Equally important sources have been my students, who lived up to the challenge to offer their perspectives, questions, or alternatives to ideas or materials used in class. A faculty member's most telling moments often emerge from points raised in the back row in a large room. My classes at City College, regularly filled with foreign-born students or children of immigrants, never failed to stimulate engaging discussions in the classroom and tantalizing ideas to consider in trying to understand this fascinating topic. I owe them for countless contributions. Last but certainly not least, I am grateful for the support of family who tolerated my obsessions, labored through successive manuscript drafts, and offered unconditional support. Any and all errors, of course, are mine alone.

1

Immigration as a Never-ending Saga

The last several years have witnessed a revival of a drama staged periodically in the United States and nations across the globe. The subject is immigration and its subtexts: shifting economies, the breakdown of borders, threats to national identity and public safety. Whenever the drama opens, the language is charged with conflicting elements of nostalgia and resentment, hope and fear, empathy and hatred. In the United States, the clash is especially painful as it portrays a country defined by immigration but still unable to manage it without rancorous debate and hostility, exacerbated by surges at the Mexican border and refugee crises. In Europe, a Union of 28 nations in fragile agreement over open borders among members is facing the supreme test of its unity with epic numbers of migrants fleeing war and chaos in the Middle East and Africa to nations with markedly different views of their obligations and one dramatically voting in June 2016 to leave the EU. The almost 65 million people defined in 2016 as internally displaced or refugees seeking asylum may represent the greatest humanitarian challenge of our time, especially to nations seen as capable of providing resettlement.

Managing population change is on every national agenda. In some, it has emerged over time as immigrants filled economic gaps and integrated into the national fabric in a long and largely successful history. For others, it manifests itself in intractable and seemingly endless ethnic hostilities; for still others, it is cast as simply the pragmatic economic solution to persistently low national birth rates. In the context of unprecedented mass migration from conflicts engulfing entire regions, it presents a humanitarian imperative not seen since World War II and its aftermath. As such, it demands that governments respond to the challenges that globalization—of people, technology, transportation, trade, communication, and civil war—has produced.

Immigration crises have few boundaries. In the last half-century, millions of Vietnamese fled postwar retaliation and violence, often to makeshift camps in Southeast Asia before settling in a number of receptive nations. Countless refugees from ethnic violence in southern and central Africa migrated to neighboring states or sought refuge through the United Nations High Commission for Refugees camps. In 1980, 125,000 Cubans were put on boats destined for the United States, in what was seen as an emptying of Cuban jails and mental hospitals. Religious minorities in Myanmar and Bangladesh sought relief from persecution, arriving but not welcomed in Indonesia, Malaysia, or other nations in the area. Even larger numbers from Asia and the Middle East left their homelands with the promise of work in nations with labor needs (Dubai, Hong Kong, even Israel, Switzerland, Spain, and northern Europe). In virtually all instances, migrants confronted suspicion, hostility, and horrific working and living conditions, as only small numbers were able to settle into steady employment and stable lives. Crises can occur almost anywhere, anytime, demanding that nations find ways of dealing with them that do not create dangerous fractures in their societies.

Immigration as a Twenty-first Century Dilemma

Examples from regions most vulnerable to immigration crisis illustrate the multiple challenges facing virtually every nation. In the United States, contemporary concern has focused on the southern border. Despite unforgiving desert terrain, increased security personnel, and 670 miles of new fencing, the almost 2,000-mile border continues to provide opportunities for illegal entry and jobs in industries that have become dependent on their labor. In 2010, the Arizona state legislature passed a bill to identify and detain those in the country illegally, and several other states followed suit with similar bills. Arizona's law and other statutes were successfully challenged in the courts as inconsistent with federal law, but the resentments that inspired them have lingered, creating deep divisions of opinion, aggressive stances in many local law enforcement forces, a growth in vigilante groups, and concerns that localities would be overwhelmed by job seekers and increased demands on their services. With increasing calls for the U.S. to accept more of the world's millions of refugees, opposition continues to be fierce.

In 2013–14, a deluge of migrants crossing the Mexican border made immigration a national issue. Increased violence and poverty in Central America encouraged thousands, believing they would be welcomed as refugees, to head north, and most sought not to elude patrols but to seek them out for assistance. Border facilities were unprepared for the numbers of mothers with children or children traveling alone, and immigration offices struggled to follow procedures for asylum hearings, but the sheer volume led to inconsistent responses. The Texas governor ordered National Guard units to the border; some local opponents organized protests and blocked buses transporting migrants; legal aid groups sent volunteers to provide representation at critical hearings. Despite passionate appeals for action by both sympathizers and opponents, state legislatures and Congress appeared to be paralyzed by indecision. Months passed with no clear policy, thousands of crossers found their way to relatives, and thousands of others began long waits in detention centers. Most strikingly, Executive Orders directing officials to delay deportations and allow those waiting for hearings to leave detention centers were immediately challenged in the courts, leaving literally millions of new arrivals, as well as the long-term undocumented, in limbo. In June 2016, the eight-member U.S. Supreme Court let stand (by a tie vote) a lower court ruling repudiating President

Obama's executive order to allow large numbers of undocumented migrants to work without fear of deportation, guaranteeing that unresolved issues will continue to challenge political leaders. Despite heightened rhetoric in the 2016 election campaigns, prospects for comprehensive policy continued to be stymied by congressional resistance to any major legislative action.

If the American case illustrates inability to deal with new arrivals, events in France illustrate both issue-specific tensions and huge general concern with migrants residing legally there. A large Algerian Muslim population has lived in France for decades, and the numbers increased even after a long and costly colonial war. In 1989, what seemed a minor disagreement—three Muslim girls refusing to remove head scarves in school—precipitated a crisis over whether the scarves violated the French commitment to separation of church and state. Localities struggled, often unsuccessfully, to devise rules acceptable to all sides of the argument. After five years of conflict, the national government issued an advisory memorandum suggesting that "discreet" display of religious symbols would be permitted, but "ostentatious" ones—such as head scarves—could be prohibited. Not surprisingly, that directive failed to resolve the issue, and frequent expulsions continued to ignite crises. Fully fifteen years after the first incident, the government approved the "Veil Law," formally prohibiting ostentatious religious symbols: veils, large Christian crosses, Jewish yarmulkes, and Sikh turbans. Resentment among Muslims reflected their belief that they have been the only real targets, a belief reinforced in 2016 by the decisions of several coastal cities to ban the "burkini," a full-body bathing suit designed to allow Muslim women to swim while observing traditions of modesty. Politicians and large majorities of the public favor the bans, indicating a deep divide between the French and the country's largest minority.

French governments have also tightened restrictions on other minorities. Although citizens of all members of the European Union are entitled to entry and residence, Romanian and Bulgarian groups known as *Roma* for their transient life style, have been driven from makeshift camps and deported. Others, including African migrants seeking work or admission to Britain, have suffered the same fate or been forced to remain in camps, leading to condemnations by the EU and United Nations. Since the Roma tend to return and immigrant groups have only grown, tensions could only increase.

They did so, dramatically, in 2015 and 2016, as Europe faced millions of refugees seeking entry and work in the EU. In January 2015, Paris suffered fatal attacks on staff at a French Newspaper and hostages in a Jewish market; in November, coordinated terrorists detonated bombs and opened fire on diners in restaurants and concertgoers in a large performance venue, killing 130 and wounding scores of others. Seven months later, a Tunisian-born man wielding a gun and driving a large truck killed 86 people celebrating Bastille Day in Nice, raising fears that France would face continuing violence perpetrated by foreigners. What had been a difficult discussion of religious practices in a secular state was eclipsed by a crisis of national security, with radical Muslims cast as a threat to French society and marginalized minorities forced onto the national agenda. As the European Union continues to struggle in efforts to craft immigration policies,

French leaders face deeply rooted resentments likely to heighten partisan divisions and place new pressures on European Union policies.

hypocracy in switz.

A striking example of immigration tension is found in historically conflict-averse Switzerland. In November 2009, 59% of Swiss voters supported a ban on the construction of minarets, the prayer towers of Islamic mosques. Since the vote was for an addition to the national constitution, it effectively created a constitutional restriction on religious freedom. As the Swiss Constitution guarantees that freedom, the force of the vote remains unclear, because it appeared to contradict rather than amend or replace existing provisions.

Still, the vote was alarming on a number of counts. Of Switzerland's 150 existing mosques only four had minarets and none conducted the call to prayer. Moreover, Muslims are less than 5% of the population, most of whom are Turkish and Kosovo migrants who do not adhere to religious codes of dress and conduct. But most remarkable was the ferocity of a campaign that consciously demonized Muslims. One image depicted the minarets as missiles emerging through the Swiss flag, with a veiled woman glaring at the viewer. Another had three white sheep standing on the Swiss flag, one kicking a black sheep over its border, with a simple "create security" caption. The ultranationalist party advocating deportation of immigrants experienced a rare surge in popularity. In a further move to restrict immigration, a 2014 referendum measure obligating the government to institute strict quotas passed, rejecting EU principles that have allowed Switzerland to enjoy EU membership benefits without actually joining the organization. The faceoff with EU leadership over immigration issues remains unresolved.

However serious the immigration issue appears in these examples, the critical nature of the problem is most evident in the post-2013 mass migrations to Europe. Increases in Middle Eastern and African migrants had been recorded since 2010, but the sinking of a boat carrying 400–500 refugees from Eritrea, Ghana, and Somalia in 2013 portended the urgency of dangerous Mediterranean passage. In 2014, two ships carrying more than a thousand Syrian refugees were abandoned by smugglers; and another several hundred drowned when an overloaded boat sank in February 2015. Italy, suddenly host to over 100,000 migrants who survived the crossings, implored EU neighbors to assist in rescue and resettlement. At the same time, two Spanish settlements on the Moroccan coast emerged as cauldrons of frustration for thousands of refugees from central Africa, creating massive camps and frequent attempts to reach the sea. Libya effectively lost control of its coast, leaving it open to more desperate voyages and casualties at sea. By mid-2016, more than 4,500 had drowned in attempted crossings.

Even larger numbers have turned to routes initiated through the Greek island of Lesbos or the Bulgarian border. By early 2016, more than 700,000 Syrians, Iraqis, and Afghanis had arrived, overwhelming small immigration offices and temporary camps. Southern and Eastern European borders became transit routes for migrants trying to reach Germany, Sweden, and Britain, and angry confrontations resulted in escalating restrictions, frequent border closures, and heightened rhetoric demanding that entry points be closed. In addition, emboldened migrants from Ukraine and Kosovo surged into EU nations to seek better economic opportunities. The UN reported in 2016 that worldwide more than 63.5 million people were displaced—eclipsing the post–World War II figure. More than half sought refuge in Europe.

The challenge to Europe is historic. Since the rescue at Lampedusa, EU leadership made numerous efforts to gain support for managing the flow of refugees, led by Germany's pledge to accept up to a million in the next year. Expanded admission/registration centers have been set up in most member nations, but no agreement reached on allocation formulas for resettlement. The EU bought time by paying Turkey to house refugees turned back at borders in Greece, but anti-immigrant sentiment remains high in several nations, encouraged by parties that insist on national prerogatives to reject any or all refugees. Such sentiment was a major factor in the near victory of a Far-Right presidential candidate in Austria in May 2016, the rise of similar parties in the Netherlands, Germany, and France, and in Britain's June 2016 vote to leave the EU.

By 2016, conditions in Africa, the Middle East, Asia and Central America culminated in what has to be seen as a continuing, even permanent immigration and refugee crisis. At stake are critical rights of destination nations to define and enforce secure borders in a time when "natural" borders are no longer sufficient to limit migration, and the critical rights of refugees to resettle in safe environments. Nations that, historically, addressed borders and immigration with short-term responses now confront pressure from both migrants and increasingly hostile public opinion, with no indication that they can or will resolve the crises. American and European responses will test their roles both as responsible national managers and as world leaders committed to humanitarian policies worldwide.

Theme and Variation in Immigration

The ubiquity of the crisis suggests that immigration cannot be explained only as related to unique national experiences. Common themes can be observed, allowing us to understand immigration more organically, as a complex phenomenon in an increasingly complex world. If that is the case, such commonalities should suggest broader explanations and, consequently, more unified responses—even multination policies addressing a global problem. Identifying such basic themes is an essential first step in that process.

Constants in Immigration Experience

Some features of immigration appear consistently over time. One is that prime movers of both immigration and national responses have been remarkably predictable over time and place. The search for safe lives and economic opportunity motivates most people who leave their homelands for the uncertainty of a future in another. The quest for such basic needs is as evident among refugees in Europe and foreign workers in the Emirates as it was in colonial America or postwar Australia.

Normally, nations accept or recruit immigrants because they need them. Regional powerhouses imported manpower essential to expansion; nations more generally have sought to balance labor demand with supply, to optimize economic growth. The direction of the flow has been consistent; people from poorer nations see opportunities in growing economies, and wealthier nations in need of labor recruit immigrants from those areas. Wars and other disruptive events periodically pry open doors that would otherwise have been closed, but the continuous forces of migration have been those of opportunity and economic need. National policies have always reflected reactions to needs and crises more than humanitarian principles, but in almost all situations immigrants have relocated, found work, and settled into permanent roles.

A corollary of this constant is that even in periods of mass disruption, immigration has almost always been incremental even as it is perceived as large and disruptively dangerous. Overall, percentages have been small relative to total population growth but initial reactions have often been strident. Most prominent has been the overarching sense of threat, reflecting fear of economic, cultural, or even physical harm. The fear of economic insecurity caused by immigrants entering the United States illegally and the millions of nationals moving freely when borders were opened within the enlarged European Union was widespread, even though the jobs they took were largely those shunned by locals. Cultural threat is a product of age-old preferences for associating with people most like oneself and seeing outsiders—especially those with different ethnicities and religions—as challenging a society's way of life. And since the first major terrorist attacks on U.S. soil in 2001, perception of physical danger has been seen as inherent in attitudes toward admitting foreigners from areas increasingly seen as hostile to the popular destinations, mostly in the West.

Underlying economic and related social fears determine how numbers of immigrants are interpreted. Growth in the number and percentage of foreign-born in the United States has varied over time. Between 1900 and 1970 the numbers remained stable as the overall population increased. After 1970 both numbers and percentages of foreign-born increased, but the percentage of the population in 2010 was still lower than that recorded in 1910. Growth has been more dramatic in Europe, mostly because it has occurred in a shorter time period. Britain saw its foreign population double (from a low base) between 1951 and 2001, then increase by another 50% in the next decade; in France, the immigrant share tripled between 1911 and 2010; in Germany the increase from 1961 to 2006 was 800% (again from a very low base) before growing by another 50% in the following five years (Figures 1.1–1.4). In all four countries, the immigrant percentage of the population remains below 15%. Those figures are part of a much larger pattern of postwar migration. Between 1945 and 1965, 15% of the world's people sought to cross national borders, mostly to enter the United States and Europe.

The 2000–2016 figures have surpassed that level of movement, creating a modern sense of crisis. Part of the massive human movement is rooted in the continuation of a postwar pattern of migration from Africa, Asia, South America, and the Middle East, reversing earlier patterns of movement to the U.S. and Europe from cultures similar to

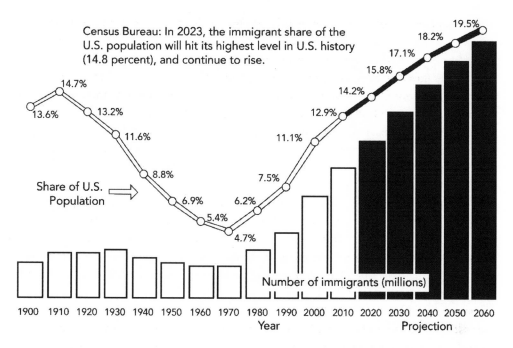

Figure 1.1. Immigrant Population as Percentage of U.S. Population. (*Source:* U.S. Census Bureau, Decennial Censuses, American Community Survey, Census Bureau Projections)

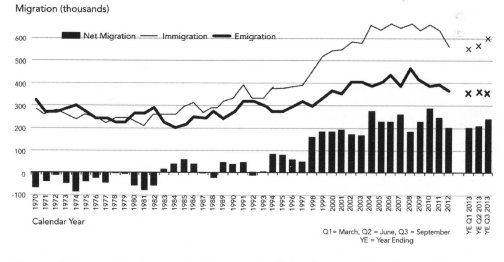

Figure 1.2. Immigration Patterns in Britain, 1970–2014. (*Source:* Office of National Statistics, Quarterly Report, 2014)

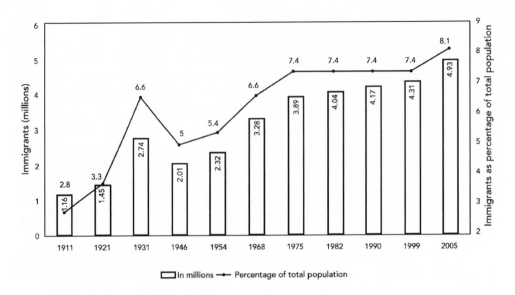

Figure 1.3. Immigrant Population in France, 1911–2005. (*Source:* National Institute for Statistics and Economic Studies (INSEE), 2006)

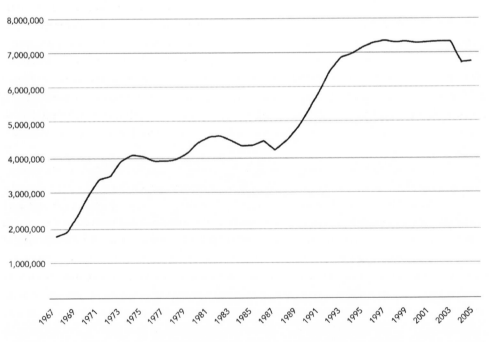

Figure 1.4. Growth of the Foreign Population in Germany, 1967–2006. (*Source:* Federal Statistical Office of Germany)

theirs or in small numbers of culturally different groups. After the postwar breakup of its empire, Britain faced immigration pressures from former colonies, whose people the British had considered dependents but not fellow citizens. For France, primary postwar newcomers were North Africans, primarily Algerians whose independence the French had unsuccessfully fought against for eight years, and in Germany the largest number were Turkish laborers. Only the United States moved to officially widen its doors to greater numbers from Latin America, Africa, and Asia, an action largely opposed by the public at that time. Opinion across all four nations was, at best, wary of the new immigrants.

But at least the United States and the European nations were in control of admission. The major reason that twenty-first-century migration has been viewed with alarm is that borders have not prevented surges of millions seeking refuge and permanent residence. The burdens of significant numbers thus fall heavily on hosts, most of whom have been overwhelmed by the challenges posed.

A second major feature of immigration experiences has been that the push to increase immigration numbers has generally come from business and industry, who have long advanced the position that economic health and growth hinged on encouraging the growth of the workforce. That claim is supported by compelling evidence that both Europe at the time of the Industrial Revolution and contemporary Brazil and China actively recruited rural populations to centers of industry and manufacturing to fuel economic growth. Where internal migration could not meet the needs of development, both nineteenth- and twentieth-century America and postwar Europe encouraged immigration to provide labor vital to replace war casualties and facilitate economic expansion. Since resilient economies regularly boast new sectors needing new workers, recruiting labor is a constant challenge. Historically, the need has been greatest for unskilled and semi-skilled workers in new industries and then for replacement workers to fill jobs opened up by upward mobility. More recently, the need for those trained in technology and the professions has expanded recruitment even further. In both settings, national debates have moved to focus more on workforce needs than generalized immigration. In the absence of long-term plans, urgency can be a critical factor in determining admission numbers and standards.

Moreover, immigrants have consistently occupied the lower ranks of occupation and status. Most immigrants enter at the bottom rungs of society's ladder. Irish, Eastern and Southern European, then non-European newcomers have all borne the mantle of scorned new Americans; guestworkers became the underclass in postwar Germany; North Africans and gypsies have been marginalized in France. Even as growth in the number of sending nations has broadened the bases of both talent and discrimination, fear of terrorism has magnified scrutiny of long-term foreign-born residents as well as new immigrants in nations across the globe. Dealing with an immigrant class perceived as dangerous in the twenty-first century is the updated version of the theme rooted in histories of hostility to foreigners in all destination nations.

Immigration issues regularly exacerbate other, deep-seated concerns. Voters may reject school budgets if they believe increased costs are due to increased numbers of migrant children. Labor unions with opportunities to organize new groups may hesitate if they worry that the presence of foreign workers encourages lower wages. Claims that capacity has been reached often mask fears of culturally different immigrants; nationalist parties in Britain, France, Austria, Israel, Switzerland, and others seek to represent silent majorities who believe that national identity is at risk. Wariness of the foreign has a long history, and recent examples of opposition across Europe remind us that it is a permanent element in immigrant experiences.

Finally, images of nations championing the world's needy or desperate are almost always dimmed by exceptions to that role. In previous eras, France and Canada had reputations as havens for refugees; Israel was initially seen as a beacon for the persecuted; Britain once proclaimed openness to all commonwealth subjects; and the United States embraced the symbol of "huddled masses" as foreigners fueled expansion and prosperity. Yet among these only Canada has offered admission to large numbers of refugees, and many have scaled back promises of relocation. In Europe, only Germany and Sweden have been proactive in accepting refugees since 2013, and that stance has threatened leadership in both. To be fair, all nations are obliged to be attentive to border integrity, security risks, capacity, and the tension between empathy and reasonable immigration limits. The inherent randomness and size of refugee crises ensure that the tension will continue to complicate rational policy discussions.

Variations on the Theme

Differences in contemporary immigration themes are also prominent in the contemporary environment. First, immigration, once a regional phenomenon, has become truly global. Somalis settle in New England, Nepalis in Korea, Mongolians in Prague, Pakistanis in Dubai. This demographic shift has not only added to the sheer volume of applicants for admission but also complicated policy options, as governments are forced to accommodate enormous cultural, linguistic, and educational differences among applicants. In their time, Irish immigrants to the United States and Poles moving to Germany were scorned for being different; today, racially and culturally distinctive immigrants almost certainly face greater obstacles than those who preceded them, wherever they settle. Nations cannot undertake policies that encourage assimilation without intervention on the part of governments inexperienced in the host's role.

A related difference is rooted in the influence of new technology. As recently as 1965, when American policies began to facilitate immigration from non-European nations, potential migrants had access to only limited information from newspapers, television and radio transmissions, or even post from abroad. With the development of myriad new forms of communication—transportation, telecommunications, and especially the internet—travel and information have become widely available; migrants seeking passage within Europe are able to receive continuous information regarding, for instance, route guidance, from others who have negotiated the trip, through cell phones. Personal communication devices such as these grant exposure to media and

theme #3: hypocracy of openness claimed by receiving nations

DIFF #1: globalization

DIFF #2: min tech. makes modern immig easier

illuminate living conditions in other nations, offering assurance of secure lives and thereby encouraging people to relocate. Globalization has also eased financial transfers, facilitating both moves and remittances.

Third, a notable change has occurred in the demographic makeup of new immigrants. Whereas the typical migrant used to be an unmarried male, who was a perfect candidate to provide labor while requiring the support of few services, nearly half of the new migrants are women, often with children. When refugees and asylum seekers are included in the mix, the proportion of needy migrants with few resources increases sharply. Such shifts involve more complicated settlement in host nations, with greater adjustments on the part of the host population and increases in the use of education and social services, all of which alter popular perceptions of migrants by defining them as draining rather than adding resources.

Fourth, there is increasing evidence that while people expect their governments to bear responsibility for immigration issues, they infrequently support their actions. That expectation is a sea change. In earlier times, immigration was largely unregulated, as businesses advised governments on whom and how many to admit, and those accepted were largely on their own. Host governments now calculate labor needs, screen applicants, manage programs for settlement, and monitor potential security threats. Governments have taken on immigration responsibilities reluctantly, as opposition parties of all stripes have portrayed such services as welfare for nonnationals and made immigration a major electoral issue in all destination nations.

Finally, international organizations have steadily increased efforts to regulate treatment of refugees and immigrants. Responding to the often horrific conditions after 1945, international standards have been codified and used to pressure regimes to provide humane treatment. However widely accepted the idea of immigration as a market function might be, the realities of exploitation have generated regional and international involvement in arenas traditionally left to national management and control. That involvement is sure to increase, as the United Nations and powerful regional associations seek to fashion unified standards and policies.

Twenty-First-Century Immigration Patterns and the Role of Refugees as Triggers of Crisis

Between 1980 and 2008, attempts were made to adapt policies to changing immigration situations. The United States granted amnesty and residency to undocumented immigrants in 1986, and France encouraged foreigners who had been allowed entry outside of official channels to seek permanent status retroactively. Britain provided funds for immigrant schooling and housing and created commissions to improve race relations. Although Germany instituted tighter restrictions on asylum, it also removed barriers to naturalization. The EU continues efforts to define common standards of immigrant treatment among its members. Still, major weaknesses exposed during the post-1945 period persist, and are especially evident in piecemeal legislation aimed at managing

managing or burden [handwritten margin note]

immediate problems rather than creating comprehensive policy [handwritten annotation]

immediate problems rather than creating comprehensive policy, and a continuing preference for keeping immigration numbers small. Across nations, official policies continue to be minimalist, apparently assuming that issues will be resolved by market forces and eventual assimilation.

Differences in who is let into what country [handwritten margin note]

Dramatic increases in the number of refugees seeking entry into both the United States and Europe have again brought the question of numbers to the forefront of national concerns. Refugees have always confounded immigration policies, since their plight and numbers can be neither predicted nor easily managed. Seventy years after the last massive surge, nations unprepared to offer more than temporary relief find themselves caught between sympathy for refugees and resistance to what appear to be unlimited numbers. Earlier crises offer little guidance. The United States was notoriously reluctant to respond to the plight of European Jews in the 1930s and '40s, but migrants from Cuba continue to enjoy automatic acceptance 55 years after the rebellion of 1959 and more than a year after new American relations with Cuba were initiated. Iraqis and Afghanis who assisted U.S. military operations expected but rarely received timely admission decisions, and refugees from civil war and famine in Somalia were required to follow application procedures for regular visas. Britain, which in 1948 proclaimed open doors for all Commonwealth citizens, moved almost immediately to

---

20th and 21st Century Migration Surges

Post–World War II: During the War, some 60 million people were displaced; by 1951, at least one million were still seeking places to live. Over 2 million Germans left Czechoslovakia; 500,000 left Poland to travel to the Soviet Union; 2 million Soviets returned to the Soviet Union; more than 600,000 resettled in the U.S.; even more migrated to the new state of Israel

Cuban Migration to the U.S: Since 1959, more than 1.1 million Cubans have left Cuba, entering the U.S. legally. In 1981, a boatlift of prisoners and unemployed brought 125,000; between 2013 and 2015, 100,000 entered, taking advantage of favorable federal policies dating to 1959.

Central Americans Entered the U.S. Requesting Refugee Status: Between 2013 and 2014, more than 315,000 non-Mexicans and 771,000 Mexicans crossed the border; 50,000 unaccompanied children have entered each year.

Middle Eastern and African Civil Strife and Poverty after 2013: In 2015, over 1 million refugees traveled by sea to Europe; 942,000 sought asylum; in 2014, 184 were granted refugee status. By 2016 the United Nations High Commission on Refugees reported that 65 million people worldwide were either refugees or displaced persons, a figure eclipsing the number following World War II.

prevent immigration from former colonies, even those beset by violence. Germany, with 400,000 applicants for asylum in 1993, revised its constitution to restrict entry. As compelling as refugee cases may be, nations confronted with unanticipated influxes have not been able to agree on consistent policies, trusting the UN High Commission on Refugees to provide temporary camps (in which by 2016 more than 10 million refugees were housed; another 25 million displaced persons were in protection programs) and negotiate for permanent homes with members. That process is cumbersome, resulting in long waits and multiple stages where applications can be denied. New refugee movements almost always lead to revival of media and political portrayals of immigration as crisis. Where immigration rarely ranked in the top twenty public concerns in most years since 1945, the 2013–16 refugee situation has inspired high-profile debates charged with divisive rhetoric. Two factors may be creating a more intense debate. One is the imagery made accessible by modern technology, which can present crises in bold relief: instant access to the world's trouble spots, demonstrations, *Media* border apprehensions, drug trafficking. Violence is newsworthy, everyday successes *Portrayal* are not, and the proliferation of outlets via news media and internet has increased viewing opportunities to an ever-wider audience. If minimal contact with people who are different has historically bred indifference to them, extensive exposure has almost certainly increased resentment and fear.

Related to universal access to information and interpretation is the fact that "hot button" issues drive politics, and immigrants push that button in a variety of ways. The 9/11 terrorists were foreigners who developed their plans on American soil; the Boston Marathon bombers were identified as disgruntled immigrants. Rioting in European cities occurred in ethnic neighborhoods; the razing of Roma camps in France highlighted their makeshift living conditions, and terrorist attacks were quickly linked to foreigners with ISIS sympathies. Through the lens of media coverage, immigrants appear dangerous or a threat to jobs and cultural identity even as the vast majority live ordinary, productive, lives. Extreme politicians and parties have news value because they are extreme, even if their electoral strength is small.

Immigration is susceptible to the "hot button" tag precisely because it differs from issues about which the public is chronically indifferent. Most foreign and domestic policies do not personally affect citizens, but immigration has the ability to touch all—how we define ourselves, how safe our neighborhoods are, what kinds of schools our children will attend, what jobs will be open to us—and thus elicits highly personal opinions about noncitizens. The issue combines central national concerns (economic opportunity and stability, public safety, social welfare) with very personal priorities. In the United States, the personal element is on display at least every two years, when candidates extol the plucky immigrants in their family lineage but still manage to disparage more current newcomers. Because immigration inspires religious, humane, and patriotic sentiments as well as economic and social interpretations of society, it is both intensely personal and provocatively complex. The question might well be not why the issue is at any given moment hot, but why there are any times when it is not.

Conflicting frameworks

Immigration is far too complex a problem to produce easy solutions to the dilemmas described here. Durable policies have to be based on an understanding of its dynamics, and comparison of nations struggling to manage it can offer important lessons. Attempts to simplify matters invite perils of their own, but three core questions can be posed to guide the analysis here. First, how have nations reconciled their economies' needs for additional workers with perceptions that foreign labor undercuts the native workforce and burdens service programs? Second, how have nations reconciled claims of openness and humanitarian ideals with pressure to restrict regular immigration and resist admitting refugees? Third, how have nations dealt with immigrants from different cultures in the face of pressure to preserve national identity and security?

This analysis compares experiences in four destination nations: the United States, Britain, Germany, and France. It builds on a basic framework that organizes a wealth of historical, economic, social, and political research to extrapolate the determinants of policy options. Within that framework, the central chapters examine the evolution of immigration policy in four nations, seeking to shed light on questions crucial to understanding governmental responses in a challenged global environment.

A Framework for Analysis

Immigration is hardly a modern phenomenon. Civilizations, kingdoms, empires, and nation-states have all experienced major population movement—borders changed by conquest or alliance; groups absorbed or expelled; native populations taking on new definition. Literature on individual cases or eras is abundant; theoretical treatments of immigration comprehensive; data readily available; and volumes including national examples rich in detail. That said, comparing modern national experiences in the face of increasing immigration pressures requires some distillation of the extant literature and a framework for analysis.

Immigration Theory

The body of scholarly literature on immigration is vast, filled with both broadly brushed and tightly focused studies in a number of academic disciplines in the social sciences and law. Historians and anthropologists document the experiences of individuals and groups in old and new societies; economists and demographers model labor flows and their impacts; political scientists and sociologists examine admission policies and immigrant assimilation; legal scholars assess citizenship rules. It is hardly surprising that noted scholar Douglas Massey and others have noted that "social scientists do not approach the study of immigration from a shared paradigm, but from a variety of competing theoretical viewpoints fragmented across disciplines, regions, and ideologies" (1994, p. 700). Moreover, disciplines differ markedly in the way they frame issues, in the units of analysis they use, and the research methods they employ (Brettell & Hollifield, 2008). An abundance of research is host to a similarly broad array of theories.

Still, disciplinary theory and research provide important guidance for those comparing immigration experiences. History and anthropology alert us to issues in earlier migrations that have shaped recent examples; political science and sociology identify policy debates and options, and document integration patterns. Within sociology, demographers define parameters of population movement; within political science, debates over critical perspectives such as realism, institutionalism, and globalization have sharpened our understanding of the challenges of traditional immigration and the growing refugee crises. A major recommendation offered in Brettell and Hollifield's *Migration Theory* is its subtitle, *Talking across Disciplines* (1994). As we argue in the following sections, each of four disciplinary approaches informs understanding of the common issues faced in the four nations examined here.

The Utility of a Cross-disciplinary Framework

Comparison of national cases requires consideration of several critical perspectives: in this volume, we focus on geography, history, economics, and politics for their ability to highlight national similarities and differences. Industrial revolutions in Europe and the United States transformed their economies but differed in the role foreign labor played and how urban centers adapted to change. Internal population movement made immigration unnecessary in some, but not all, areas; language and cultural barriers arose in some but not others; the political influence of business varied widely. To understand how immigration shaped host societies and their orientations to nonnatives, attention to the complexities of place, time, economics, and politics is basic and informative.

The framework used here is meant to facilitate one course of theory building suggested by Brettell and Holifield and others, by building bridges based on common questions asked in different settings by different disciplines. It sets out certain variables as central in most, even all, national experiences with immigration. It directs readers to those variables as they influence the timing and size of movements, obstacles, and policies that emerge. Frameworks are not theories in themselves, but set the stage for both specific and general hypotheses about immigration, thereby contributing to the creation of theories. Organizing information within the kind of framework offered here provides a basis for consideration of broader theories of sociopolitical accommodation and change critical to effective immigration policies.

Why Compare American and European Experiences?

Immigration is a ubiquitous phenomenon, fascinating in its breadth but requiring focus to make its study manageable. We have selected the United States, Britain, Germany, and France for three reasons. First, a primary goal of this study is to explain the challenges facing destination nations, primarily advanced industrial democracies. Our four nations offer choices for workers at all skill levels, and all have current and project future gaps in their supply of available labor. All are signatories to international conventions that mandate support and fair treatment for refugees and minorities in situations they might well prefer to avoid, setting up prime situations for examining their responses.

Second, the four nations have all seen immigration become increasingly salient as a political issue, often challenging traditional party governance. Leaders and legislatures are expected to manage tensions between solving economic problems and protecting national identities. All are currently confronting refugee crises that threaten to strain resources as well as political tolerance. In the European setting, the issue is compounded by the question of how much authority the European Union should have in areas traditionally reserved to national governments. The future of the EU may well depend on how it balances national needs and the goals of an ever-greater economic and political union.

Third, a host of extensive studies on immigration in the four nations have provided data that can be compared with minimal distortion. Economic indicators and population censuses use comparable measures; election cycles are similar; public opinion institutes structure surveys according to common standards. Comparisons can thus be made with relative confidence. Those undertaken here seek to define both national cases and immigration itself, utilizing a framework based on four individual but related elements.

Geography and Its Limits

Like real estate, immigration is influenced greatly by location. For individuals, the potential for improving one's lot, situation, prospects, essential services, and security furnishes important criteria regarding relocation decisions. At a national level, geography sets natural parameters for immigration, especially regarding ease of entry, but also in structuring border relations and the capacity to serve inhabitants' needs. Nations defined by natural barriers—large bodies of water or difficult terrain—enjoy a degree of geographic isolation that has historically meant protection from foreign intrusion and development of homogeneous populations. Borders that divide similar neighbors serve as latent natural boundaries, loosely policed simply because there is little pressure to leave one country for the other. The British Isles have long been favorably isolated by geography, and the United States experienced similar security for 200 years before the porousness of its southern border created routes for uninvited migrants. In contrast, most European nations live with the effects of histories replete with border-changing conflicts. Across the continent, territorial claims and ethnic animosities linger, straining internal and external relations. Borders are only partially successful in restricting entry, and nations within the European Union have had reason to worry that variations in size, resources, and population density must necessitate differences in how populations are managed.

However critical geographic characteristics have been historically, some have become less significant over time. Population movement once limited to land crossings and dangerous sea travel has access to faster, safer, and more elusive routes. Air travel facilitates visits that are difficult to monitor. Densely populated areas appear able to absorb new and uncounted foreign nationals, defying many analyses of capacity. The reality of a smaller globe serviced by advanced transportation and communication has reduced the role of traditional barriers. Still, Britain developed a perception of immunity from immigration by its physical isolation; others believed their size and unpopulated areas would make overpopulation unimaginable; the United States continues to focus on its southern border even as those entering by air pose a larger threat to remain illegally. Still, even with physical barriers less relevant to population movement, the rhetoric of secure borders continues to define both perceptions and political debate.

History as Guide to the Present

Although the 250-year existence of the United States has been brief by comparison to the histories of the European nations, all have long and cumulative immigration narratives, which have defined appropriate roles for foreigners. Most simply, history helps us understand how nations came to be who they are and how, therefore, they are likely to deal with current and new immigration issues. The cases studied here have distinct histories but can be compared with respect to three important themes.

RELATIONS WITH NEIGHBORS

Most obvious here are differences between Britain and the United States, on the one hand, and continental France and Germany, on the other. What is now Germany comprises areas formerly controlled by other states. Over time, many of those were conquered and their citizens forced to work to support the industrial economy, during both the nineteenth and twentieth centuries; their only value was as wage labor. After 1945, a Germany desperate for workers turned once again to foreign labor despite being inexperienced in dealing with them as potential citizens. The period since 1960 reflects both the historical biases the nation encountered and its attempts to overcome them. France had more stable borders prior to 1945, having welcomed workers attracted to industry in the north and agriculture in the south since the early nineteenth century; at one point, France had the largest percentage of foreign-born residents in either Europe or North America. The number of immigrants of all backgrounds increased throughout the first half of the twentieth century, building an image of France as a haven for refugees. Since most of the new residents were motivated by either economic opportunities in France or untenable political conditions elsewhere, or both, they were welcomed as loyal new citizens. France's disastrous war against its favored colony in Algeria abruptly changed that perception to one that reflected fear of the cultural and security threats posed by immigrants whose loyalties were not guaranteed.

Despite some early conflicts with Europeans—with Portugal over control of the seas; with France over potential royal alliances—actual border conflicts did not trouble insular Britain in its early and modern history. By the early nineteenth century it was truly a nation of emigration, having established a pattern of sending not only troops but also administrators and merchants abroad to create and rule the empire. The government's antipathy to immigration, however, was never in doubt, rejecting the idea of nonwhite entry to Britain in 1905 and retaining that stance for 200 years before facing twemty-first-century changes, with inevitable difficulty.

Finally, early American history was one of territorial expansion, without extended conflict, and such growth encouraged settlement by immigrants in sparsely populated areas as well as rapidly growing cities. Conflict with other nations over territory ended with the Mexican-American war, and even there disputes over travel or relocation did not reach the level of major concern until the second half of the twentieth century, when postwar immigration demands forced the revisions of U.S. policies discussed in the next chapter.

COLONIALISM

The histories of Britain and France have been significantly influenced by colonialist experience. In each case, empire created a relationship of domination based on the conviction that colonies were incapable of either self-governance or independent economic development. In each case, colonial rule led to local resentment, most notably of the French in Algeria and Indochina and of the British in East Africa and South Asia. The end of World War II hastened the end, of colonialism and both controlling powers struggled with transitions to independence in more than 50 colonies and territories. Thousands of citizens of former colonies sought to migrate to Britain and France, creating unanticipated challenges for both. As a lens through which Britain and France viewed those seeking entry, colonialism can explain much of the resistance to all immigration. Both avoided responsibility for colonies as parents might deal with children not ready for adulthood but too costly to support, much less house, and in both the repercussions were severe.

Neither Germany nor the United States had a comparable history. Germany lost its few colonies in the World War I settlements, and the U.S. expanded territory without creating colonies even as it took over Native American land and acquired territory from other nations. However aggressive many of those campaigns were, they never instituted a structure of foreign rule without incorporation. In this important historical experience, legacies of colonialism would be critical for France and Britain but not Germany and the United States.

IMMIGRATION HISTORY AS PLURALISM OR SEGREGATION

Immigration has been assigned very different national definitions in the countries studied here. Among them, only the United States has had a long history of large-scale immigration, in cycles dominated initially by Europeans before shifting to include natives of

[Handwritten margin notes: "end of wwii / sent people / former colonies / to brb/france / fast influx / hard to deal / w/ — is not a / problem for / germany / U.S."]

other continents. Despite persistent hardship and considerable discrimination, immigrants persevered to assume roles in a society seen as a great melting pot. Skids were greased for them by opportunistic political parties, and they inhabited urban centers where jobs were plentiful and citizenship easy to attain. As new nationalities arrived, older ones were accepted; and, increasingly, younger generations consistently embraced an American culture with a hybrid population and widespread mobility. Despite contentious periods, the longer pattern has been one of general assimilation, leading to the retrospective boast that the U.S. is a "nation of immigrants."

Experiences in Europe have been less positive. Britain and Germany officially insisted for decades that they were not immigrant nations, and newcomers were marginalized socially and politically there, and later in France as well. Multiculturalism as a goal has been rejected by native populations increasingly supportive of nationalist parties, and claims of geographic limits have resonated with all, adding tension to already fractious political environments. Whether the bases for hostility are common or variable, their historical roots are central to the framework utilized here.

Like geography, history can play both direct and indirect roles in defining immigration issues. The most obvious direct roles are evidenced by the legal agreements by which Britain and France defined their relationships with their colonies during and after independence. Independence documents revised definitions created during the colonial regimes that had granted a sort of subaltern citizenship to subject peoples, changing favorable classifications that at least implied access to England and France to categories that rendered the newly freed subjects not eligible for entry into either nation. Indirect roles appear in the histories of all four of the countries examined, primarily in perceptions that have persisted over time and perpetuated beliefs that immigrants—especially those who are racially, ethnically, and culturally different from their hosts—are poor candidates for a future in the West.

Economic Factors in Immigration

Many analysts argue that whatever other factors may exist, economics is always trump in the game of immigration. Provided with evidence that demand for labor exceeds available supply, governments reverse or temporize previous positions, politicians play to the needs of the day, and citizens accept policies they previously opposed. From the perspective of migrants, economic opportunity has been a universal magnet for relocation, over time outpacing even forces of natural and man-made disasters.

Economics as the foundation of human relocation is at the heart of basic push-pull theories of immigration. People are pushed to move when work is scarce or nonexistent; nations accept or even "pull" them when their own workforces are insufficient to meet the needs of their economies. Stephen Castles and Godula Kosack allude to the simplicity of economic forces with the observation that "[l]abor migration is a form of development aid given by the poor countries to the rich countries" (1985, p. 428). Economic factors that define this relationship are the most straightforward elements in our framework. In most simple terms, both long- and short-term labor demand are calculated regularly by governments and businesses in all developed nations. Contributions to the economy are easily estimated by productivity of industry, immigrant spending, and taxes; costs are quantifiable expenses in training, education, and public services.

Germany relied on such an economic calculus in defining its postwar guestworker programs, reasoning that temporary workers contributed significantly to economic growth while consuming few resources. Only after a generation did the limits of the simple economic model become evident (as was also documented in earlier programs in the United States). Mandatory rotation of workers after arbitrary lengths of employment was resisted by employers in strong economic times and proved embarrassingly difficult to apply when recessions hit. Single workers recruited without dependents sought permits for relatives or started families in their new home. As workers stayed for longer periods, questions about competition with local labor, costs of instruction and support services, and what rights their children should enjoy all revealed that issues of long-term employment, mobility, and integration had not been anticipated, making what had been simple policies politically controversial.

Although economic variables are by nature precise in definition and measurement, they are commonly generalized in political discourse (immigrants depress working-class wages) or cast as broad patterns in unspecified contexts (immigrants overwhelm localities with their need for services). Economics is also often cited when the underlying concern is cultural (immigrant ghettos are incubators of unemployment and crime). Far from being simple push and pull forces, economic factors are used to bolster all manner of social and political arguments. But even as they are conflated with social and cultural issues, economic variables remain central to understanding immigration and its policy alternatives. We thus include review of economic patterns—market and supply conditions, costs and benefits to the host economies, role in sustaining workforce numbers—in our comparisons. If immigration is at base about economics, other variations among nations should be less influential in defining policies.

Political Actors and Alignments

However important geography, history, and economics are as influences, policies are ultimately the responsibility of political institutions. Politics is the crucible within which the needs of competing groups are weighed, national and regional differences balanced, and the enthusiasm or limits of public acceptance registered. In this arena, formal institutions (political parties, legislatures, executives) as well as an array of nongovernmental forces (lobbies, citizens' groups, public opinion), play roles, often decisively. Their ability to define policy is thus essential to the framework employed here.

FORMAL ACTORS: INSTITUTIONS OF GOVERNMENT AND THEIR PARTISAN BASES

In all four nations the center of decision making is the national legislature. In Britain and Germany, parliamentary and executive leadership are constitutionally linked;

leaders of the party winning the most seats form a government, comprised of either a single majority party or a coalition assembled by the party with most votes. France has a semipresidential system, with separate elections for president and members of the National Assembly. The presidential winner names a prime minister, and forms a governing coalition only if it is needed to control a majority in the National Assembly. In the United States, the president and members of both houses of Congress are elected separately, but the legislature officially initiates and passes all laws before the president finalizes action. The consequence of different forms of governance for legislating is significant. Unified governments (Germany and Britain by electoral law, France by tradition) routinely enact laws formulated by the majority party. The American separation of executive and legislative branches requires agreement to enact law, often delaying, preventing, or compromising laws strongly endorsed by one branch. That difference can be decisive in crafting policy and is critical in understanding variations in policies across nations.

Although efficient lawmaking is expected from strong central governments, policy does not always emerge easily. Across all nations, immigration issues have created uneasy alliances within and between parties. In Europe, where parties are more often defined by traditional Left-Right ideologies, immigration typically defies placement on that spectrum. Nationalistic conservatives wary of working-class agendas have been pressured by businesses to support increased admissions. Liberals traditionally advocating for working and lower classes have confronted opposition from unions resenting a competitive labor market and increasingly diverse workplace environment. Even when one party has a clear majority, agreement on policy is often elusive.

Compounding these obstacles are regional variations, where provincial and local governments often disagree with the national majority. In the United States, state immigration laws have dramatically contradicted federal law, forcing the federal Justice Department to bring suit to void them. Education, constitutionally controlled by state governments in Germany, varied so much from state to state that federal courts were forced to intervene. The European Union has taken the lead in codifying common immigrant rights, but progress has been uneven as member states have resisted supranational control. The varying roles will be explored in the framework utilized here.

INFORMAL POLITICAL FORCES: INTEREST GROUPS AND PUBLIC OPINION

In all political systems, official institutions are guided by the interests of those they serve and develop processes through which citizens and groups may influence decision making. The nations examined here differ in the array and power of such groups within their systems, but all are sensitive to their positions on immigration issues. The most visible are those groups that serve as bases for the major parties. In all four of our cases, the bases of the main conservative parties (Republican in the U.S., Conservative in Britain, Christian Democratic/Christian Social Union in Germany, Union for Popular Movement in France—now the Republican Party) have been business interests and the upper-middle and upper classes. The major liberal parties (Democrats in the

U.S., Social Democrats in Germany, Labour in Britain, Socialists in France) define their bases by organized labor, lower-middle and working classes, and the poor. In all, racial and ethnic minorities have identified mostly with liberal-to-left parties. In Germany, a frequent coalition partner has been a third party, adding its business (Free Democrats or FDP) or environmentalist (Greens) supporters to the mix. Minor parties have attracted more attention than electoral success in all four nations, but they cannot be dismissed, as they draw disaffected voters from across the ideological spectrum. What is important for our purposes is to examine how the various groups articulate and pursue policy preferences, and here immigration issues have created strange bedfellows. Businesses needing a reliable supply of labor have often been more sympathetic to immigrants than others on the political Right. Labor unions have distanced themselves from immigrant-friendly proposals favored by liberal parties. Cross-cutting immigration issues have, in short, created variations among the positions of powerful interests and in so doing have increased internal party conflict and governmental gridlock.

Pressure on decision makers also comes from single-issue groups that have arisen to oppose immigration and support fringe parties. FAIR (Federation of Americans for Immigration Reform) has attracted funds and members to pressure legislators, and groups such as the English Defence League have organized protests and campaigns in Britain. On the other end of the spectrum are immigrant support organizations, many which are church based and most of which are low profile. The intensity displayed by these groups can be a critical factor in understanding ultimate immigration outcomes.

Finally, a major source of influence is generated by public opinion. No democratic government could survive committing a major deviation from electoral sentiment, and all cultivate popular support. In the current context, public opinion may be even more important, because postwar governments effectively avoided public discussion of the immigration question for decades while they fashioned narrow or stopgap policies. The issue and its avoidance have caught up with them, making the call for decisive policies more urgent, as immigration crises show no signs of resolution or letting up.

The historic tendency of officials to downplay immigration issues is understandable if we recall that even in nations where immigration has been continuous through history, public opinion about it has often been wary or negative. Some have attributed that guarded view to a basic human aversion to change, but recent opposition more resembles widespread fears of massive immigration of people from different, even hostile cultures, and has shown no signs of reverting to the indifference that characterized long periods in earlier times. We suggested earlier that public opinion may be decisive simply because citizens see immigrants as impacting their lives. That phenomenon, and the intensity that candidates generate during the course of political campaigns, are likely to keep the issue close to the surface for voters and the elections they decide. As Gary Freeman and his co-editors have noted in *Immigration and Public Opinion in Liberal Democracies*, "Public opinion may not determine policy outcomes but rather set boundaries—sometimes wider, sometimes more narrow—within which policy makers find opportunity or constraint" (2013, p. 3).

public opinion in policy making

To document the critical role public opinion often plays in shaping government policies (and their avoidance), this analysis utilizes a wide array of opinion surveys generated by the most rigorous organizations, many of them associated with university centers: the Eurobarometer series, institutes at the University of Michigan in the United States, the University of Essex in Britain, and the University of Mannheim in Germany. Other surveys quoted are from the Pew Research Center in the U.S., an organization dedicated to scientific survey and analysis of American and global opinion. Although all surveys run the risk of simplifying opinion or tapping it only during particularly volatile periods, their attention to representative sampling and repeated measures offer the best evidence of the distribution and intensity of opinion in the nations studied. Together with geographic, historical, and economic data, they provide a comprehensive picture of the factors critical to understanding variations in attitudes and policies regarding immigration across nations.

The framework outlined here is constructed to give order to the comparison of immigration in four nations and to allow modest testing of common hypotheses about what policies are adopted and how. To apply it, we turn to four case examples before returning to basic questions in the final chapter.

For Further Reading

Caroline B. Brettell and James F. Hollifield (EDS). *Immigration Theory: Talking Across Disciplines.* 2nd Ed. New York: Routledge, 1994.

Eytan Meyers. *International Immigration Policy: A Theoretical and Comparative Analysis.* New York: Palgrave Macmillan, 2007.

2

The United States

Immigration Model or Nation of Continuous Conflict?

However varied the American immigration experience has actually been, the predominant popular images it invokes are those of the United States as a national beacon, a destination for millions, with a historic record of adjustment and assimilation. In 2014, there were 3.8 million immigrants in New York City alone, representing 36% of the population of the metropolis and 48% of those employed there. Throughout its history, the United States has attracted more people, from more cultures, than any other nation, while building a diverse society in which *E Pluribus Unum* (out of many, one) is a living reality. It has also experienced serious conflict, exclusion, and discrimination in a frequently fractious culture. As the current American political climate descends into acrimony and legislative standoff, one might easily wonder whether it constitutes just one more chapter in a tale that will end happily, or a set of skirmishes leading to major changes in national policy, or a sign that the country is ready to curtail immigration permanently.

The political divisions that have emerged in the last ten years have been especially severe. In 2016, an estimated 11.3 million undocumented immigrants resided in the United States, up from 3.5 million in 1990. Despite the clear need to address failures in the system, it took six years for the Senate to agree on a comprehensive bill in 2013, only to watch the House of Representatives refuse to consider it—promising but not producing specific bills of its own, and later deciding to postpone any discussion until a new president was in place. In the summer of 2014, a new generation of undocumented immigrants—more than 60,000 Central Americans, including unaccompanied children and mothers with minor children crossing southwestern borders to seek U.S. protection—gained national attention as political leaders decried the numbers but still offered no solutions beyond deportation in procedures delayed or prohibited by laws requiring administrative or judicial hearings. Frustrated by legislative inaction, the president ordered immigration offices to focus on criminal activity and border security, effectively delaying deportations, moving opponents to challenge his actions as unconstitutional. In 2016, immigration occupied a front and center stage position in a presidential election in which

[handwritten marginalia: 1990 → '16; 3.5 Mil → 11.3; immigrants; undoc]

foreigners were depicted as dangerous and a threat to U.S. workers and radical changes in policy were promised. The temperature of the debate has risen, with little effort to bring it down through normal lawmaking procedures. How the United States responds as a nation will surely define the size, shape, and color of the country for generations to come.

Immigration as Defined by Geography: The Physical Context

America's geography has itself been defined in important ways by the history and evolution of its political and economic systems. Initial settlement in North America was small in scale and concentrated in what is now New England, increasing gradually as new arrivals moved south and west. In 1776, the original thirteen colonies covered only about 10% of the current American land area. As the nation expanded, it forcibly occupied land owned by Native Americans and negotiated territorial acquisitions from Britain, France, Spain, and Mexico to fill out the borders that, leaving aside noncontiguous Alaska and Hawaii, have defined all but one boundary (Arizona became a state in 1912) of the nation's physical outline since 1853. Compared to the great conflicts over borders in Europe and elsewhere, the United States has enjoyed generally harmonious relations with Canada and Mexico. Although borders were permeable, migration was uncontroversial and rarely the focus of broader debates on immigration policies.

The eastern and western borders of the country have been geographic protectors, by definition. The Atlantic coastline is more than 2,060 miles long, the Pacific 2,093, and the Gulf Coast 1,631. Distances between the U.S. mainland and even the nearest foreign ports are large: 3,100 miles to Europe and 5,500 to Japan. American physical isolation has been real, discouraging conflict for more than 200 years.

As geographic distance and good neighbors insulated the country from foreigner incursion, its resources were only beginning to be tapped. The most obvious was its vast area. The nation was underpopulated when Europe began to run out of arable land, and continues to enjoy low population density even with crowded metropolitan centers taken into account. It has also benefited from abundant natural resources, from fresh water to forests, minerals, gas, and oil. The Southwest is ideally suited for solar power, and hydropower is generated by major rivers and the Great Lakes. By any standard, the country continues to be resource rich. With 85 residents per square mile, the United States ranks among the least densely populated nations, far below the others studied here (Britain: 679, Germany: 591, and France: 306).

Ample land facilitated varied settlement patterns. For the first 150 years, newcomers arrived and stayed in areas near the coasts. Some ethnic groups gravitated to the Midwest, initially in and around Chicago, then found comfortable homes across the country. In 1910, immigrant populations were still concentrated mostly in coastal New England, New York, Pennsylvania, and New Jersey in the East, in San Francisco, Los Angeles, and Seattle in the West, and in Illinois and Michigan in the Midwest. At the turn of the twenty-first century the foreign-born still tended to cluster in California,

New York, and Massachusetts. Mexico also became a major corridor for migrants from Central America, increasing percentages in the Southwest. The midsection of the country is still comparatively sparse in migrant settlement, although clusters have followed job opportunities: meatpacking in the Midwest, construction in Colorado, small farming in Minnesota. Though they are still found mostly in border states, undocumented immigrants have become significant populations in others as well (Table 2.1).

Geography and resources were important facilitators of immigration until the emergence of two post-1945 developments. First, modernization of equipment disrupted traditional agricultural employment in Mexico, leading large numbers to abandon farming and seek opportunities in the United States. Western and southwestern border states have enjoyed the benefits of Mexican labor for years, legally through the "Bracero program," and then illegally, although tolerated, after that program was ended, but the numbers entering after the 1965 immigration reforms set off alarms. What had been a sleepy, trouble-free border turned into a geographic liability: almost two thousand miles of permeable territory, with loosely patrolled points of crossing and terrain that, though difficult to navigate, offered literally thousands of paths of entry.

The second significant development was the growth of affordable air transportation, as noted in chapter 1. New routes and lower fares served a larger market, facilitating travel by working- and middle-class immigrants. Unlike many other nations, the United States did not develop systems to track entrants to enforce visa limits; nor did it create effective permits for work or residence. As a result, overstaying visa limits and finding work proved to be relatively easy for those without documents. Control of the southern border became an issue after a very long period of relatively open immigration and easy naturalization. Borders thus emerged as problem areas for immigration in the late 1900s.

Table 2.1. Estimated Number of Undocumented Immigrants in the Labor Force by State, 2010

State	Labor Force Population	Estimated # Unauthorized Immigrants
California	18,811	1,850
Texas	12,261	1,100
Florida	9,064	600
New York	9,742	450
New Jersey	4,679	400
Illinois	6,719	375
Georgia	4,777	325
North Carolina	4,658	250
Arizona	3,116	230
Maryland	3,100	190

Source: U.S. Department of Homeland Security, Office of Immigration Statistics, Population Estimates, February, 2011.

Immigration in American History

Immigration has been more or less continuous in North America since the late eighteenth century, as open space and opportunity presented a compelling alternative to destinations known for their historic conflicts and religious divisions, and lured populations who would define the new nation. Histories of the migration are numerous and varied, but they tend to employ common themes.

Immigration as a History of Surges and Ebbs

Students of immigration have identified three periods during which major surges occurred: from 1840 to 1860, 1880 to 1914, and 1965 to the present. Figure 2.1 illustrates the numbers and countries of origin in each. Britain and Ireland were the major source of immigrants in the first period, Germany, Austria-Hungary, Italy, and Russia in the second, and Mexico, Central America, and the Caribbean in the third. The end of each period was hastened when political forces united in their hostility to newcomers and pressured Congress to halt the flow. The years between surges, which often involved war or domestic conflict, slowed immigration, as national borders were more closely monitored and the number of potential migrants reduced by war casualties abroad. But the flow never stopped completely, as the lure of opportunity was constant and the supply of potential migrants plentiful.

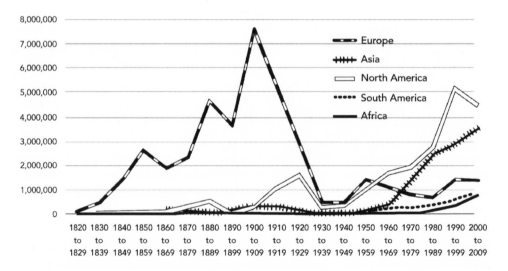

Figure 2.1. Number and Origins of Immigrants to the U.S., 1820–2009. (*Source.* U.S. Department of Homeland Security, *Yearbook of Immigration Statistics*, 2010)

Conditions of sending countries that lead to immigration surges in U.S.

The United States / 29

By the time the American colony separated from Britain and established a government, one hundred years of voluntary, unregulated immigration had already passed, creating an implicit template for much of the next century. In all three periods of surge, conditions in sending countries led to migration. In the first, the Irish famine was a prime mover. Some 250,000 people had already emigrated between 1750 and 1800; another 1–1.5 million followed between 1800 and 1845. The 1845–1852 famine devastated the native population, and one million emigrants left for America. Other European nations also suffered as the Industrial Revolution, which had brought millions of rural residents into urban areas, proved unable to accommodate all who sought employment. Crop failures and insufficient land increased risks of bankruptcy, pushing desperate Europeans to migrate. Even a devastating Civil War in the United States caused only a temporary lull in transatlantic relocation.

The second wave drew more continental Europeans and Russians, Jews, and Catholics. American industrialization followed its European counterpart by only two decades and, unlike Europe, created immediate opportunities for foreign labor to fuel its growth. Rapid development of major cities in the East and agriculture in the South and Midwest lured more than 30 million immigrants, effectively doubling the population. That increase fundamentally defined urban life as one with strong ethnic concentrations. The first period witnessed fear of newcomers who were as white and Anglo as most of those who had settled before them; the second period, also mostly white, revealed the enormous power of any kind of difference—ethnic, geographic, religious—to create friction and political opposition. The face of America changed during this period, inspiring theories of assimilation and pluralism central to its new identity.

The third wave came after the lull created by two twentieth-century wars and the worldwide depression between them. At the end of the second war, in 1945, new pressures to increase immigration levels emerged. After decades of calls to admit more refugees and non-Westerners, supporters of major change mobilized in Congress to pass the Immigration and Nationality Act of 1965. The act introduced a global vision of immigration with higher quotas for Asia, Latin America, and Africa and a shift to emphasize family unification over national origins. Followup legislation in 1976 and 1978 replaced Eurocentric formulas with allocations of 400,000 visas for the Eastern Hemisphere and Latin America, and since then the majority of those admitted have been from Asia and Latin America, with a marked increase in families united under provisions of new laws. The Refugee Act was passed in 1980 to facilitate an increased commitment to those groups. An unanticipated surge in undocumented migrants from Mexico and Central America led to amnesty legislation in 1986, but the flow continued despite increased border security and penalties for hiring workers without documents. Since 1986, the number of undocumented immigrants has continued to increase (with a brief decline during the 2008 recession), raising concerns about border control and the impact of uncontrolled entries, which have continued to frame if not resolve national debates.

Migration does not occur randomly. Disruption of some kind is almost always a prime mover: population growth and insufficient opportunities for work in nineteenth-century Europe undoubtedly influenced millions to move, adding 17 million new residents to the United States between 1890 and 1914 and securing an immigration tradition in the U.S. The continuation of this pattern was evident in the 1965–1995 period, when the population of Mexico tripled and its domestic economy grew at twice the rate of its equivalent in the United States. Migration to the United States included 5 million Mexicans even as 10 million moved from rural areas to Mexico City. The U.S. experience provides ample proof that positive as well as disruptive forces are constant and reliable predictors of surges with the potential to redefine national identities.

Immigration as a History of Loosely Regulated Indifference

Even with widespread resentment of new immigrants, America's early history reflected mostly indifference to them. During the colonial period there was no effort to count and little to control immigrants, as the influx between 1776 and 1880 grew to include more and more diverse settlers. Even when the flow of foreigners increased dramatically with industrialization in the late nineteenth century, federal and state governments paid scant attention, responding only to pressure to restrict Chinese entry. Overall, movement to the United States was essentially one of large-scale voluntary relocation.

With cities growing and Americans moving steadily into undersettled areas in the West, immigrants presented no real danger of overpopulation. Newcomers were economic additions, even in areas where they caused ethnic friction, and there is little evidence that local residents saw immigrants as part of some larger national issue. American census records indicate population growth from almost 4 million in 1790 to more than 50 million in 1880, including almost 22 million immigrants and their children or grandchildren. Given that 40% of the total population were immigrants, it is indeed odd that so few laws addressed them. Congress did pass legislation prohibiting further importation of slaves in 1808 (after some 375,000 had been brought forcibly to America), but essentially ignored other questions related to entry. In establishing and tinkering with naturalization rules, the government had the opportunity to define admission but did not act on it. In the 1860s, legislation was passed encouraging immigration (the Homestead Act of 1862, opening up land outside the original thirteen colonies, and the 1863 Contract Labor Law, which authorized payment of passage to the United States by companies recruiting workers). However, it was not until 1875 that hostility to Chinese immigrants in Western states led to passage of the Page Act, the first attempt to define as "undesirable" candidates for admission (Asian men brought in as forced labor, Asian women entering to work as prostitutes, and criminals). Political leaders who had abetted the railroad industry's recruitment of Chinese to build the transcontinental railroad were pressured to restrict further entry when California fell into economic recession and the Chinese were cast as unwanted competition for jobs. Seven years later, Congress passed the Chinese Exclusion Act, the first law to deny entrance to a specific national group.

In 1891, lawmakers at long last moved to recognize the importance of immigration nationally, imposing a 50 cent tax on each immigrant and establishing a Commissioner of Immigration within the Treasury Department. That act officially defined immigration as the responsibility of the federal government, but even a continuous increase in immigration in this period did not result in significant federal legislation until 1924. Between 1880 and 1920, 35 million Europeans and another million from Mexico, Asia, and Canada migrated to the United States. That workforce drove industrial modernization and new urban infrastructures, but it also produced open resentment, which expressed itself in segregated neighborhoods and lower wage levels for immigrants. Congress continued to focus on exclusion, extending the ban on Chinese immigrants, setting quotas for Japan and Korea, and in 1917 banning immigration from all of Asia except the Philippines. In 1919, it finally passed the nation's first comprehensive immigration legislation in the National Origins Act of that year, reducing new admissions to 2% of the number already in the United States from any country and empowering American consulates to judge applications. The onset of the Great Depression and World War II significantly slowed immigration, mitigating the more restrictive terms of the Act until the late 1940s. The one piece of significant legislation passed during this period was the Bracero Program, authorizing temporary admission to Mexican farmworkers. Under this program, 4 million Mexicans entered between 1942 and 1964; at its conclusion, the workforce was declared unnecessary, even as 75% of those admitted continued to live and work in the United States.

The postwar period brought economic growth throughout the U.S. and Europe, but attention to immigration was slight until 1965. A small number of programs assisted people displaced by the war, but were either embarrassingly late (1948 to assist victims of Nazi rule in Germany), small (a total of 250,000 visas over two years), or focused on the emerging Soviet threat (refugee relief to Eastern European political refugees). The McCarran/Walter Act of 1952 made an elliptical attempt to identify undesirable immigrants by specifying desirable qualities (refugees and those with family or skills) but retained quotas specified in the 1924 act. Only creative actions by President Eisenhower allowed admission of Hungarian and Cuban refugees in 1956 and 1959 after Congress failed to act on their behalf.

The comprehensive immigration law passed in 1965 differed from all previous legislation in liberalizing a system that had favored Europeans for 200 years. It abolished the 1924 national origins formula, allocated almost half of the annual visas to Western Hemisphere nations and prioritized family entry. It posed no real barriers to Europeans, but growing economies there translated into fewer people seeking entry. Others, however, were on the move. Between 1971 and 1986 more than 7 million migrated to the United States, and by 1990 60% of U.S. population growth was due to immigration. That period also witnessed steady increases in the number of persons entering illegally, especially from Mexico, prompting passage of the Immigration Reform and Control Act, which bolstered border security and mandated fines for hiring those without official status. Believing that the problem of illegal entry would be solved by the new measures, the bill's supporters also offered amnesty to undocumented immigrants who had resided in the United States for at least four years. The 1965 bill was seen as historic but passed only after encountering intense opposition and requiring assurances by proponents that it would not create drastic shifts in immigration patterns.

The acts of 1965 and 1986 were major commitments to define and control the flow of immigrants, but in general, proactive government action has been rare. Before 1965, political leaders relied on market mechanisms to regulate labor flows, usually with remarkable success. When popular sentiment brought issues to the fore, political leaders most frequently opted for narrow policies, including exclusion, leading many analysts to conclude that the laws of 1965 and 1986 were responses to a system badly needing revision, not conscious blueprints for immigration in the decades to come. There is a case to be made that debates since 2008 have been substantively different, engaging a broad spectrum of views and constituencies. But the continued inability or unwillingness to produce a comprehensive law suggests that leaders still prefer piecemeal responses, with the hope that broader issues will resolve themselves.

The predominant pattern in immigration legislation has thus been one of frequently reluctant reaction to both acute and continuing problems. The few laws passed before the early twentieth century were expressions of hostility toward specific nationalities; none created comprehensive policy and none addressed issues of immigrant protection. The major changes embodied in the 1985 and 1986 laws were similarly responsive to increasingly apparent flaws in existing laws. Over long periods, political leadership was largely silent on immigration issues. Remarkably, that system at least allowed intergenerational mobility, indicating that immigrants' children and grandchildren might well enjoy opportunities unavailable to first arrivals.

Immigration as the Great Urban Experiment

A powerful force in immigration's favor emerged with the arrival of industrialization and the rapid growth of cities, following the Civil War. As in Europe, industrialization in the United States initially drew people from outlying areas to work in expanding industries. But unlike the pattern in Europe, the needs of industry soon outpaced the labor supply in an underpopulated nation with seemingly unlimited opportunities for people seeking new or better lives on the expanding American frontier.

One immediate answer to labor shortages could be found among the large numbers of foreigners ready to relocate to American cities. Only one American city had a population of over 250,000 in 1850, but eleven reached that number by 1890 as the nation's urban population increased sixfold. Twenty-five million immigrants arrived between 1860 and 1914. For businesses, the situation was ideal. The new immigrants were usually young, desperate to work, and unlikely to object to low wages and long working hours. Newly organized political parties moved quickly to capitalize on that situation, offering housing, social services, and guidance in obtaining citizenship—all in exchange for loyalty at the ballot box once the immigrants were legally able to vote. When they had acquired experience, parties helped them improve their positions as factories expanded, more local businesses emerged to provide infrastructure and services, and still more immigrants took positions made available by the mobility of their predecessors. As long as industry grew, more immigrants were necessary and desirable, a situation benefiting both them and their patrons. It is difficult to overstate the influence that industrialization, and its political henchman the urban political machine, had on immigration in the 1880–1920 period. Immigrants were both the oil of industry and the engine of the party machine at a time when sheer numbers meant blunt political power. Immigrants were critical to both enterprises, even as they lived and worked in conditions that were often unsafe and for which they were undercompensated. Their vulnerability kept them in the lowest jobs and poorest slums, but offered at least the chance for better futures.

It was inevitable that the symbiotic immigrant–political party coalition would draw the attention of reformers outraged by the corruption within party machines. Their exposes mobilized public support for crackdowns on abuses and laws to eliminate electoral fraud. But by far the most important reform was establishment of a merit-based civil service system in 1883, effectively stripping party machines of their most effective resource, patronage jobs for their followers. Without the power to expand projects and payrolls at will, the machines and their partners in business lost the ability to reward supporters and thus their attractiveness to immigrants. Still, the legacy of the urban machine was huge, facilitating the development of a politically active working class, which would become a critical force in the twentieth century. *Urban machine*

Immigration as Historical Inconsistency

Even as the United States avoided major national conflict over immigration, it created a history in which inconsistency was common. Most obvious have been instances when a national avoidance of predictable problems has led to policy reversals. Chinese workers were recruited for railroad construction projects, then excluded when public opinion proved hostile to them. Federal policy was mostly silent on qualifications for immigration, but reacted to an oversupply of labor by specifying particular nationalities for exclusion (Mexicans and Filipinos during the Depression). Historic constitutional amendments outlawing discrimination were passed in the middle of the nineteenth century, but immigrants of different nationalities continued to receive differential treatment in basic areas of voting, residence, and employment.

A second inconsistency was the 200-years-long Eurocentric bias in immigration policy, which persisted long after Asians and Mexicans had established themselves as important economic contributors. The Chinese exclusion Act was not repealed until 1943, and Japanese Americans and legal immigrants were sent to internment camps during World War II. Mexicans were considered white and made citizens when large areas of the Southwest became part of the United States after 1850, but many were coerced into leaving during the Depression.

A third major example of inconsistency was the American position on admitting refugees, particularly during and after World War II. The most telling case was the reluc-

Gross reluctancy

tance to support victims of Nazi oppression in Germany. Neither the United States nor its European allies responded to the increasingly perilous situation of European Jews before 1939; those who left early or escaped were aided mostly by underground resistance networks and charitable organizations. As many as 20 million Europeans, including survivors of death camps, were displaced after the war, but American legislation provided entry for only 450,000 refugees. A more positive response was crafted after 1973, when the United States accepted 125,000 Vietnamese whose association with American forces during the war there put them at risk, and another 531,000 facing persecution by the victorious government were admitted between 1981 and 2000. But American assistance to Iraqi and Afghanistan refugees has been tepid. Congress passed Special Immigration Visas legislation in 2008 to expedite admission of those who aided U.S. forces, but by 2016 only 6,000 applications for entry had been processed, most after two-year waiting periods. The United States continues to resist admitting those fleeing violence in Central America and the Middle East, accepting only 11,000 of the 5 million Syrians in refugee camps or awaiting decisions in Europe in mid-2016. On the other hand, Cubans fleeing the regime in their country have been freely admitted, not only after the communist takeover in 1959, but 55 years later. In the first eight months of 2016, 44,000 Cubans were admitted. Although there are variations in these situations and current law reserves 70,000 admissions to refugees, response to crises has often been spotty and burdened by resistance.

A broad array of groups have settled and thrived with bearable levels of friction, and immigrants have been firmly linked to economic growth. Initial public wariness has most commonly been followed by gradual assimilation and ultimately a celebration of cultural diversity. But despite decades of experience with immigration, strikingly common fears have reemerged as new groups arrive. What is constant is the inconsistency of ideals and acceptance deeply rooted in American history.

Immigration as Historical Myth and Current Reality

Related to inconsistency in dealing with immigration is the role of myth in guiding policy decisions. Many of the inconsistencies just discussed can be fairly easily explained as action and reaction, as policies proved unworkable and had to be revised. In that context, it is remarkable that even as contradictory policies were being tested a mythical history was being developed. In it, huddled masses emigrated to find a home free of persecution; the immigrant poor pursued opportunities unthinkable in their lands of origin; vast new lands with few limits facilitated new lives. America as a land of opportunity and the fulfillment of dreams became an image as pervasive as royalty in Britain and musical genius in Germany.

The immigration myth is in fact a collection of partial historical truths. Americans recall the real struggles of their ancestors as heroic preludes to their own success, when the actual circumstances under which the forerunners lived were likely those of hardship and marginalization. Those who extoll the pride of ethnic communities often neglect to mention the violence that made living in them horrendous for previous generations. For every immigrant who recalled an environment of supportive neighbors, teachers, and employers, thousands of others carried painful memories of stigmatization and hostility. As Elisabeth Hull has noted, "Americans traditionally have greeted newcomers with half-open arms. Periods of fulsome generosity have alternated with ones of xenophobia and intolerance" (1983, p. 215). In the electoral arena, the appeal of terms such as the "big tent" (under which distinct ethnic, socioeconomic, and racial groups unite to promote common interests) has dimmed repeatedly when confronted by the reality of competing interests and political conflict. Successful pluralism exists when groups interact on a level playing field to argue their positions and craft compromises with others; most immigrants have seen that field as distinctly un-level, producing outcomes that favor groups other than their own.

A consideration of myth and reality in immigration needs to be part of the discussion of the U.S. case because the moniker "Nation of Immigrants" is so central to the nation's sense of self. American political tradition claims much more than simple acceptance of diversity in its continuous celebration of cultural difference. None of the other countries included here has had either a history of or a notable commitment to immigration as part of its national image. Truly multicultural societies are rare, making their study critical to understanding the vast challenges that immigration presents.

US hypocracy

However varied circumstances were in the 200 years that followed American independence, the period since the early 1970s has been distinctly more challenging. The most obvious reason is the breakdown in border control, most prominently that with Mexico but also the larger system, which has allowed millions to enter but lacked the ability to ensure their departure. Some of the breakdown was due to an unrealistic quota in the 1965 law. That provided only 120,000 slots annually for the entire Western Hemisphere at a time when Mexico was experiencing major worker dislocation and Central American poverty and violence were on the rise. By the mid-1990s the number of illegal entrants from those countries rose from 500,000 to 1 million annually, prompting partial construction of the controversial border fence. In addition, undocumented immigrants moved into states with little exposure to foreigners but growing labor needs in agriculture, food processing, and construction. No other nation experienced such volume, even if the percentages were lower when measured against the larger base population in the United States. In 2005, an estimated 1.3 million entered, more by far than legal immigrants to Spain (569,000), Italy (225,000), Canada (208,000), Germany (200,000), or the United Kingdom (190,000). The overall immigrant population doubled between 1990 and 2013—from 23 million to more than 46 million, a large demographic change even for a nation of 280 million inhabitants.

Modern challenges

Employment patterns among legal immigrants changed as well. In 14 of the 25 largest metropolitan areas, between 51% and 80% of new legal immigrants held white-collar jobs; women outnumbered men in jobs in the health and childcare industries, local restaurants, and shops; fewer found work in agriculture. Immigrants also moved into smaller cities, often revitalizing urban ghettos and expanding both occupations and local development.

in employment status

Accompanying the larger numbers of immigrants has been a resurgent concern that recent immigrants will not assimilate as earlier generations did. Such views appear in obvious places—communities with large concentrations of new immigrants, right-wing partisan forums, conservative publications—but also in the writings of respected observers. In a provocative 2004 treatise, one argued that unlike earlier immigrants from non-English-speaking nations, Mexicans were particularly poor candidates for assimilation and hence poor choices for admission. He attributed that anomaly to a culture of willful difference, in which families insist on maintaining an ethnic identity with no commitment to the common language or core American values of pride and undivided loyalty (Huntington, 2004). Those sentiments have been echoed by resentful citizens and championed by political leaders claiming to discern a growing threat to the traditional, white, American majority.

Most scholars disagree with such pessimistic conclusions, pointing out the striking similarity between current critiques of Mexicans and arguments aimed at virtually every group that has migrated to the United States. Their analyses project Mexicans as following the patterns of yesterday's Irish, Germans, Chinese, or Cubans—all seen as deliberately separatist until their children and grandchildren moved into the economic and social life of the mainstream. German immigrants were outspoken in their insistence on German language instruction in the nineteenth century; Asians were loath to intermarry well into the postwar years; yet both groups have assumed the values and social profiles of American citizens. Cultural festivals once seen as defiant in emphasizing their differences are commonly orchestrated by second- or third-generation ethnics who speak only English but celebrate the traditions of their parents and grandparents. Few differences that are genuinely separatist survive among ethnics who have known only American norms.

Huntington and others also assumed the existence of a clear and unchanging American culture, which could be used as the metric of assimilation of new immigrants. Beyond respect for political processes and a commitment to democratic values, an American "core identity" would be hard to define, especially within the context of a well-established American pluralism. One historian argues that assimilation itself has not been fully appreciated, if one understands it as "not simply a process of the immigrants becoming Americans, but ultimately of mutual accommodation, in which society changes alongside the changing individuals and groups that compose it" (Gerber, 2011, p. 108).

For our purposes, the question is, How does history frame the current debate? First, American immigration history conditions current options precisely because it has been so integral to national definition. If immigration made the United States what it is, it almost certainly must be at least part of its future. Despite its tensions, immigration in American has been a force for innovation, an impetus for urban regeneration, a source of cultural variety and strength. Continuation seems inevitable, even if a changing society demands revisions, certainly a reasonable expectation in today's climate.

Second, multiculturalism is a demographic reality in the United States due to the country's history and evolution as a nation committed to acceptance of geographic and ethnic diversity of admission. That evolution created a population of diverse groups now acculturated by generations of residence, and those groups reflect the success of standards that value family and talent. The option of returning to some state of ethnic homogeneity exists only as fantasy in a society of immigrants whose numbers increase annually.

How Diverse Is the United States Due to Immigration?

The United States has historically been defined as a "nation of immigrants." How central are immigrants to the current and future makeup of the country?

—In 2013, the U.S. population included 316,497,531 people, of which 41,347, 946, or 13.06%, were foreign-born. Between 1965 and 2014, the U.S. population increased by 72 million more people than would have been the case without growth due to increases in immigrants and immigrant births.

—By 2015, that percentage had grown to 14%; by 2065 it will reach 18%, making foreign-born and their descendants the main driver of population growth since 1965.

—Although the American heritage was distinctly European, the largest sources of immigrants in 2014 were Mexico, India, the Philippines, China, El Salvador, Vietnam, Cuba, Guatemala, the Dominican Republic, and Korea—but they accounted for only 55% of the total. In fact, more Mexicans left the U.S. than entered in 2015, reversing a 40-year pattern of increases.

—By 2056, there will be no ethnic majority in the U.S.

—In 2014, the U.S. remained the largest source of refugee resettlement. The largest numbers of refugees were from Africa, Asia, and the Middle East.

Finally, the United States cannot escape the perception and reality of capacity rare in the world of advanced nations. Two hundred years of immigration to open territories and experiences with unanticipated newcomers have demonstrated an enviable ability to absorb outsiders. What makes current discussions about legal and illegal immigrants especially difficult is the fact that Americans have historically resisted monitoring any residents. Borders have always been porous and mechanisms to track foreigners minimal or nonexistent, yet those who have entered have historically become part of the fabric of society. If history defines a nation's comfort level with immigration, the American version has established a foundation for seeing immigrants in ongoing and important roles. As this component of our framework aids understanding national options, it dictates recognition that immigration has consistently strengthened its economy and enriched its culture—even if its population has just as consistently been an initially grudging audience.

Economic Factors in American Immigration

In the often heated debates about immigration policies, recent or projected increases in admissions are commonly linked to grim economic forecasts. Communities fear unemployable hordes; workers worry about keeping their jobs; public agencies project hopeless outlooks for schools and health facilities. Casting immigrants as costly to those who admit them is hardly new, but continues to require examination of economic issues over time and circumstance in both the United States and Europe.

Basic Economic Drivers of Immigration

During its long history of immigration, the United States has experienced all of the forces defined in classic "push-pull" theories of population movement. In the "push" category are circumstances that have driven mostly desperate people to leave their homelands for uncertain futures. Famines in Europe motivated millions in the mid-nineteenth century; insufficient arable land forced farmers to choose between working in overcrowded cities and hoping to find unclaimed land in the United States. Aiding in the decision to leave was the reality that workers would outnumber jobs in Europe, creating a surplus of labor with no safety net. In the first half of the twentieth century, fascist regimes and two devastating wars created surges of dislocated Europeans who would seek resettlement in any safe environment. Well-educated young people in Asia and Africa facing bleak job prospects moved to pursue opportunities abroad, particularly in the United States, and the specter of poverty and violence drove many to attempt long and dangerous journeys for a chance at a better life. Economically or socially disrupted lives defined literally millions of immigrants.

"Pull" factors were also at work. America represented both an idealized and a concrete future. Many migrated with only a generalized idea of opportunity—new lives, fortunes, space—all of which assumed the availability of work. American business and government actively promoted opportunities, many tied to vast, underpopulated areas in the Midwest and West. Word of huge lodes of gold in unexplored mountain ranges lured thousands of Chinese, as well as American frontiersmen. Railroad developers recruited them as construction workers, who braved bad weather and dangerous terrain to complete the first transcontinental railway line in 1869. Between 1852 and 1880, the Chinese population in the United States increased from 20,000 to more than 300,000, and American industrial growth in the late 1800s and early 1900s promised still more jobs consistent with a vision of unlimited opportunity. Powerful political machines in Eastern cities encouraged new immigrants to bring family and relatives, creating both immediate and future workforces with heavy concentrations of the foreign born and their descendants. A half-century and a severe Depression later, World War II opened up new possibilities in factories, construction, and infrastructure projects. Despite periodic slowdowns, labor shortages in a large range of industries have attracted workers from a growing number of countries. As recently as the end of the 2008 recession, the need for workers in fields such as agriculture, technology, and health care outpaced the supply of available nationals.

As noted earlier, full integration into the economy was not always smooth. Immigrants in surge periods accepted work with long hours, dangerous conditions, and no job security, and vulnerable workers were frequently mistreated by employers. Child labor limited opportunities for schooling until a law banning the practice was adopted in 1938 (The Fair Labor Standards Act). Overall, the economic prosperity of the 1880–1910 period was made possible by immigrants whose rewards would be the greater opportunities available to their descendants.

Some of that pattern has continued to define the economic lives of immigrants. Although the percentage of legal immigrants recruited for higher-level jobs has risen, large numbers entering with few skills have had to follow the earlier path, starting in jobs with minimum wages, few benefits, and little mobility. The poorest of them cluster in occupational sectors that fail to attract Americans even in distressed economic times. When Alabama and Georgia enforced background checks and deportation penalties in 2011, thousands of agricultural workers left for states with more forgiving systems of enforcement. Despite widespread unemployment, farmers could not retain local labor, bringing dire estimates of lost agricultural and tax revenues from the more than 120,000 undocumented workers. One study by the University of Alabama's Center for Business and Economic Research estimated the costs of losing 40–80,000 immigrants as 70–140,000 jobs, $1.2–5.8 billion in lost earnings, and $57–264 billion in lost income and tax revenues (Addy, 2012). By the summer of 2013, word that the laws were no longer being enforced brought undocumented workers back and normal agricultural cycles were restored. In Ohio, economists found that a widely dispersed undocumented population of 25,000 workers continued to fill essential positions in local industries, generating an estimated $1.8 billion in economic output and even more in consumer spending (Gerber, 2011). What is notable is the persistent role played by the demand for labor in attracting immigrants willing to accept work in poorly paid and onerous jobs. The axiom that new labor gravitates to areas of demand consistently trumps laws that aim to limit the supply of workers.

demand trumps aim to limit immigration

Finally, one important corollary to immigrant work in the United States and elsewhere has been the expansion of revenue to homelands in the form of remittances. Direct aid worldwide reached a remarkable high of $500 billion in 2012, with 25% ($123 billion) of that sent from immigrants in the United States. Remittances to Mexico in 2015 were almost $25 billion, or more than the nation received from oil revenues. The amounts have always been substantial, even crucial, to home economies. The figures also bolster the claim that rather than being economic liabilities, immigrants direct sizeable shares of their income to both their former and their adopted homes.

Economic forces encouraging migration have coexisted with the tensions that accompany arrival in a new land to encourage the decline in friction as immigrants ease into an absorbent economy. That process has lent support to a general equation in which economic growth is a function of both population increases and increased production and services to accommodate the needs of more people. Historically, population growth in the United States has depended on both native births and new immigrants, and the economy has generally grown—through good times and bad—by adjusting supply and demand in both labor and production. Even with dramatic shifts in major industries, few economists suggest that capacity has been reached.

policy idea: adjust push-pull demographics

The Role of Immigrants in the Economic Structure

Immigrants have played key roles in facilitating economic growth, most basically by adding labor to the workforce where it was needed and becoming active taxpayers and consumers. Labor shortages appeared when mobile younger populations created vacancies in industry or agriculture, but they also emerged in growth professions such as technology and health care. As long as immigrants accepted whatever work was available, they filled voids in an economy whose health thrived with their presence.

The key term here is *economic health,* with its basic assumption of balance between demand and supply of both labor and consumers. A healthy economy adapts to changes arising as methods of production improve, popular preferences shift, or new products are developed. New industries arise, production is refined, and popular demand creates jobs that did not exist in previous years. In the United States, automation and competition have reduced the need for some workers (assembly line positions) but created jobs in new industries, including a larger financial management sector, and greater demand from increased numbers of two-income families for goods and services. In some instances, the pattern is defined by true technological development and associated job shifts; in others, it derives from an evolving social structure in which working or single parents need more care facilities, household help, or local services; in still others, it is simply more people requiring more goods, more schools, more services. As long as the economy supports such change, immigrant labor is in demand.

Immigrants—both legal and unauthorized—continue to play crucial roles in specific sectors of the economy. The example of Alabama farmers unable to recruit workers is instructive for the larger phenomenon it illustrates. Of roughly one million farm workers in the United States, a majority are foreign-born, with as many as 60% unauthorized. The breakdown is similar in other industries, including meat packing, home care and domestic services, construction, and warehousing, all of which have experienced difficulties in attracting sufficient numbers of native-born workers. Where factories are still operating, large percentages of the workforce are foreign-born. At the other end of the skills spectrum, immigrants have steadily increased their presence in high tech industries and health care. The U.S. Chamber of Commerce, usually a stalwart supporter of conservative policies, has consistently argued that immigration is crucial to the survival of American business and agriculture simply because it provides workers when shortages appear.

In the United States, immigration has consistently been linked to labor needs. The Great Depression, less severe recessions in 1980 and 2008, and World Wars I and II reduced jobs and the flow of immigrants declined. The number of border crossers dropped significantly and the number of immigrants returning to Mexico increased during the 2008–2012 recession. For those without documents, unemployment is especially punitive, as they are ineligible for government assistance and afraid to seek help from other organizations—situations approximating a self-regulating marketplace. The presence of millions of undocumented workers in even a depressed economy lends credence to the claim that they continue to meet market needs.

The Appeal of Temporary Immigration

A purely economic model of labor demand and supply would include "flexible labor," or workers available when demand is high but expendable when it falls. That model has been the basis for seasonal work permits adopted by other nations in the postwar boom years. It was also the rationale for the American Bracero program created specifically to allow Mexican workers to harvest crops in California. The program was extended to workers in railroad maintenance (only through 1945), adding thousands to the initial quotas, and at its peak in 1956 it covered 445,000 temporary workers. Despite the large number of workers admitted legally, thousands of others entered without documents, inspiring the Eisenhower administration to carry out massive raids in agricultural and industrial sites and deport more than 100,000 Mexicans in the mid-1950s under the unfortunate codename of "Operation Wetback" (a program praised by presidential candidate Donald Trump in 2016.) Tension between the two governments over the deportations, wages, and treatment of workers ended the Bracero program officially in 1962, even as thousands remained without documents and even more followed.

Temporary visas for unskilled and skilled workers to fill labor force gaps have had an uneven history. The current program (the H-2B visa category) imposes extensive restrictions, and recruitment is typically outsourced to private subcontractors with an unsettling record of citations for exploitation of participants (fees averaging $2,000–$2,500, crowded housing, deductions for services, and paychecks rejected by banks). Evaluations of such operations have often concluded that they are largely agents of "subcontractor servitude" (Gordon, 2013), but others support the many legitimate firms that work in sectors dependent on temporary workers (*New York Times*, March 30, 2014). One pattern is undisputed: temporary worker programs in both Germany and the United States have been singularly unsuccessful in ensuring the return of workers to their homelands, suggesting that the programs might better be cast as probationary work permits which most often result in permanent residence for those with steady employment.

The Key Role of Population Maintenance and Growth

Historically, economic expansion in the United States has required population growth. Even in times when the American population increased by national births in successive generations, the power of additional numbers to provide innovation and manpower has been essential to growth. In the years since 1965, a slowing of population growth among nationals has been at least partially offset by increases in the numbers of children born to immigrants. By 2012, however, even with higher birthrates among immigrant women (particularly Hispanic and Asian), the U.S. birth rate overall had experienced a five-year decline of almost 10%. That has raised concerns about the economic stress being placed on smaller numbers of workers as older cohorts retire and become dependent on the tax contributions of younger cohorts. A birth rate of 2.1 children per woman is commonly accepted as necessary to replace current populations, and the U.S. rate been below that figure since 2007. Even with significant economic pressures felt by immigrant groups their birth rate was almost 50% higher than that of their American-born neighbors; of the 4 million children born in 2010, 930,000—or 23%—were born to immigrants representing only 12% of the overall population.

This pattern points to two relevant economic consequences. First, larger percentages of people living in nations with aging populations need to worry about the security of their retirement. Among 21 nations surveyed by the Pew Research Center in 2014, only respondents from countries with high birth rates and the United States had positive outlooks on their future. Second, the fact that the U.S. shares the optimism of nations with higher birth rates suggests either unawareness or denial of the economic consequences of a falling American birthrate. The United States, like its European counterparts, is in a position requiring attention to the roles which immigrants play in the national economy and must devise policies to maintain balance in its labor force.

Lingering Economic Questions

Even as most of those who debate policy acknowledge the economic roles immigrants have played, a vocal opposition argues that current conditions are sufficiently different to make immigrants a drag on a healthy economy. The Federation for American Immigration Reform (FAIR), for example, advocates a reduction in legal admissions to around 300,000 per year, or about 25% of the most recent target. The case can be summarized in three major arguments. The first is that in times of both prosperity and slowdown, immigrants compete with Americans for jobs. In the worst case, they take positions that could be filled by nationals, leaving the latter unemployed and likely dependent on welfare. This argument assumes employment to be a zero-sum phenomenon, or one in which there is a fixed number of jobs and when a job is taken by an immigrant, it is necessarily lost to a native citizen. Labor dynamics, however, do not work that way. In a broad spectrum of jobs (agriculture, service, and others) immigrants and native workers are almost never interchangeable. Immigrants, especially the undocumented, rarely compete for the same jobs as citizens, even in a depressed economy. On the macro level, the American Immigration Council has reaffirmed findings of a 2009 study concluding that there was no correlation between immigration levels and unemployment, across all U.S. counties in all periods before and during the economic recession of 2008–10 (Camarato & Ziegler). More recent is the 2016 report of the American Academies of the Sciences, Engineering, and Medicine, reviewing the work of 14 leading economists and demographers. That report found no overall negative effects of immigration on the employment of nationals, even those with less than a high school education. In response to the related claim that immigrants take jobs from minorities at the lowest levels of employment, the council's report also found no correlation between percentages of immigrants and unemployment levels of African Americans (American Immigration Policy Center). In cities with high concentrations of Latin American immigrants, unemployment among African Americans was actually lower than in cities with smaller immigrant populations. Across all variations in economic climate, most immigrants compete primarily with other immigrants for low-level jobs. Moreover, when a weakened economy reduces employment opportunities, the rate of immigrant return to home nations increases. Despite constant claims that American jobs are being taken by immigrants, almost all studies agree that such competition rarely if ever exists (Chokshi, 2013).

A second argument made by those who believe immigrants pose an economic threat is that immigrants depress wages of American workers by their willingness to work for lower pay. Evidence for this claim is often anecdotal, pointing to lower prices offered by immigrant contractors or lower wages accepted by immigrants in agriculture and the service sectors. To the extent that wages paid to workers in these sectors are frequently not reported—especially if the workers are undocumented—the data are difficult to collect and estimates necessarily suspect. The American Academies 2016 report, however, found no evidence of wage disparities in the most comprehensive review of quantitatively based research. But the real context for this question remains the reality that much of the work in most of the examples is not that sought by nationals. When immigrants compete with other immigrants, any depression is necessarily limited to their wages, not those of nationals.

The low wages paid to immigrants at the bottom of the American economic scale are primarily a function of the daunting educational deficit most recent immigrants bring with them. In 2008, the average income of legal Mexican immigrants was $22,300, less than half the average of native-born workers and $15,000 lower than the average of all immigrants. It is true that the Mexican subset represents competition for unskilled Americans with similar skill sets, and also true that higher concentrations in the Southwest might put pressure on competition for lower-level jobs there. But since Mexicans at all levels of education comprise only 4% of the U.S. workforce, it would be difficult to label them a threat to the workforce generally. At the same time, the importance of education in determining income is well known, and it affects all groups regardless of ethnicity or citizenship status. College graduates still earn almost three times as much as high school dropouts and more than twice as much as those with only a high school diploma. In addition, other factors—the decline of unions and a stagnant minimum wage, to name just two—would have to be included in any discussion of why wages are so much lower for unskilled labor, but the presence of immigrants would at best be a rare correlate.

Residents in communities experiencing increases in immigrants are likely to fear economic consequences, especially as they involve employment capacity. A true experimental test of this threat was provided by the unanticipated surge that occurred in 1980 in southern Florida, when more than 125,000 Cubans were allowed to leave Cuba and arrived in Florida as refugees. The so-called *Marielitos* (from their point of origin in Cuba) joined an established Cuban community, adding about 7% to the workforce there from one day to the next. Several studies followed the newcomers' work experience and compared the Miami data to similar cities that had experienced no comparable influx of migrants (Tampa, Atlanta, Houston, and Los Angeles). They found that unemployment increased for the first two years in both Miami and the other cities. By 1985, however, unemployment declined for the *Marielitos* in Miami, and also fell below 1979 levels among African Americans (Card, 1990). Like experiences in American cities through-out the nineteenth and twentieth centuries, this surge of immigrants gradually found or created work, frequently adding new business (shops, restaurants, services), with no notable depressing effect on local wages.

The third argument raised by immigration opponents is that newcomers strain allocations for unemployment insurance and local resources—especially schools and health care services. The first point is quickly dealt with by a historical review of unem-ployment patterns. Immigrants have frequently had higher unemployment rates than the American-born, but differences have been neither consistent nor large. Between 2007 and 2014, the period of the most recent recession the rate was virtually identical for both groups, and by 2014 it was lower for immigrants. But the more important question asks what happens to immigrants and their children after their entry into the U.S. as they search for work, places to live, and schools. That question has been extensively studied by demographers at the Pew Research Center, whose full report is detailed in *Second Generation Americans: A Portrait of the Adult Children of Immigrants* (2013). The study revealed that the 20 million U.S.-born adult children of immigrants are economically much more secure than their parents on all measures of achievement—higher incomes, college degrees, home ownership (Figure 2.2), making their economic status remark-ably similar to the American population as a whole. Contrary to charges that current immigrants are taking a larger share of the nation's jobs than in previous periods of influx, the Pew Center's analysis indicated that the first and second generations' share of the overall population in 2010 was actually lower than in 1900. The U.S. Census projects the Hispanic share to rise to 28% in 2050 (Figure 2.3, page 46), largely due to the higher birth rate among immigrants. The issue of cost to communities is thus generally a transient one, as people move in, struggle initially, but watch their children achieve incomes that resemble those of their neighbors. The issue of costs to communi-ties, even if it is not permanent, is still real as it entails local expenditures not funded by federal revenues, and raises a legitimate question of economic capacity. As immigrants find jobs in new settings, the more central question is whether those costs outweigh the contributions they make as taxpayers and consumers.

Some of those contributions (diversifying the retail sector, revitalizing inner city neighborhoods, creating attractions for locals and visitors) as well as some of the costs (additions to school classes, wear and tear on local infrastructure or services) are hard to quantify, inviting competing assessments of the net costs or gains. But some costs

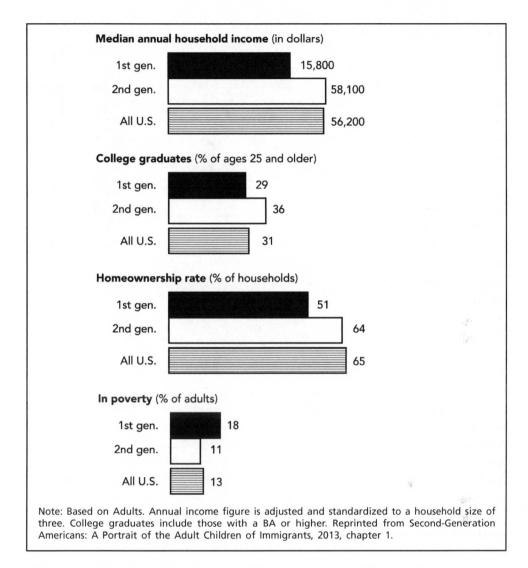

Note: Based on Adults. Annual income figure is adjusted and standardized to a household size of three. College graduates include those with a BA or higher. Reprinted from Second-Generation Americans: A Portrait of the Adult Children of Immigrants, 2013, chapter 1.

Figure 2.2. Comparing Immigrants, the Second Generation, and All U.S. Adults. (*Source:* Pew Research Center, Current Population Survey, Integrated Microdata)

are more easily assessed, especially as they differ from those exhibited by earlier groups. Compared to the majority of immigrants entering during the period of industrial expansion in the 1880–1920 or post-1945 periods, for example, new immigrants today are more likely to bring their families with them or start them in their early years in the United States. They are thus more likely to make use of public services, particularly public schools, where the increase in new students may require additional staff. Immigrants and their children also add drivers to streets and passengers to buses; they need security

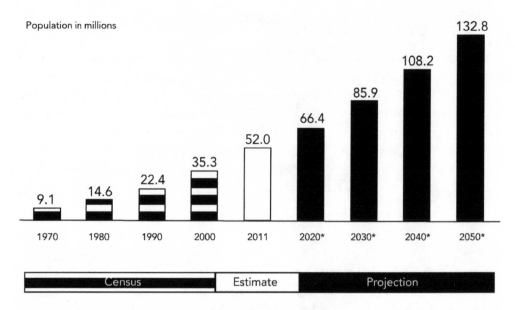

Figure 2.3. Hispanic Percentage of U.S. Population, 1980–2050. (*Source:* U.S. Census Bureau, 1980–2010 Decennial Censuses, July 2013; Population Estimates, 2012 National Population Projections)

provided by local law enforcement, all of which may require higher budget allocations. At the same time, they make less use of health services—sometimes because there are limits on the benefits they may claim—and there is no evidence that their numbers are linked to higher rates of crime. In fact, their rate of criminal acts is actually lower than that of the native-born.

The real costs of accommodation associated with schools, libraries, and public services need to be measured in relation to the economic benefits of taxes paid, money spent locally, and productivity raised by a steady labor force. If, as the Pew Report suggests, children of immigrants are as or more motivated than nationals, they contribute to greater economic growth. The American Academies 2016 report found that although first-generation immigrants cost states and localities up to $57 billion in annual expenditures, the second generation actually generates $30 billion in taxes and pending, and by the third generation the positive contribution exceeds $223 billion. Precise estimates of the monetary value of a thriving subset are difficult to make, but most economists agree with the Academies report and argue that immigrants are a positive—and necessary—force for prosperity in the United States. As Giovanni Peri wrote in his conclusion to a report of the Federal Reserve Bank of San Francisco, "Immigrants expand the U.S. economy's productive capacity, stimulate investment, and promote specialization that in the long run boosts productivity. There is no evidence that these efforts take place at the expense of jobs for workers born in the United States" (2010).

Political Climates and Alignments in Deciding Immigration Issues

Immigration questions are raised, debated, and ultimately resolved within the contexts of all levels of American politics. At the front end, numbers and rules of admission are defined by acts of Congress and implemented by the executive branch, primarily the Immigration and Naturalization Service (INS). State and local governments are expected to ensure equal treatment, often with federal program assistance, improvising as local situations require. All political leaders take cues from the public and organized groups as they call attention to real and perceived problems, but also channel requests, from businesses and ethnic groups, to support further immigration.

The Setting: Social and Cultural Elements in the Political Debate

Our overview of the American immigrant experience has exposed recurring patterns based in how foreigners arrived, settled, and were viewed by their often reluctant hosts. From the outset, suspicion and discrimination were widespread. Ben Franklin characterized German immigrants as "the most ignorant stupid sort of their own nation," unable to understand liberty and unwilling to learn English (Gerber, 2011, p. 17); newspapers routinely parodied the Irish, Germans, Italians, and whoever succeeded them. Ethnic identity was a ready source of conflict, encouraging groups to stake out neighborhoods, which came to define the cultures of cities across the nation.

Arguments that the social climate changed with the passage of the 1965 Immigration and Nationality Act are rooted in the belief that assimilation has stalled with the influx of Asians, Africans, and Hispanics from Mexico and Central America. Some of those were in fact different; they were unskilled or lower-skilled nonwhites, from areas which had sent few immigrants historically. Large numbers of them lacked proper documents and tended to clusters in the shadows of urban ghettos and day-labor jobs. Those characteristics led many to fear that new immigrants would not fit into the American culture.

Most studies, however, indicate that immigrants arriving after 1965 followed the pattern of their predecessors, even if at a slower rate of assimilation. A major study of Cuban and Mexican immigrants in the 1970s documented the use of ethnic enclaves as bases from which immigrants gradually moved into the broader circles of American life, especially in the second generation (Portes & Bach, 1985). More recent research by the Pew Hispanic Center reported that second-generation Hispanics and Asians are twice as likely to think of themselves as a "typical American," are more educated, earn almost 30% more, and are less likely to live at the poverty level than the first generation (Table 2.2, page 48). They are also less likely to have engaged in criminal activity than other immigrant groups or the general population. While they lag behind other immigrants in some respects, their pattern of eventual assimilation still resembles that of previous groups.

Other evidence indicates adaptation under adverse conditions. Lewiston, an overwhelmingly white mill town in Maine, lost thousands of jobs when textile and shoe

Table 2.2. Characteristics of Adults by Immigrant Generation, 2012

	1st	2nd	3rd	Total
Population (in millions)	37.4	19.71	177.7	234.7
Share of Population	16	8	76	100
White Share of Generation	20	46	78	66
Black Share of Generation	8	4	13	11
Hispanic Shared of Generation	47	35	6	15
Asian Share of Generation	25	12	0.5	5
Median Age (in years)	43	38	47	46
Married	63	42	53	54
Fertility (Women ages 15–44)				
Gave birth in the past 12 mos.	9	6	6	7
Of these, % unmarried	23	41	40	36
Educational Attainment (ages 25+)				
Less than high school	28	10	9	12
BA or more	29	36	31	31
Average household size (persons)	3.1	2.4	2.4	2.5
Home ownership p	51	64	68	65
Persons in poverty (%)	18	11	12	13
Median household income	48,800	58,100	60,600	58,200

Source: Pew Research Center, Analysis of Current Population Surveys, Integrated Public Use Microdata Series; Fertility data from 2004–10 and all other data from 2012, Center for Political Studies. *Second-Generation Americans: A Portrait of the Adult Children of Immigrants,* 2013, Chapter 1.

factories closed in the 1960s. Despite attempts to recast the mills in urban renewal projects, high levels of unemployment prevailed in 2001, when a group of 1100 Somali refugees relocated there. The contrast of cultures could hardly have been greater. The Somalis came from a rural society with poor housing, few schools, primitive health care, and a stubborn civil war, which motivated one group (the Bantu) to flee. Their initial experience was harsh, in a lackluster economy where locals saw them as permanent dependents. In time, however, the state opened a language center, and the Somalis settled into unwanted housing near the mills and built small businesses, which sparked a modest inner city revival. In 2004 *Newsweek* named Lewiston a "place to do business," and a *New Yorker* article described the success of the Somali relocation in "New in Town" (December 2006).

There is no doubt that post-1965 experiences have varied. But the argument that contemporary immigration reflects a negative sea change is an exaggeration, with one important exception—that the numbers of illegal entries has mushroomed to levels unprecedented in the United States. The Department of Homeland Security reported that the recession beginning in 2008 saw a drop in the undocumented population between 2007 and 2012, followed by a small uptick in 2011. By 2016, the total number of undocumented immigrants was an estimated 10.9 million, almost 10% fewer than the 12 million reported in 2006. Still, the volume of illegal entry from Central America is sufficiently new and serious to focus most attention on border issues rather than economics.

It is hardly surprising that so much of the focus of the American immigration debate is on Mexico. A border too long to monitor easily, a large area in the contiguous United States whose population shares Mexican roots, and the obvious disparity in wealth between the two nations have created an environment that, for decades, has encouraged Mexicans to attempt illegal entry and more recently prompted Central Americans to do the same. The Pew Research Center reported that by 2014, Hispanics represented 48% of the state residents in New Mexico, 39% in California and Texas, and 31% in Arizona. Most Mexican immigrants enter the United States for economic reasons, and they consistently seek to bring family after finding work. Beginning in 2008, however, recession, stricter employment controls, and a more heavily fortified border has sharply reduced the Mexican share of undocumented entries. As importantly, growth in Mexico's economy has shifted the immigration flow, so that Mexico is becoming more a destination than a departure point for immigrants. In September 2016, *New York Times* economic reporter Eduardo Porter cited studies showing that Mexicans were no longer coming north in large numbers, and the Pew Research Center confirmed a steady decline in the number of Mexicans entering illegally. One consequence has been that those immigrants who have remained in the United States have lived longer as American residents; by 2014, 66% of undocumented Mexican immigrants had lived in the United States for more than a decade (compared to 41% in 2005). As transportation and labor costs in Asia have increased, Mexico has become more attractive to industry and manufacturing companies in other countries seeking outsourcing and relocation, and growth in those sectors was higher than that of the United States, Canada, or Brazil in 2010–12. While ineffective government and the continuing threat presented by violent cartels still motivate people to migrate north, a reduction in the numbers of illegal immigrants from Mexico, and an increase in the number of Mexicans leaving the United States rather than entering are clear evidence of a shift away from problems still cited by candidates in 2016.

Partisan Bases of Division on Policy

As noted earlier, decades passed in American history without major attention to immigration. Congress paid scant heed to issues beyond citizenship rules, before passing selective exclusionary legislation and voicing general preferences for Europeans—already the predominant group. Only one party dedicated to restricting the admission of immigrants was actually formed, in 1852. Deriving much of its support from the aptly named "Know Nothing" organizations in the East, the American Party campaigned exclusively on a nativist platform written by respected men more concerned with educating foreigners than opposing immigration per se. Its ally (the Know Nothing Party) had some early success in Philadelphia and Massachusetts, but was largely ignored by 1856. Neither party was able to attract support in the environment dominated by the Civil War, and both organizations effectively disappeared from the national stage by 1870.

Until 1965, immigration was discussed as it affected other issues, most commonly those associated with business expansion. In this context, immigrants were nonpartisan subjects, and Republican as well as Democratic machines profited by capturing their loyalty. New Deal Democrats had successfully built a national coalition around working-class voters, including large numbers of immigrants; after 1945, both parties vied for their support in areas with significant concentrations, correctly valuing them as fuel for both business growth and electoral power.

Congress did set quotas in the early twentieth century, but for decades national attention was distracted by two world wars, the Great Depression, and, after 1945, the need to provide enough workers to sustain the high levels of industrial production generated by the wartime economy. Finally, in 1965, comprehensive reform legislation was passed in Congress with overwhelming support from both parties (the House approved it 320–70, the Senate by 76–18), even as the majority of public opinion opposed increasing the diversity of future citizens, a concern hardly noted in congressional debates. Key party leaders on both sides of the congressional aisle (Democrats Senator Ted Kennedy and Congressman Emmanuel Celler, Republican senators Hiram Fong and Alan Simpson) spoke out to reassure doubters that the bill would not significantly change the mix of immigrants or result in a deluge of poor immigrants into American cities. The bill was supported by President Lyndon Johnson, who also promised that the law would not affect the lives of millions of Americans. Given the magnitude of changes embraced by the law, it is remarkable that the bill passed so easily.

The other major post-1945 legislation was also passed by a bipartisan coalition, responding to appeals from Republican president Ronald Reagan. Initiated in reaction to increases in illegal entry between 1965 and 1980, the legislative process took five years, from 1982 until 1986, to complete. Disagreement over terms of legalizing the status of the undocumented was intense, but the final bill authorized both an amnesty program with paths to citizenship and sanctions on employers who knowingly hired undocumented workers. The law incorporated protections for Hispanic workers and assured business owners that background checks would not be costly. The ultimate bill passed with solid majorities in both houses of Congress, and thus, within a 20-year span, both parties had agreed to the most comprehensive immigration legislation in history.

New issues did emerge in the 1982–1986 congressional debates as a growing Hispanic presence began to be felt in districts where changing demographics could affect upcoming elections. Democrats invoked their historic commitment to the working class, which immigrants most often joined, even as organized labor was wary of new workers; Republicans attempted to reconcile their concern that illegals might get a free pass with the party's historic support for looser regulation on businesses wanting to hire them. Both parties were torn, as neither could construct a clear basis for its position. The conflict thus evolved into its current version, wherein a majority of Democrats disagree with a majority of Republicans despite inconsistencies within both camps. The greater opposition in the 1986 vote (compared to that in 1965) anticipated the emergence of this issue as one more likely to be defined by overriding partisan, if not ideological, differences, which would come to paralyze attempts at immigration reform in the years to follow.

Legislators seeking to revisit the issue after the turn of the twenty-first century encountered an arena changed by passions rooted less in ideology than in the recognition that the United States had neither effective border controls nor systems to monitor those who entered legally on temporary visas. Both parties knew that immigration controls were not working but allowed themselves to be drawn into the immigration drama, downplaying areas of agreement to portray each other as either soft on lawbreakers or lacking any compassion for those who sought only better lives for their families. Prominent analyst Wayne Cornelius has highlighted how misplaced the focus on borders has been, arguing that almost no level of expenditure on enforcement efforts would be cost efficient, while the issue's partisans would rather keep the debate "mired in implausible possibilities" (*New York Times*, September 20, 2016). Thus, the reforms proposed by President George W. Bush in 2007 died from an inability to agree on how to deal with those already in the country. The battle lines were not those that had defined the parties since the New Deal: fervent Republicans took stands inimical to their traditional friends in business, insisting that workers without documents be deported, while liberal Democrats opposed the plan as being too harsh on immigrants. Ultimately, the Republicans rejected their president's bill. Although sentiment in both houses of Congress conveyed the appearance of a Left-Right conflict, in the debate that distinction was blurred by both regional complexities and the subtexts of parties seeking support from affected ethnic groups.

Inspired (or embarrassed) by attempts by states to create their own immigration policies, the Senate resurrected the effort to address the issue in 2012. A group of eight senators with seniority and experience with immigration issues crafted a comprehensive bill that included enough of each party's positions to attract support in the full body. The bill did not satisfy those on either end of the political spectrum, although opposition was strongest from conservative Republicans, especially those defining themselves as Tea Party Republicans. The debate was contentious, but the bill passed in June 2013 by a 68–32 vote (14 Republicans joined a united Democratic majority). Among the Republican senators defying party leadership to support the bill were two from Arizona, and one each from Florida, South Carolina, and Utah—states with either large numbers of immigrants, recent attempts to pass restrictive laws, or both.

No spirit of bipartisanship emerged in the Republican-controlled House of Representatives. The House leadership refused to consider the Senate bill, preferring to consider separate bills dealing with individual components of the issue. The debate was acrimonious on each such proposal, with conservative Republicans insisting on major new funding for border security and resisting the adoption of paths to citizenship for undocumented immigrants, both of which promised to make any such bill unpalatable to the Senate. With that stalemate, debate ended.

Legislative action was also complicated by positions taken by prominent leaders, past, present, and future. Supporting the Senate bill were former presidents Bill

Clinton and George W. Bush, who was joined by his brother Jeb, the former governor of Florida and 2016 presidential candidate, who had argued arguing for compassionate reform in his provocatively titled *Immigration Wars*, coauthored with Clint Bolick in 2013. The latter Bush's two sons founded Political Action Committees echoing their father's proposals. Republican 2012 presidential nominee Mitt Romney called for conservative actions including "self-deportation" by the undocumented. Republicans have drawn firm lines against legalization and citizenship, making compromise difficult if not impossible. Those aligned with the Tea Party have mounted attacks on immigration liberals, ensuring that elections will continue to be battlegrounds for the issue.

Similar polarization has characterized congressional response to the unprecedented influx of unaccompanied children and mothers with minor children, beginning in 2013 and 2014. Although laws enacted during the Bush administration required that minor children be turned over to the Department of Health and Human Services' Office of Refugee Resettlement for temporary shelter and assistance in locating relatives in the United States until panels could hear their cases, many in Congress called for immediate deportation and rejected requests for additional funds to process applications. Inability to prevent or control the deluge further aroused public sentiment, inspiring both volunteer efforts to aid border crossers and protests against those awaiting hearings. In 2017, thousands of asylum seekers and their families remained in detention centers awaiting hearings, often without legal representation or assistance.

Responding to congressional inaction, in November 2014, President Obama issued a seies of executive orders to curtail deportations and provide temporary protection for large groups of undocumented immigrants. Interestingly, that action, which prompted several state-based lawsuits seeking to overturn the orders as unconstitutional (and put at least a temporary hold on them in 2016 when the eight-member Supreme Court could not reach a majority decision regarding a relevant case), contrasted with the administration's extraordinary push to deport undocumented immigrants. During his two terms in office, more than 2.5 million person were deported by mid-2016, earning Obama the nickname of "Deporter-in-Chief," reflecting decisions made in the absence of any action by Congress. The Speaker of the House of Representatives actually vowed to take no action before 2017, when Obama's tenure as president would end. Disputed presidential actions and court cases constituted the only official responses to a crisis acknowledged by all. The debates on immigration appeared mostly as drama without end, hinting at a fundamental breakdown in the federal policymaking system far more serious than simply disagreements over any one issue.

Parties and Governments Responding: State Immigration Laws

One explanation for congressional inaction is, as earlier, that immigration issues are complicated by intraparty disagreement at a level that reflects basic philosophical differences. While liberals favor a welcoming orientation to immigrants, they are reluctant to strain the tolerance of their working-class constituents. In border states, even immigrant-friendly partisans appreciate the concerns of locals. Similarly, the most ardent conservatives oppose what they see as the dilution of American culture, even as their business leaders argue the need for more foreign labor in the workforce. As a result, neither party has been willing or able to craft a bill with majority support, leaving the 1965 Act as the most recent comprehensive legislation.

In this environment of gridlock, states continue to deal with immigration issues directly. Since mid-2012, 43 states and the District of Columbia have enacted 146 *DACA* laws and passed 231 resolutions, most of them designed to restrict immigrant activities or rights. In early 2017, many states were refusing to participate in the Refugee Resettlement Program, by which federal funds are distributed to nonprofit organizations that assist refugees in adapting to their new homes. Many states have challenged presidential decisions such as the Deferred Action on Children Arrivals, which granted temporary reprieves to undocumented immigrants brought into the United States as children. Most states have allowed them to get driver's licenses, attend public universities, and receive public services; fourteen have granted them access to in-state tuition; and several have created official identification documents. But others have reacted by reaffirming restrictions, denying scholarships even to those covered by the DACA declaration, and refusing to process driver's license applications. In June 2016, the Supreme Court announced a 4–4 vote in a case challenging President Obama's directive (Deferred Action on Childhood Arrivals) protecting as many as five million undocumented immigrants from deportation. The tie vote effectively let stand a lower court decision to halt the Obama plan, putting off clarity in the fate of almost half of all undocumented immigrants to a time when a new Supreme Court justice is confirmed and the issue reaches the Court for decision. Such legislation followed the initiative of the Arizona legislature, whose laws, noted in chapter 1, mandated aggressive actions to identify and prosecute those without documents. Other states (Alabama, Georgia, Indiana, South Carolina, and Utah) have adopted similar provisions; still others passed at least some restrictive laws. Federal district courts were consistent in either rejecting laws or delaying their implementation until the Supreme Court had ruled on a challenge to the Arizona law. The June 2012 decision threw out several provisions of the state law that were inconsistent with federal law and only allowed local law enforcement personnel to check the status of those under arrest for other violations. Other states (Missouri, Florida, Mississippi, North Carolina, Tennessee, Kentucky, Michigan, Illinois, Nebraska) continued to consider proposals that would meet the Supreme Court's standard but still stiffen restrictions. Thirty-one states, fearing infiltration of refugee groups by radical Islamic terrorists, challenged the administration's decision to accept 10,000 Syrian refugees, despite State Department assurances that extraordinary vetting procedures are in place. In March 2016, a federal district judge blocked Indiana's attempt to refuse residence to those refugees.

How Extensive are American Vetting Processes for Political Refugees?

Syrians seeking resettlement in the United States must pass through multiple UN and American screening stages, often taking two years to complete. The stages include:

1. Four steps conducted by the U.N.: Registration, Interviews, Granting of refugee status, and Referral for resettlement in the U.S.

2. Seven steps conducted by State Department contractors: Interviews, 3–4 background checks, 3 fingerprint screenings.

3. Three or Four steps conducted by U.S. Homeland Security: 1–2 case reviews, including one by a U.S. Citizenship and Immigration specialist and an optional review by Homeland Security's Fraud Detection Unit, a final in-person interview with a Homeland Security officer.

4. Two compulsory requirements; screening for contagious disease and a cultural orientation class.

5. Match with an American resettlement agency.

6. A final multi-agency security check before leaving for the U.S.

7. One final security check at an American airport.

Not all state action has been restrictive, as indicated by the 39 cities and over 300 counties identified either as sanctuary counties or as setting limits on local cooperation with federal immigration authorities. State laws vary widely, and have often evolved in immigrant-friendly directions. In California, where in 1994 the state struggled to provide education and health care for its large immigrant population, Republican governor Pete Wilson proposed an initiative limiting the access of both unauthorized immigrants and their children to public services. The initiative was approved by voters but quickly overturned as discriminatory by a federal court. Since then, the state has worked to accommodate 3.5 million legal immigrants and almost as many without documents, recognizing both the costs of services and the importance of the workforce they support. The state legislature approved drivers' eligibility for licenses and in-state tuition rates for the undocumented, and in 2013 voted to allow noncitizen legal immigrants to sit on juries and serve as election monitors. It also agreed that undocumented immigrants who had been brought into the country as children and graduated from law school would be allowed to practice law in California. The law in Florida is similar, and in June 2015, an appellate court hearing a New York case ruled that states cannot bar law school graduates from practicing—a decision with broad implications for other restrictive laws.

California's actions reflected not only the dominance of Democrats in state politics but also the reality that the futures of seven million residents could not realistically be ignored. The need to deal with this important bloc has also influenced California's representatives in increasingly diverse districts. In 2015, more than half of California's fifteen Republican congressmen served districts that are more than 30% Latino, and several from the Central Valley have distanced themselves from leadership opposed to legalization. Kevin McCarthy, the party's majority leader in the U.S. Congress, whose district includes a large numbers of Hispanics, has been pressured by both leadership and his delegation, creating the bind which makes consistent voting a practical impossibility for many in both parties.

Continued attempts by state legislatures to pass restrictive laws despite a Supreme Court ruling that immigration is the preserve of the national government illustrate frustration with congressional inaction. But they also highlight that immigration conditions can be locally addressed, by officials who feel compelled to respond to their constituents, and that, therefore, the problems surrounding immigration issues may defy widely accepted federal solutions. State and regional divisions make the task of Congress even more difficult in confronting an issue challenged by both ideology and the dynamics of federalism in a uniquely American system.

Opinion Leaders: Interest Groups and Immigration

Immigration-focused interest groups were largely peripheral until well into the twentieth century. The ill-fated American Party was at base a collection of cultural protectionists seeking to turn immigrants into loyal Americans, who possessed scant ability to influence elections. In 1887, the American Protection Association attracted more than two million members by targeting the increasing numbers of Catholic immigrants, but never created a real political presence. In 1894, an Immigration Restriction League resembling the American Party of academics and reformers was formed but could generate little enthusiasm for a platform based on returning government to the custody of Anglo-Saxon elites.

Anti-immigrant activity was largely local during the surges of the late nineteenth century, making life unpleasant but not impossible for newcomers. In 1911, an official report by the respected Dillingham Commission actually reinforced stereotypical views of immigrants, at first refuting myths of Europe's unloading only its poor and praising the immigrant work ethic, but going on to invoke crude racial and ethnic terms to distinguish among European groups. It also endorsed restrictions that would later be included in the 1921 Emergency Quota Act, but never grew to establish itself as a permanent voice influencing national policy.

Formal groups were not prominent during the interwar period or after 1945, in part because the New Deal coalition united supporters of traditional immigrant groups—humanitarian associations, labor, Catholics, Jews, as well as big-city ethnics. After 1965, however, opposition to new admissions prompted creation of what would become the largest anti-immigration group in the nation's history, the Federation for

American Immigration Reform (FAIR), which was formed in 1979. It described itself as an organization "of citizens who share a common belief that our nation's immigration policies must be reformed to serve the national interest," and called for (1) a reduction in the number of legal immigrants to 300,000 annually, (2) strict border control and an end to illegal immigration, and (3) rejection of amnesty for undocumented immigrants, temporary work programs, and most asylum applications. Currently, the organization claims a membership of 250,000 but is most noted for the reports its two major research arms (the FAIR Congressional Task Force and the Immigration Reform Law Institute) issue on a regular basis. It maintains a lobbying presence in Washington and regularly mounts media campaigns to promote restrictive legislation and oppose liberal candidates for office. Most recently, attorneys associated with FAIR have provided models for state anti-immigrant laws, including the legislation passed in Arizona in 2010. Two similarly inclined groups, Progressives for Immigration Reform and Numbers USA, provided materials and media presentations for use in the 2012 elections.

Pro-immigration groups have also been active. The most prominent are Hispanic organizations headed by the National Council of La Raza. Chapters in states with significant numbers of Hispanics pressure local and national legislators and are often joined by an eclectic cast of like-minded organizations. The AFL-CIO officially supports comprehensive immigration reform, undercutting persistent claims that immigrants take jobs from and depress wages of American workers. The U.S. Conference of Catholic Bishops, a constant supporter of protections for immigrants and their families, highlighted reform proposals for an entire month in 2013. Their sponsorship of local sanctuary organizations—providing assistance to migrants facing deportation—has inspired humanitarian causes but has also suffered from backlash, as when a chronic deportee fatally killed a bystander in California in 2015. Even though that incident contrasted with both a miniscule rate of terrorism-related arrests and an overall low crime rate among immigrants, a major theme of anti-immigrant groups has been the danger immigrants purportedly pose. More recently, online groups with wide-ranging programs have emerged. They include ImmigrationWorks, a national coalition of small and medium-sized businesses, America's Voice, an organization collecting and reporting opinion data to political leaders, and notably FWD.US, founded by Facebook CEO Mark Zuckerberg to create online vehicles to pressure lawmakers. Dozens of coalitions stretch across demographic boundaries to support reform, as in the work of Bibles, Badges, and Business—a group founded by the National Immigration Forum to communicate the combined voice of religious organizations, law enforcement, and businesses to state legislators.

Businesses, including agribusiness, have also weighed in to support proposals facilitating a steady supply of labor. The National Chamber of Commerce supports regularization of the status of undocumented immigrants and admissions tailored to economic needs; industries as varied as construction, meatpacking, and tourism have taken similar stands across states with long-term or recent dependence on foreign labor. An example is found in the agricultural Central Valley area of California where the

Western Growers' Association has lobbied Republicans to support reform and campaigned for sympathetic candidates.

It is worthy of note that many groups are internally divided or take positions inconsistent with public opinion. Most Americans, both supporters and opponents of reforms, agree that border security is essential, but law enforcement officials are not uniformly in favor of the measures proposed. For example, some local forces aggressively pursue suspected illegals; a 2013 Supreme Court decision found that Phoenix, Arizona, law officers led by a popularly elected sheriff had systematically discriminated against Mexican Americans. At the same time, other local police refused to enforce the 2010 Arizona law requiring officers to check the status of people who might be undocumented. Law enforcement agencies across the country are crucially involved with immigrants but have been conspicuously silent in the debate over divisive and vague mandates.

[margin note: want something but disagree on how to achieve]

In addition, these agencies, as well as environmental and humanitarian groups, have serious concerns about further fortification of the 1,100-mile-long southern border. To them, the wall has potentially negative effects on water flows and migratory animals, and symbolizes a barrier more reflective of the Cold War in Eastern Europe than a relationship between two friendly nations. That image has been reinforced by the sheer bulk of American military force along the border, supported by helicopters, drones, and weapons designed to combat armed forces rather than desperate refugees and job seekers. The massive wall proposed by Donald Trump in the 2016 presidential campaign emerged as a polarizing issue, and the plan to forge ahead with the wall continues to raise concerns about its cost, effectiveness, and symbolic message to an important neighbor and trading partner. A bill introduced in the Senate would pose similar concerns as it would stiffen the border by widening the patrolled zone to one hundred miles into Arizona, New Mexico, Texas, and California, necessitating a permanent military presence of thousands of soldiers.

[margin note: concerns about the wall]

Public Opinion

The history reviewed earlier illustrated both a wide range of public opinion and, except in times of crisis, an overall indifference toward immigrants. Given how harsh conditions often were for newcomers, their assimilation was testimony to their perseverance, but also to a public that ultimately accepted them. That environment has almost certainly muted deeply rooted ethnic hostilities of the sort that have plagued other nations, and facilitated the reality of the United States as a nation of immigrants. Clashes between rival ethnic groups have been tragic, but they represent deviations from an overall pattern of group coexistence. Bad treatment of neighbors, in family feuds or small towns shunning new immigrants, has been an embarrassing sign of narrow-mindedness, but has not escalated into the pattern of full-fledged assault that has divided multiethnic societies elsewhere.

Public opinion in earlier periods can be only imperfectly estimated, but it is fair to say that opinion on immigration did not rise to the level of dominating elections for most of American history. Exclusion of Asians in the late nineteenth century and narrow definitions of acceptable immigrants that were applied prior to 1945 were evidence of scapegoating and a general aversion to multiculturalism, which were both ironic to consider in a country in which many people heralded the successes of a nation of immigrants, even while reserving the right to complain about them. That contradiction persists, allowing judgments that simultaneously exhibit tolerance and prejudice, commitments with caveats, generosity with exceptions. But given the joint existence of both restrictive quotas and the ongoing assimilation of newcomers, it is reasonable to assume that American opinions were most likely as lukewarm to immigrants before as they were after polls began to measure them more systematically.

The Gallup Poll, begun in the 1930s to project election outcomes, started collecting trend data in opinions about immigration in 1965, repeating questions about immigration levels, policies, and immigrants themselves. The initial questions asked respondents to define an ideal level of immigration, and the percentage favoring larger numbers of immigrants did not exceed 10% until 2000, with overall opinion predictably guarded about their role. Similar patterns were recorded by Roper polls between 1955 and 2011. Those are consistent with the opposition lawmakers feared might derail the 1965 bill as they pushed it to passage. A similar pattern was found in the 1980s, when amnesty legislation promoted by President Reagan was opposed by congressmen and senators fearing backlash from their constituents.

The resistance that reformers faced in 1965 and 1986 certainly suggested that opponents would eventually succeed in passing restrictive legislation, but the trend data do not lead to that conclusion. While support for increasing immigration levels hovered around 10% throughout the 1990s and then dropped still lower after the attacks on the World Trade Center and Pentagon in 2001, they gradually increased to 23% in 2013. The percentage of those favoring a decrease was 33% in 1965 and gradually grew to 65% in 1995, but declined sharply to 35% in 2013. After the 9/11 attacks, the percentage in favor of reducing the number of immigrants grew before dropping gradually in the next four to five years. The "keep current levels" option started and ended at 40% (Gallup Polls, 1965–2013). Although there was continuous resistance to widening the gates through 2000, the percentage wishing to maintain or increase the number of immigrants has exceeded 50% since then.

Other data buttress that general pattern even as contradictory sentiments appear in particular areas of concern. In 2013 a large majority (75%) reported that on the whole immigration is a "good thing" for the country, compared to 52% in 2002. At the same time, almost as many (72%) felt it extremely or very important for Congress to pass laws to address post-1986 issues. Even more (88%) favored paths to citizenship, after payment of fines and taxes and demonstrated competence in English, for the undocumented. Only two years earlier, Gallup had found 64% agreeing to that same proposal, with another 13% preferring only to let them stay to work. By 2013, 48% of all respondents found their positions to be closer to those of the Democratic Party, sponsor of the most liberal proposals. The steady increase in support for permanency for those without documents appears to reflect the realization that deportation would cause logistical nightmares, create massive suffering, and disrupt an economy dependent on immigrant labor.

At the same time, surveys have identified categories that elicit negative views within the generally positive orientation. In 2006, before recession and the influx of Central American children and mothers, 81% agreed with a statement that illegal immigration was out of control. In 2008, a majority of respondents believed immigrants were making the nation's crime problems worse, and an equal number agreed that immigrants were the cause of higher taxes. At a more general level, three-fifths believed that immigrants cost American taxpayers too much; only one-third believed that they were paying their fair share. Gallup polls asking respondents to name groups they would not like to have as neighbors found that negative views about foreigners in general and Muslims in particular increased dramatically between 1995 and 2006 (doubling for both groups). During the same period, negative views of homosexuals dropped by 11 percentage points, indicating that hostility was specific to immigrants.

Other surveys have found similar patterns of sympathy coupled with suspicion or hostility. The 1984 National Social Survey asked respondents what circumstances would justify the admission of potential immigrants, and found affirmative responses to a wide range of hypothetical cases: refugees from national crises, but also Mexicans seeking better lives for their children. Humanitarian needs were especially likely to evoke sympathetic responses, even when they reflected specifically economic motives. Still, in 1986—when Congress was debating amnesty for undocumented migrants—polls revealed considerable confusion about who such immigrants actually were. Majorities thought that illegal migrants and refugees were the most numerous groups, and large percentages of the poll respondents expressed positive views about immigrants in general but offered negative characterizations of Asians and Latin Americans. By 2015, majorities representing all party groups favored paths to citizenship for undocumented immigrants (Table 2.3). Since 2010, the number of respondents who believe that immigrants strengthen rather than threaten American society grew from 44% to 58%; a 60% majority believed that immigrants bring strong work ethics and talent; and only 19% of those who were informed that by 2050 whites would be a minority were bothered by that idea (Jones et al., 2014).

Table 2.3. American Policy Preferences on Immigration: Support for Allowing Undocumented Immigrants to Remain in the U.S., 2016

Pew Research Center, March	73
PRRI/Brookings, April-May	78
Gallup, June-July	84

Sources: Pew Research Center; Public Religion Research Institute; Gallup Poll.

The border crisis of 2014 continued to evoke mixed feelings toward immigrants, even those who were bona fide refugees from violence in their home countries. In June of that year, almost two-thirds of respondents in a Rasmussen poll were dissatisfied with the administration's handling of immigration policy, yet Gallup and Brookings polls conducted in February and June of the same year found majorities of both Republican and Democratic voters favoring eventual citizenship for those without documents. In real crises opinion can be both generous and contrary to congressional stances, suggesting frustration with cautious or slow government responses. A 2004 survey that oversampled ethnic and racial minorities provides additional insight into the dynamics of opinion, most strikingly in its conclusion that, contrary to popular and some academic claims, American national identity has not been changed by an increasingly diverse population. Nationals and immigrants alike claim a primary identity that is American, not muted by country of origin. As was the case in earlier periods, immigrants value both the work they find and the national identity they have acquired (Schildkraut, 2010).

Variations in public responses suggest several dynamics at work. The easiest to identify are those related to how questions are worded. Respondents may not understand the difference between immigrants and refugees, or the distinction between undocumented immigrants and those in the United States who fulfill the requirements of one of the many categories of nonresident visa. But deeper explanations are almost certainly at work as well. A number of scholars have observed duality of opinion among respondents who embrace conflicting views with ease. They are able to take pride in the nation's immigration history but want to restrict new entries; they may be sympathetic to individual cases but reject the category they represent. Immigration is enticingly susceptible to principles with exceptions. It is thus not surprising that a mixed portrait has emerged, in which Americans are magnanimous but stingy, broad-minded and myopic, ideologically pure and pragmatic, all at the same time. The "nation of immigrants" includes millions of older immigrants wanting to close to door to the new arrivals, with no recognition of the irony of that position. Ignorance and misinformation, both abetted by a dizzying array of news and media outlets, also contribute to a confusion as many masquerade as neutral forums but shade truths in the quest for audience. Faced with inconsistency and hyperbole, political leaders use information that justifies positions they already hold, almost certainly retarding progress on issues that are anything but simple.

The United States in the Throes of Immigration Dilemmas

American history has been so thoroughly defined by immigrants that the nation's future is inevitably linked to decisions about who will enter, and under what conditions. Unlike more homogeneous nations, the United States must ask not whether immigrants will change the character of society, but how they will fit in with the many varieties of humanity that have already come to coexist and thrive within its borders. A history of pluralism necessitates a debate different from those in other nations.

Several themes should be noted before moving on to European cases. The first is the importance of geographic and historical context in the development of American immigration. Those who arrived in the eighteenth, nineteenth, and even twentieth centuries found a work in progress, one advantaged by physical separation from older nations, huge in area, and in many places sparsely populated. Entry was simple and room to settle ample. Given those parameters, friction was insufficient to cause unending violence or sustain rivalries comparable to conflicts elsewhere. Colonial powers with claims in North America were bought out or defeated, and border issues with neighbors generally resolved by negotiation.

Second, immigration issues were almost always dealt with on an ad hoc basis, with national governments preferring local solutions and reacting more to the needs of expansion than identity in a nation not yet defined. Immigration policy was skeletal for decades on end; the federal government did little but adjust rules for citizenship and react with limited measures to assuage nativist biases—even during the great surges in population that accompanied the nineteenth-century Industrial Revolution. The government's limited role was most essentially to quietly support a system that was operating reasonably well and which only infrequently sought to restrict groups found annoying by citizens. Even the transforming Immigration and Nationality Act of 1965 was mostly a reaction to both market needs and the awkward truth that existing policies patently discriminated against refugees, non-Europeans and nonwhites. Given a generally wary public opinion stoked occasionally by polarizing events and strident political leaders, the tendency to react to single issues or targeted groups continues in a system increasingly resistant to bold changes in policy.

A third theme is rooted in the question of how a nation of immigrants could have tolerated continuous patterns of scorn and exploitation, which counted on immigrants being satisfied with minimal accommodations and rights. Both the myth and the reality of the immigrant experience recognize the centrality of the concept of hardship, in which newcomers suffered in difficult jobs, poor housing, and hostile neighborhoods. The system's basic hierarchy may have promised them work and the chance to improve their—or at least their children's—lot, but the prerequisites were always hard labor and acceptance of difficult conditions.

Two aspects of this theme are remarkable. The first is how pervasive the pattern of ranking and delayed mobility has been over 200 years of immigrant experience. Starting at the bottom was an unchanging expectation, as even those with desirable skills often found doors closed to them in their specialties and were forced to resort to menial work. Even more notable is that the American narrative transformed this hardship—and its corollaries of discrimination and social inequality—into a cultural virtue. Overcoming bad circumstances has been and continues to be the heartwarming version of immigration; extolling the struggles of one's ancestors is a constant refrain of politicians, successful businessmen, even teachers imploring students to continue the tradition with hard work. The odd coupling of fond reverie surrounding the downtrodden immigrants of the past and doubts about those of the present is entirely consistent with a dual-sided American orientation deeply rooted in its history.

 A fourth theme is the use of economic rationales for both continuing immigration and curtailing it. Opponents of immigration most frequently worry that immigrants will take jobs away from nationals while at the same time they claim those migrants to be chronically unemployed and a drain on welfare funds. The continuous problems that farmers face in finding labor to harvest crops defies the claim that system capacity has been reached, and unemployment rates among immigrants continue to be lower than those for nationals. Even opponents of paths to citizenship concede a continuing need for foreign labor, a need compounded each year by the decline in the American birth rate. Latent and overt hostilities are a constant element in immigration debates, but economic rationales have always been and are sure to remain central factors in determining the ultimate policies defining labor recruitment.

The resilience of the economic arguments for reducing quotas even when increased numbers are crucial to the economy points to the fifth theme, which is the now-predictable condition of political stalemate among intransigent political groups. Like other outsized aspects of the immigration debate, politicization of national and state-level debates continues to direct focus upon related but not central issues. In the current setting, that has meant a furor over immigration failures (ineffective borders and ineffectual enforcement of visa limits), which then overshadows discussion of real national economic needs. Live-and-let-live solutions of the past offer no realistic guide for the present, wherein high-pitched anger has threatened both to derail attempts to deal with humanitarian immigration issues and to fuel the polarized stances assumed by political leaders that make lawmaking impossible. Such political discourse has created hyperextended divisions, promoting what many observers of the 2016 presidential campaign have called the "normalization of bigotry" at the expense of seeking solutions to fundamental problems (*New York Times*, September 5, 2016).

 A sixth theme has emerged as a widespread concern that accepting refugees or even regularly screened immigrants will increase the risk of terrorist attacks in the United States. Amplified in the 2016 election campaigns, such concerns raise fears that new immigrants, as well as long-term residents, will become victims of discrimination or even hate crimes, tolerated or encouraged by political leaders. The challenge may well be the greatest task facing administrations attempting to reconcile a history defined by immigrants with a future clouded by security concerns.

 Finally, it is striking that in the current conflict the distance between public and leadership response is so large. Polls reveal widespread support for addressing the issue of immigration, and majorities of those polled consistently support some kind of legalization being granted to immigrants without documents, neither of which has been embraced by national lawmakers. Political leadership in previous decades (and centuries) was inclined to weigh in with selective restrictions but generally let the market determine ultimate numbers. The admission by the United States of far more immigrants than other nations (in 2005, the U.S. admitted 1.29 million legal immigrants, more than the next five nations combined) and additional pressure to accept refugees from a host of regional conflicts have produced a need for commensurately greater leadership to deal with them.

An important question raised in this debate is whether it can be informed by the experiences of other nations grappling with similar issues in different contexts. To answer that, we turn to a comparison to three European states in the throes of similar dilemmas.

For Further Reading

David Gerber, *American Immigration: a Very Short Introduction*. New York: Oxford University Press, 2011.

Deborah J. Schildkraut, *Americanism in the Twenty-First Century*. New York: Cambridge University Press, 2011.

Jennifer Hochschild et al., *Outsiders No More? Models of Immigrant Political Incorporation*. New York: Oxford University Press, 2013.

3

Great Britain

Reluctant Parent to the Former Empire

If the United States is the classic example of a nation built and developed by immigrants, modern European states represent the anti-model. Dominant native populations were established centuries earlier, after monarchs gave up trying to expand their realms by marriage and war, and national identities have been defined by endurance and homogeneity. Despite long colonial associations with dozens of nations, the British have mostly resisted policies that would encourage immigration. Since the end of World War II, the nation has reduced its international role, trading global responsibility for cautious membership in a European Union that began removing internal borders in 1985 and committed members to assist in resettling thousands of refugees in the 2014–16 crises in the Middle East and Africa.

Immigration issues, hotly contested throughout the postwar period, have inspired major responses in Britain. The ultra-Right UK Independence Party has shown unusual strength since 2008, surprising most observers by winning 27.5% of the vote in the European Parliament election, gaining 24 seats, and outpolling mainstream parties. In the 2015 national election, it received 13% of the overall votes, although only one parliamentary seat, but its strong anti-immigrant, anti-EU positions were a critical factor in the June 2016 British vote to leave the European Union, surely the most dramatic turn of national politics in decades. Despite a similarity to America's geographic insulation and interests common to those in Europe, the British experience has been sufficiently different from both to make it a compelling case for comparison.

The Geography of Insulation and Foreign Conquest

Britain has a long recorded history dating from 6000 BC, with international conquests starting as early as 55 BC. The years since the Norman Conquest in 1066 included extended periods of European conflict, with intermittent changes of rule and more than seventy invasions worthy of the name, as kingdoms maneuvered to consolidate territory and power. Since 1700, however, actual encroachment into British territory has been incidental, with raids by assorted pirates lonely examples of foreign threats. During World War II, the Germans occupied the Channel Islands for five years before relinquishing them at the end of the war. Overall, a general history of secure borders has persisted for the better part of 1,000 years.

It is easy to appreciate how the history and location of Britain combined to build a foundation based on both isolation from proximate neighbors and dominance in territories across the globe. Although separated from continental Europe by only 22 miles, early development of armies and a superior navy have prevented invasion of the British Isles for centuries. To the north, east, and west, greater sea expanses served as effective borders, and the more remote and underpopulated nations of Scandinavia to the east presented no real threats of encroachment or emigration of their nationals to Britain.

Although the United Kingdom has a limited land area suitable for large-scale agriculture, it exploited, and depleted, natural reserves of coal and iron for over 300 years. Discovery of oil and natural gas in the North Sea allowed Britain to become a net exporter as coal and iron declined in the 1970–2000 period. As those reserves have fallen the nation has had to resume importing both oil and gas, but maintains an active ownership and production industry in both.

In most of its modern history, Britain's main source of natural resources was its global network of trading partners, many of which were first occupied militarily and then absorbed as colonies or dominions between 1850 and 1914. Each area had proven value as either a rich source of imports, an outlet for exports, or a key location along the greater trade routes Britain had developed since the late seventeenth century. Britain's colonial reach was nothing short of breathtaking. At its height in 1914, the British Empire spanned all the world's continents, including land and loyalty in North America, South Asia, East and West Africa, the Middle East, Australia, and New Zealand, as well as smaller outposts in South America and Southeast Asia. At the Empire's peak, Britain ruled 458 million people, almost 20% of the world's population.

As Britain demonstrated to the world of the time, trade and empire constituted a critical symbiosis upon which economic and global power would be based for 200 years. From the early 1800s to 1945, Britain established a world stature far greater than its size and resources at home would have predicted. From Africa alone it controlled vast resources of metals, minerals, precious stones, gold, oil, cotton, and rubber, as well as raw agricultural products. With the occupation of former German territories in Africa after World War I, Britain was able to increase agricultural production to ease postwar shortages in the homeland. India, Caribbean nations, and the dominions of Australia and Canada became prime markets for British products. Even after the breakup of the Empire following World War II, Britain managed to retain trade relations with most of its former colonies and continued its prominence in commerce, development of natural gas and oil reserves, and international finance. Even without colonies, it maintained its position as the third largest economy in Europe (after Germany and France).

With a population of more than 65 million and a residential density of 679 persons per square mile, Britain is one of the developed world's most space-limited nations. Population projections are for minimal growth with a low native birth rate and a heavily white, British-born populace (85.4% in 2011). Despite major immigration influxes since 1965, the combined black, Indian, Pakistani, and Asian population comprised less than 15% of the total population as late as 2011. Within immigrant groups, a significant proportion of Indians and Pakistanis have been in the country since the mid-twentieth century or earlier, and they are by any measure long-standing residents. By American, and even European standards, illegal migration into the country is low. The largest concentrations of minorities and immigrants are in London, followed by the large, manufacturing cities of Manchester and Birmingham.

More recently, Britain has experienced an influx of immigrants from the eight nations that joined the European Union in 2004, with largest numbers from Poland. Britain accepted those with job prospects immediately, in numbers estimated at between 5,000 and 13,000 migrants annually. More than 521,000 Poles arrived between 2004 and 2011 (the total number of Poles rose to 831,000 in 2016), causing enough concern that when Romania and Bulgaria joined the EU in 2007, Britain and others limited the entry of migrants from those nations until January 2014. The net migration between 1997 and 2009 totaled 2.2 million, sharply increasing numbers from what had been a relatively low base during the long period between 1970 and 1995. Facing new pressures to accept African and Middle Eastern refugees, Britain has staunchly resisted, claiming a lack of capacity beyond the current immigrant minorities.

The Tangled History of Colonialism and Contemporary Immigration

The history of Britain from the mid-nineteenth century to 1945 was dominated by relations within the Empire, even during times of war. As Europe's preeminent naval power, Britain ventured into Africa, Asia, and the Caribbean with little or no competition from rival states. Local resistance in Africa and Asia was subdued, even with significant casualties on all sides; only in its American colonies did the British encounter opposition ultimately leading to independence. Since many of Britain's conceptions of immigration were based on reports from the colonies and secondhand knowledge of experiences elsewhere, that history created both traditions and expectations in the postcolonial era.

Early Stages of Colonial Expansion

Although Britain enjoyed the security of isolation in its early history, it coveted the spoils of conquest gained by Spanish and Portuguese naval forces in Asia and the Americas. Recognizing the advantages of trade routes protected by British-fortified posts, forces were sent to establish relations, first in the Caribbean and later in excursions into Canada's Hudson Bay, Newfoundland, Gibraltar, and Menorca. The most ambitious successes were in India, where British forces took on the Dutch and gained control of the textile trade, then fought off Bengal forces to establish a permanent foothold there. By the late 1700s, Britain assumed the role of leading maritime power, engaging in both commercial and slave trade as it prepared for further expansion.

With the unexpected loss of the American colonies in 1783, Britain concentrated on solidifying Canadian territory, aided by as many as 100,000 British loyalists from the new United States, then moved to formalize claim to Australia and New Zealand—two nations forcibly occupied and utilized as both sources of resources and as penal colonies for British citizens deported as undesirable. A major boost in non-Anglo acquisitions during this period followed victory over Napoleon in 1815; Britain was rewarded with control over Malta, Mauritania, St. Lucia, and Tobago from France, Trinidad from Spain, and Guyana, Ceylon, and the Cape Colony from the Netherlands.

The Imperial Century

With impressive gains made without major military losses, Britain was ready to extend its colonial dominance even farther. Between 1815 and 1922, it added more than 13 million square miles of territory and 500 million people to the Empire, moving to establish control over Argentina and China and join forces with the East India Company in South Asia. The combined powers moved into Singapore, Malaya, Burma, and Hong Kong, followed by suppression of rebellion in India and direct control in 1858. Soon thereafter Britain moved aggressively into Africa, starting by purchasing 40% control of the Suez Canal in 1875, then occupying Egypt seven years later. Combined British and Egyptian forces defeated a Mahdist army to take control of the Sudan in 1896. Completing this stage of expansion was the takeover of Rhodesia in the 1890s and the defeat of the Boers—the Dutch and their Afrikaner descendants—in South Africa in 1902. Although this period did include lessening of colonial control in Canada, Australia, and New Zealand—redefining their status to that of dominions with substantial governing autonomy—those nations retained strong Commonwealth ties. Stricter control, built on the belief that governance by a British elite was necessary and proper, was adopted in nonwhite colonies.

Britain did not enter World War I to increase its colonial holdings, but ended up doing so. The victorious allies sought to weaken the German Reich in the postwar settlement and saw Britain as a natural heir to German colonies. The Treaty of Versailles awarded Britain control of the Ottoman Empire, Palestine, Transjordan, Iraq, parts of Cameroon and Togo, and Tanganyika; the South African dominion took control of Southwest Africa; Australia acquired New Guinea.

At that point the Empire was at its most extensive, even as the seeds of independence were being sown. In 1919, Ireland was granted dominion status; semi-independent statehood was granted to Iraq in 1932 and Egypt in 1936. The famous Balfour Declaration of 1926 formalized the autonomy of Britain's dominions. Even as the British reveled in the victory of 1918, it began to recognize the importance of powerful, largely independent forces within the Empire. More ominously, the war also revealed that the home country could not assure the protection always promised to its colonies, foreshadowing global change and the eventual end of empire.

Breakup of the Empire

World War I clearly revealed the limits of British power. Even regional conflicts strained its resources, making it clear that its forces would be insufficient to fend off greater threats in distant locations. As significantly, the war revealed major fissures within the Empire, but before Britain had time to deal with growing calls for independence it was forced to confront mounting hostilities in Europe. Its leaders turned their attention to aggression by Germany, and sooner than it ever anticipated, England was pushed to declare war in 1939. It was joined by Australia, New Zealand, Canada, and South Africa, but the Irish Free State refused and remained neutral throughout the war. Soon thereafter, Singapore fell to Japan in the early stages of the Asian hostilities and the British were unable to move forces to aid in its defense. However impressive the global British military presence had been in earlier times, it had barely enough resources to confront military challenges in its own neighborhood in 1939, foretelling the loss of power it would face when that conflict ended.

Although Britain was one of the victorious allies, World War II had laid waste to its cities and infrastructure, devastated its economy, and removed any doubt that its imperial days were over. Any plan to resume its role as colonial master was eclipsed by the need to rebuild the homeland. Billions of dollars in American aid under the European Recovery Program (better known as the Marshall Plan) were concentrated in Britain, which received more than 25% of the total postwar U.S. aid (followed by France with 16%, Germany 11%, and the Netherlands 8%). The reconstruction program went into overdrive, with government and the private sector partners in a multiyear demolition and rebuilding program, which would include new infrastructure and an industrial base for an economy with a national rather than international scope.

As Britain turned its attention inward, independence movements and civil conflict grew throughout Asia, Africa, and the Caribbean. The postwar Labour government under Clement Atlee firmly supported decolonization with minimal entanglement in the troubled nations. After announcing a 1948 date for independence in India, the government actually moved the date forward to facilitate the break in 1947. Britain avoided commitments to any governance role in a Middle Eastern region made even more volatile by the redrawing of borders and establishment of the state of Israel in 1948. Britain recognized new governments in Egypt in 1952 and the Sudan in 1956. When the Egyptian president nationalized the Suez Canal in 1956, Britain joined forces with France and Israel to maintain control there, but the United States opted to lead a United Nations force, compelling Britain and its allies to withdraw and cede control over the canal. In Asia, Malaya, which had fought communist insurgents on its own and gained independence in 1957, joined with Singapore, Saraweh, and North Borneo to form the state of Malaysia. Throughout the Empire the British acceded to independence demands, repeatedly learning that acquiring colonies had been far easier than freeing them. Too often the liberations were bitter, foreshadowing hostile relations after independence.

By the early 1960s, independence movements were unstoppable and Britain gradually withdrew from its remaining possessions. In many, the processes took place without incident, but others experienced violent upheavals either against the British or based in long-standing rivalries that had been suppressed under colonial rule. A bloody uprising of Mau Mau in Kenya marred the exit of British forces and expatriates; a persistent civil war in Rhodesia continued long after the English left. Mediterranean colonies fared only slightly better, as conflicts arose in Cyprus and Malta when they set up governments and tried to reconcile competing interests without effective military or police forces. In the Caribbean, transitions were generally accomplished without violence, and some of the island nations even maintained some ties with Britain (Barbados, St. Lucia). The final and dramatic end to the Empire came after protracted negotiations for the withdrawal of British authority over Hong Kong. The actual transition took place with relatively minor disagreements, and in 1997 Hong Kong formally became part of mainland China.

The sheer magnitude of acquisition and devolution of colonial possessions was the largest example of international control and breakup in the 1,400 years since the end of the Roman Empire. Historians have seen the politics of empire as partly jockeying for competitive advantage with European rivals, partly realization of the need for trade and resources to guarantee British prosperity, and partly a drive to guide the future of those seen as incapable of ruling themselves. When the acquisitions gained after World War I are added, the Empire was more a collection created by force and accident than the product of rational national policies. In hindsight, it is easy to understand that the Empire had insufficient common beliefs and interests to keep it together, even if the British had been willing to engage local populations in governance and national development. The system persisted for more than two centuries before moving from a greater commonwealth controlling the fate of more than 700 million people to one overseeing fewer than 5 million (3 million of whom were citizens in Hong Kong, which became independent of Britain in 1997), and that experience will assist in explaining how the British dealt with immigration issues after World War II.

The Immigration Consequences of Colonialism: Relations with the Former Empire

Most important in understanding the British struggle with contemporary immigration is the fact that throughout most of its history Britain has been a land of colonial emigration. Most of its non-American emigration consisted of upper-class military, political officials, and businessmen who assumed positions of status and control in colonized territories. In the eighteenth and nineteenth centuries, almost 2 million Britons left England and Ireland. Most went to the American colonies and later the independent United States, but a large number traveled to trading posts, dominions, territories, and colonies of the Crown. After important centers were secured, major businesses opened in India, East Africa, Pakistan, Asia, and Australia, and later in South Africa and the Caribbean. The government provided passage and promises of positions in the Crown government or local industries. Throughout the period of imperial growth emigration was continuous; even during and after World War I, when independence movements emerged, some 2 million British citizens emigrated. After the end of World War II, another 720,000 left for prosperous possessions which were only a few years from independence.

Although there were many variations in the relationships between emigrating Britons and local populations, most reflected British interests and deeply ingrained views. The primary interests were economic. Britain set up shop in India to promote trade and ultimately control development of profitable industry and commerce there; its motivation in Africa was access to rich supplies of natural resources; possession of Hong Kong, Malaya, and Singapore assured dominance in Asian trade. The British provided capital for development and controlled the resulting production and trade; its political officials negotiated terms of growth and recruited managers from their own ranks. Although colonial leaders interacted with the upper strata of the host societies, economic and political power were the preserve of British elites. Wherever the Empire put down roots, it took control of the economy. Whether the British could have established secure trading centers without colonizing territories cannot be known, given the absence of real examples. In the imperial age the allure of resources was irresistible and the rationale for ruling an undeveloped world compelling to ambitious leaders. Colonialism came to mean economic service to Britain, and military control was required to preserve it.

The economic formula was simple. Resources as well as cash generated in the colonies flowed to Britain. Except in the dominions, the ruling regime was a small group of expatriates supported by local business and taxes. Maddison describes the economic behavior of the British in India as "rapacious" (1971). In addition to lavish salaries and benefits provided to administrators, colonies were charged for London offices overseeing policy in the Empire. Between 1858 and 1947, payments of such "Home Charges" grew steadily, amounting to 40–50 million pounds by 1930. During World War I, India paid for more than a million troops and made cash contributions totaling 730 million pounds to Britain. Direct and indirect transfers of money and resources were a steady source of revenue from all colonies.

If economic gain was the root of initial colonial expansion, competition among European powers fueled it. Despite its insular location, Britain continuously worried about European alliances as it expanded global conquests and the naval forces required to maintain primacy. Even if trade and control over resources had not been an obvious prize for strong expeditionary forces, challenging European powers promised power, and thus security, in itself.

Exporting British nationals to rule the new settlements was essential to maintaining that power. It also created an emigrant class that would shape British views of the nations and people it dominated for almost 200 years. The Empire took on an identity of its own, defined not only by an expansion far greater than that of European states but by the rules it established to manage millions of people far from British soil. Given the rapid and often unchallenged control over such large territories and disparate cultures, it is easy to understand how the British developed a sense of destiny in their control of the fates of populations across the globe.

British conceptions of colonies and their residents were thus in many respects products of political and social institutions created in the colonies. Governance was assigned to British officials appointed by the Crown; in each colony a British viceroy was in charge of establishing whatever administration was needed to govern. In India, a warlord aristocracy was replaced by a civil and military bureaucracy staffed by Britons charged with optimizing exploitation of resources and maintaining order. That administrative monopoly continued into the 1920s, when a civil service system was set up to allow a small number of nationals to serve. In most colonies, governing councils made economic decisions and built the infrastructure needed to modernize agriculture, mining, and some industry. In all, the primary objective was profitable growth in production and trade, for the benefit of British overseers and the Crown.

Although there were attempts to introduce a British system of education in several colonies, efforts were limited by both the sheer magnitude of the task in populous countries and the opposition they encountered. Britain had little interest in taking on massive projects—and their costs—in the face of such resistance and the likelihood that they would produce educated dissidents. Lacking the religious or cultural zeal to reform entire societies, the British undertook only modest changes. In India, for example, religious opposition undercut early initiatives in 1857, prompting creation of only a small number of English schools. Three universities were also set up, but served mostly as examining bodies for students needing limited academic programs to qualify for middle-level jobs. British children were educated in separate schools and sent home for university training. Providing even minimal schooling was never a priority (88% of the Indian population were illiterate at the time of independence in 1947). Those who did manage to attend select schools rarely became part of the national elite, at best joining the pool of government clerks or teachers. For the most part, the British maintained or increased the enormous gap between rulers and ruled, leaving investment in mass education to postindependence governments.

The lives of Britons in the colonies were thus kept separate from locals in virtually all spheres. Emigrants were heavily subsidized by the central government in London and the local political authorities or businesses that employed them. Costs of living with elaborate services were low, and most British families enjoyed lifestyles they could never have afforded in the homeland. The social structure of colonial rule was highly segregated. Historian Angus Maddison concluded that in India,

> The elite with its classical education and contempt for business were quite happy establishing law and order, and keeping "barbarians" at bay on the frontier of the raj. They developed their own brand of self-righteous arrogance, considering themselves purveyors not of popular but of good government.

The word "British" lost its geographic connotation and became an epithet signifying moral rectitude. (1971, p. 16)

The pattern was similar in all colonies, with authority exercised by a remarkably small colonial class. In 1931, the British in India numbered 168,000. Ninety thousand held jobs in business, 60,000 were in the army and police, but only 4,000 occupied government positions—less than 0.05% of the population. By standards of the times, that figure was remarkably low, as it reflected both the absence of the British in areas such as education and the relative ease with which a small central government controlled a larger population that did not share its culture.

Although the British were aggressive in their control of colonial governments and economies, they were unlike other conquerors who, motivated by religious zeal, insisted on remaking or converting indigenous cultures. Essentially opportunists, the British supported investments in infrastructure, and those investments represented some positive consequences of colonial rule. In modernizing transportation to improve the movement of materials and products, they left behind roads, railways, water and sewage systems, industrial and even residential construction, which would serve the postindependence populations. To support a dependent colonial population that grew to almost 400 million in the 1930s, the British increased arable land area by 800%, turning desert areas into productive fields. But they also restricted local industries that would have competed with British counterparts (especially textiles), delaying development of local businesses needed after independence. Overall, industrial output per capita was flat under colonial rule; failure to improve education and other services meant mammoth challenges for governments after independence was achieved.

Any review of the British colonial legacy would be incomplete without discussion of the role race played in imperial policies. In the early years of expansion, Britain established its presence in North America, Australia, and New Zealand and consciously encouraged settlement there. Between 1800 and 1850 the European population in Australia increased from 0.3% to 58.6%, creating a majority able to subdue native resistance and manage a form of self-rule. Instead of imposing homeland-based control, the London office instituted systems of self-governance. Almost certainly guided by their American experience, the British granted Canada the right to national rule in 1839; in 1852, the New Zealand Constitution Act endorsed a form of local governance. Canada was allowed to develop its own currency, and in 1867 the British North America Act authorized a national parliament and prime minister for Canada's new status as a dominion. Australia was granted a similar form of self-government in 1901 and, in 1926, the Balfour Declaration assured that the dominions would henceforth all enjoy equal status in the Commonwealth. The stark contrast between governance in white Commonwealth nations and that maintained in colonies in Africa, Asia, and the Caribbean reflected a conviction that the latter were incapable of self-rule. Although required to use military force to gain control in Africa and Asia, the British did so with confidence that superiority in both military might and culture would ultimately guarantee acceptance. That indigenous populations submitted to foreign rule for so long strengthened the British sense of moral right and cultural superiority, convictions which remained strong long after breakup of the Empire.

Finally, it should be noted that even as British policies provided dramatic examples of the economic exploitation and control of native populations, all of the colonial powers exhibited similar patterns of rule before the breakdown of those systems in the mid-twentieth century. Britain, controlling the largest empire in modern history, was assured of both the fame and the infamy associated with that outsized role. As will be evident in the French case, one common consequence would be lingering animosities toward former colonials rooted, at least in part, in the histories created by colonial rule.

The Decline of Emigration and Rise of Immigration

Given the long period of colonial rule, it is not surprising that British planners did not anticipate shifts in migration patterns after 1945. For 200 years. net immigration into the United Kingdom had been negative, as Britons served as roving explorers, conquerors, and settlers of outposts across the world. A large number had become permanent expatriates, establishing businesses and comfortable lives. There had been some migration by citizens of the colonies into small ethnic enclaves in English cities, but the flow was small, never suggesting that it would grow. Migration from the developing world had been effectively restricted by laws discouraging relocation, as well as the high cost of transportation.

Those circumstances changed with the end of the war, the beginning of a communications and travel revolution, and the realization that colonialism was at an end. Facing the reality of a nation devastated by war, large numbers of Britons opted to emigrate; between 1946 and 1950, more than 700,000 skilled workers and professionals left for the United States, Canada, and Australia. Although an English economic boom would soon develop, thanks to massive American aid, Britain lost a critical part of its workforce, creating labor shortages whose obvious solution lay in the availability of foreign workers. The world of emigration was turned on its head, forcing the British government to construct immigration policies with little forewarning or planning.

Restrictive Immigration Laws

The legal basis for postwar British policies on immigration had been established forty years earlier. In 1905, Parliament passed the Aliens Act, defining the "undesirable" immigrant as destitute, diseased, or criminal and authorizing deportation at the discretion of the Home Office. The Act was passed when population movement was minimal, and the targets were poor Jews from Eastern Europe. Subsequent laws (the 1914 and 1919 Alien Restrictions Acts) required foreign nationals to register with the government and limited their rights to employment. Ostensibly aimed at seamen trying to remain in British ports, the law covered the large number of Commonwealth citizens from Africa,

India, and the Caribbean. They singled out groups seen as unworthy of permanent residence, but at base established a clear opposition to immigrants who could not trace their genetic stock to Britain, a theme that would be repeated over and again in later discussions of fundamental policy.

Antipathy to non-Anglos seeking to settle in Britain reflected widespread negative views of the residents of areas that had been ruled by Britain for decades. That made the postwar British Nationality Act of 1948 especially anomalous. Introduced with a fanfare for an obviously crumbling Empire, the law granted literally millions of Commonwealth subjects the right to entry and settlement in Britain. Supporters saw it as the symbolic bond that would keep the Commonwealth alive, clearly not grasping the potential it opened for the wholesale reconstruction of British society. Critics who foresaw the implications of the open invitation immediately called for restricting actual British citizenship to those with British ancestors. The 1948 Act was a blunder of monumental naiveté, illustrating how extensive the lack of comprehension of the issue was.

The consequences of empire for immigration policy were staggering. Christian Joppke concluded that "[t]he legacy of empire has afflicted British immigration policy with the enduring curse of racial discrimination" (1999, p. 101). The bias in British attitudes toward black colonial subjects presented political leaders with challenges that had, to that point, only been discussed hypothetically, and the national debate was predictably shallow. Significant divisions existed within and between political parties over how to define citizenship in the Commonwealth. Casting some as eligible for citizenship and larger numbers only as transients would signal racial distinctions inconsistent with the laws of Britain's allies and the charter of the newly established United Nations. Political leaders responded to the dilemma mostly by ignoring it and hoping that it would somehow resolve itself. Although the two major parties initially coalesced around the principle of free movement within the Commonwealth, Labour tentatively supported future citizenship for those who entered. Conservatives were opposed, anticipating quite correctly that an amorphous commitment to citizenship would necessitate internal classifications certain to be unworkable and increase the resentment already apparent in the colonies.

For ten years after passage of the 1948 Act, relatively low levels of immigration from "New Commonwealth" nations (a term applied to mostly nonwhite colonies after they became independent) preoccupied with establishing independent governments kept the issue from demanding immediate attention. The respite was short-lived, as any hope that the immigration issue would sort itself out, or that citizens of the former colonies would not seek admission to Britain, was dashed by two developments. First, the numbers of New Commonwealth immigrants increased steadily. In 1953 only 2,000 arrived, mostly from the West Indies; by 1955 the count had risen to 42,000, and to 136,000 in 1961, including large numbers from India and Pakistan (Table 3.1). Although the numbers were small compared to those in the United States and Canada at the time, they were dramatic for a nation that had never experienced net population growth due to

Table 3.1. Estimated New Immigration from New Commonwealth Nations, 1953–1962

	West Indies	India	Pakistan	Others	Total
1953	2,000	——	——	——	2,000
1954	11,000	——	——	——	11,000
1955	27,500	5,800	1,850	7,500	42,650
1956	29,800	5,600	2,050	9,350	46,800
1957	23,000	6,600	5,200	7,600	42,400
1958	15,000	6,200	4,700	3,950	29,850
1959	16,400	2,950	850	1,400	21,600
1960	49,650	5,900	2,500	−350	57,700
1962*	66,300	23,750	25,100	21,250	136,400

*First 6 months

Source: House of Commons, Library Research Paper No. 56, Commonwealth Immigration to the UK from the 1950s to 1975—A Survey of Statistical Sources.

immigration. Moreover, the entry of new migrants was rarely smooth. Race riots broke out in several cities, and the concentration of black immigrants in poorer urban areas portended continued unrest. The simultaneous appearance of racially based violence in the United States provided grist for public fear and calls by Conservative politicians to curb all immigration.

Debates over laws passed between 1962 and 1981 illustrated the dilemma for British leaders in both major parties. On some level, they all recognized the need to restrict immigration in the context of a full-employment economy and a public resistance to immigrants from nonwhite nations. Seeking to mute charges of racism, Conservatives cast their bills as generally curtailing immigration, but admitted those "persons who in common parlance belong to the United Kingdom" (from the Home Secretary, quoted in Joppke, 1999, p. 108). "Belonging" was defined by birth in the UK, effectively excluding those from New Commonwealth nations. Although Labour leaders strongly objected to what they claimed to be the racist intent of such laws, they themselves were responsible for the Commonwealth Immigrants Act of 1962, a bill restricting immigration to those with specific job offers. In 1965, Labour arbitrarily limited the number of immigrants by abolishing the category of those without explicit job-related qualifications.

In 1968, the Labour government passed another hostile law, rescinding the right of entry for more than 200,000 East African Asians who were being marginalized or even threatened in Kenya, a former colony. That action led the European Commission on Human Rights to condemn the British law for using race to deny entry to those with clear ties to the United Kingdom. Undaunted by the commission's rebuke, Britain continued to enact restrictive legislation. Having campaigned on a pledge to halt immigration from the third world, a Conservative government passed the Immigration Act of 1971, an act that would set standards for the next 40 years. Where earlier laws had tried to distinguish among Commonwealth nations on the basis of birthright, passport status, or familial ties to Britain, the 1971 Act defined potential immigrants as one general group, excepting only a subset labeled as *patrials*—those with either UK citizenship or a British grandparent—to facilitate reentry of British residents from former colonies. A full decade later, under the more strident Conservative leader Margaret Thatcher, the British Nationality Act finally phased out the concept of partial right to residence by subjecting all foreigners to severe restrictions. The most controversial provision of the 1981 law was its rejection of the principle that anyone born on British soil had a basic right to UK residence. Tory leaders applauded the law for providing the legal basis for denying rights to parents whose children had been born in the UK. After more than twenty years of debate, the 1971 and 1981 laws finally renounced any Commonwealth claims to citizenship.

The focus on Commonwealth rights to entry sidestepped difficult but related issues such as secondary immigration. The 1971 act virtually halted new immigration from New Commonwealth nations but left unclear the entry rights of family members of immigrants living legally in Britain. Unlike other nations (Germany and the United States in particular) where family rights are embedded in constitutional provisions and immigration statutes, British laws delegated decisions on family applicants to immigration officers. Administrative discretion was broad and applications by even close family members were widely rejected. Hearing officers focused on eliminating those with false claims to family status, demanding documents often not used in home countries. Even harsher standards were set for fiancés, including proof of jobs in Britain. In an extraordinary case of international review of policies discriminating against men applying to join wives, the European Court of Human Rights ruled against the British standards, only to see immigration agencies redefine their refusals as rejection of marriages they deemed motivated by immigration. To facilitate this shift, in 1988 Parliament passed legislation that revoked the commitment to family unification, which had been included in the 1971 Act, thus ensuring that administrators could reject the relatives of legal immigrants. Decisions by midlevel officials were routinely affirmed by appeals boards and courts.

British reliance on state-level administration to define policy by their admission decisions is itself remarkable. Joppke concludes bluntly that "[t]he primary-purpose rule encapsulates the essence of British immigration law and policy: unfettered state discretion" (1999, p. 125). The rule placed the burden of proving the legitimacy of a marriage on naive and ill-prepared applicants, allowing British courts to ignore both legal contradictions, which European commissions had identified, and the plight of the immigrant. Friction between governments that had earlier heralded world citizenship and foreigners who faced legal barriers to that ideal was, in this context, inevitable.

A final element of postwar immigration history can be found in the history of the British experience with asylum seekers and refugees after 1945. Any openness to those fleeing persecution was beaten back by hostility toward Commonwealth immigrants, and asylum seekers were quickly redefined as ordinary applicants for admission subject to the zero-immigration imperative embraced by all parties. When British courts were asked to weigh in on refugee cases, they regularly deferred to immigration officers empowered by national laws. After years of rejecting appeals from refugees and asylum seekers, Parliament finally passed legislation specific to those groups in 1993, agreeing to consider applications but maintaining a high bar for acceptance. Britain's reputation as unreceptive to asylum claims resulted in the lowest number of applicants among European nations; over the 1980–88 period, fewer than 38,000 applications were received.

Despite rules that defined asylum as one immigration category with restrictive standards, high-profile cases involving Tamils fleeing persecution in Sri Lanka attracted national attention in the late 1980s. A series of deportation cases involving Tamils, Turkish Kurds, and a Zairean leader were reviewed by the European Court of Justice, ending with specific instruction to the British to allow relief when the dispute involved violation of European law. The British responded with the 1993 Asylum and Immigration Appeals Act, which added one provision for appeals but also stiffened requirements for students and short-term visitors and instituted a fast-track procedure to expedite decisions on claims the government viewed as "manifestly unfounded." Rather than bringing the process closer to the standards used by European states, the British law facilitated swift, negative decisions.

Myth and Reality under Colonialism

A colonial history as extensive as that of the British would have to include some element of myth. Political leaders encouraged the belief that the Crown protected and nurtured subjects everywhere, leading easily to a narrative where the world was destined to embrace the English culture. That little of the colonial empire actually developed or thrived was probably recognized by those controlling its fate but accepted as the legitimate condition for colonies, whose primary role was service to the realm. As a combination of myth and reality, British rule rewarded its own citizens with real economic benefits and pride in the apparent spread of their culture. With the breakup of the Empire and the realization that Britain would no longer control the fate of its colonies, what remained was at least some part of the national myth that the Empire had made unparalleled contributions to regions which otherwise would not have experienced the advantages of living as part of the Commonwealth.

The legacy of colonialism was never far from the minds of those dealing with immigration after World War II. A view of the largely nonwhite third world as inferior to its former rulers was prominent in the struggle to define who might have access to residence and work in Britain. Political leaders can easily be faulted for the transparency of their prejudices and the awkwardness of their rationalization of racial exclusion, but the challenge to build workable immigration policies after centuries without immigration would have been enormous under any circumstances. Economic and political forces added to the challenge, as we will discover in the next sections.

The Economics of Immigration in Britain

Britain's lack of a real immigration history was remarkable on at least two counts. First was the long pattern of emigration of British nationals to the United States and colonial territories, creating an anomalous tradition of outward movement. As importantly, labor adaptation in Britain successfully accommodated the needs of changing markets for the better part of the nineteenth and early twentieth centuries, fostering an unusual degree of stability in British industry with its enduring socioeconomic class system. That system became the basis of a two-party system in which control of the government alternated between parties over long periods of time. Only a small number of migrants arrived and remained through the end of World War II, and although discrimination undoubtedly existed, it was part of a system in which those with lower class status simply did not have access or aspire to the privileges of the upper classes. Economic and social mobility was rare, class the defining variable for a wide array of issues that would affect immigrants as well as the population generally.

Immigrant Labor in the Aftermath of World War II

During World War II, the demand for both personnel and services for the armed forces outpaced Britain's capacity to deliver either. One hundred and twenty thousand Poles joined the Allied forces, and they remained in Britain after the war. In addition, more than 10,000 West Indians were recruited to service planes and equipment for the Royal Air Force, and thousands of citizens from colonies in West Africa and Asia served in either the military or support industries. When the war finally ended, both physical damage and the loss of working-age men in the war created an unprecedented need for additions to the work force. Even under these circumstances, labor unions and their supporters initially opposed allowing Poles and other foreigners to remain in the country, and the government established a "working party" committee to ease the process of recruiting workers from colonial areas. That committee concluded, remarkably, that since black workers would find it difficult to assimilate, no systematic immigration effort should be adopted, foreshadowing the mindsets that would influence debates for the next 75 years.

Even as postwar groups resisted changes in labor recruitment, the push-and-pull forces of immigration were already at work. Operating entirely within the purview of British declarations and laws allowing free access across Commonwealth borders, thousands of West Indians, Indians, and Pakistanis migrated to Britain, where jobs were plentiful. Between 1953 and 1962, more than 500,000 immigrants arrived from these nations alone, providing badly needed manpower for the recovery effort. Financial aid from the United States created vast opportunities for work in reconstruction projects and basic industries, where foreigners quickly came to outnumber nationals. As in migration patterns elsewhere, the newcomers typically took positions as unskilled and semiskilled laborers with low wages and long hours, subtly creating job mobility for locals. In the postwar economy of replacement and growth, they became a critical component of the reconstruction economy.

British governments during those years were forced to deal with both reconstruction and the daunting process of defining terms of independence and future relations with dozens of colonies. The two problems were intertwined, since the immigrants who were beginning to arrive in Britain were often from colonies with whom delicate negotiations were being held. Government leaders were keen to avoid conflicts in or with these colonies and thus put off proposing restrictive entry measures as the first wave of immigrants arrived, found jobs, and settled in for permanent residence. Despite being worried that an unsettling process of immigration was underway, political leaders delayed direct action or legislation for 17 years, until the passage of the 1962 Commonwealth Immigrants Act. By then, a significant if not huge foreign labor force had established roots in Britain.

Most analysts identify three distinct stages of British immigration policy. The first is the 1945–1962 period just described, one distinguished by largely unregulated flows, mostly of former colonials who provided essential labor and established an ethnic and racial presence in the country. The second stage, through the late 1980s, saw increasingly restrictive legislation. Laws passed in 1962, 1968, and 1971 tightened controls on entry, and the British Nationality Act of 1981 strictly limited prospects for citizenship. As recessions during this period slowed economic growth and reduced the need for labor, leadership in a long period of Conservative rule (1979–1997) legislated permanent reductions in immigration to protect the local workforce as well as the British social order. At the same time, there was a growing if reluctant realization that immigrants with long tenure in the United Kingdom were there to stay, even in the face of continuous experience of discrimination and opposition to reunion with family members.

With the advent of the third stage in the early 1990s, officials began to recognize a change in population growth, in which immigration was a major engine. Between 1991 and 1998 net immigration averaged 104,000 persons per year, compared to a net increase of 107,000 among the British-born; by the end of the century, the shift was dramatic, with net immigration reaching 194,000 and native population growth falling to 72,000. Most immigrants in that period were from outside the European Union, leading the Labour Party's immigration minister, Barbara Roche, to affirm what would be a major evolution in the government's position: "The UK is a nation of immigrants. Immigration is a very good thing and has benefited the country" (*The Guardian*, January 25, 2001). After years of denying the possibility that Britain could tolerate—much less embrace—a multicultural society, the government came to terms with both the reality of a significant ethnic minority presence and the need for a source of youth and future workers to offset what had become a chronically low national birth rate.

Real changes in the economic role of immigration came only with the return of a Labour government to power in 1997, after almost twenty years in opposition. Between 1997 and 2009, Labour passed six major pieces of legislation aimed at redirecting policy to accommodate workers of all nationalities. Most significant was the 2002 law facilitating immigration based on skills, job offers, and anticipated shortages of unskilled and semiskilled labor, a policy change that effectively overrode decades of limited entry. The system adopted in 2008 allocated immigration slots according to a system based on labor needs. It did restrict the route to permanent residence to the highly skilled and those with confirmed positions, but it also bought into EU rules facilitating the entry of less skilled immigrants to work without real restriction. Britain and other EU members monitored the movement of migrants from states joining in 2004 (ten members, eight from Eastern Europe) and 2007 (Romania and Bulgaria), reserving the right to restrict entrants until January 2014.

Changes in policy, and EU enlargement, contributed to important shifts in immigration and demographic patterns. Between 1991 and 2008, net in-migration increased steadily, from flat levels at the beginning to almost 200,000 in 2007 and 2008 (noted in chapter 1, Figure 1.2). In 2015, the number was even larger (330,000). As a result of both migrant origins and higher birth rates among ethnics already in Britain, diversity increased markedly. A population that was over 94% white in 1991 became 89.9% white in 2008. In the latter year only 80.1% of those under the age of 16 were white. Where Asian, black, and mixed-ethnicity groups constituted only 5.2% of the population in 1991, by 2008 they amounted to 8.3% of the total and more than 18% of persons under 16. As in the postwar period, immigrants became crucial as a replacement generation, this time filling the gap created by lower national fertility rates. Indians, Poles, and Irish became the largest foreign-national groups living in Britain. Whereas immigrants in earlier years had clustered in industry and lower-level services, by 2004 most were concentrated in finance and health sectors, often with backgrounds similar to those in Europe. Those from EU nations were less likely to pursue citizenship, as they possessed unrestricted rights of entry and work. By the end of the first decade of the twenty-first century, Britain appeared to have evolved from a bastion of resistance to a nation joining its European neighbors in a utilitarian approach to immigration, one based on active recruitment of needed labor and a commitment to social assimilation.

Still, many Britons remained hostile in general and skeptical of varying estimates of economic benefits. For example, the Labour Party had forecast a fiscal benefit of 6 billion pounds per year—an amount close to predictions for the much larger American economy—and an influx of 20,000 immigrants from Eastern European nations joining the EU in 2004—not the 700,000 who would actually enter. The stage was thus set for the reemergence of conflict after the 2008 economic downturn and, more ominously, during the crisis of refugees that hit Europe in 2013, which still shows little prospect of resolution.

Economic Drivers of Immigration

Although economic recessions and racially based hostility to immigration defined a significant segment of the postwar years, basic economic drivers of immigration were still evident in the British experience. An economy based on revenue and resources from the

Empire disappeared, and its replacement developed around industries requiring diverse skills and manpower. Labor shortages attributed to radically different origins (wartime casualties, diversification of the economy, declining birthrates) necessitated searching for workers outside the United Kingdom. In spite of widespread native hostility, the contributions of foreign labor in both the postwar and post-Conservative periods were obvious and substantial. Their role in the reconstruction effort helped facilitate the economic boom that accompanied repair and building programs through 1961. Large sections of London and other urban centers were restored, transport updated, and military facilities developed for the new defense alliance (the North Atlantic Treaty Organization). Not surprisingly, by the time British legislators began to restrict immigration, large numbers of immigrants and their families had settled into permanent residence.

As in the United States, early waves of immigrants found the sort of work nationals preferred to avoid: manual and unskilled laboring positions in textiles, mining, shipbuilding, service industries, and the National Health Service. At least initially, the rate of employment among immigrant men was higher than that of the general male population. Among women, Muslims had lower rates of employment than adult British women, but other ethnic groups were more likely to occupy jobs than their British counterparts. Immigrants displayed high levels of union membership, a full 15 percentage points higher than native workers. Still, recessions in the 1970s and early 1980s caused higher levels of unemployment among immigrants and longer periods without work, driving many of the foreign unemployed into even lower level jobs and losing much of the job mobility they might have gained in better times (Smith, 1977).

After 1977, the higher unemployment level among immigrant men persisted. After immigration reforms that made skills a prime criterion for admission were implemented in 2002, the gap narrowed, and by 2009 it had disappeared entirely. Almost identical unemployment rates continued through the four years of recession that began in 2008. A 2015 report by the Center for Economic Performance of the London School of Economics and Political Science found no overall direct relationship between migration rates and unemployment among nationals; in fact, unemployment levels decreased over much of the 1991–2014 period even as immigration numbers increased sharply (Wadsworth, 2015). Moreover, recent immigrants have been, on average, better educated than their British counterparts, unlike the patterns of earlier periods. Just over half of British-born members of the working age cohort had left school by age 16, compared to only 10% of immigrants entering under the skills-based system. More than half of the new immigrants were in school at age 21, compared to only 20% of their national counterparts. That breakdown existed across a wide spectrum of skills and positions across all sectors of the economy. Industries with higher proportions of foreign workers also exhibited higher levels of productivity, especially in manufacturing and real estate.

Because the points-based immigration system favors educated and skilled applicants, opponents have claimed that new arrivals compete with and depress the wages of British nationals. A large body of research concludes that such has not been the case, however. As in the United States, skilled immigrants to the UK resemble immigrants elsewhere in that they compete mostly with each other for positions for which there are insufficient numbers of national applicants. When the skills-based system is working efficiently, immigrants complement the work force that is already in place, an argument confirmed by studies of the impact of European Union immigrants on local economies.

A rough measure of economic replacement—that is, the degree to which immigrants fill gaps in the workforce—is the percentage of immigrants in the working population. Since 1975, the share of the working population filled by immigrants has risen steadily, reaching an all-time high of 15% in 2014. Immigrants are distributed throughout the labor force but overrepresented in both professional and what economists label "elemental" occupations—in service positions, healthcare, and basic industry. Like their counterparts in other advanced societies, overqualified immigrants often take work in lower-level occupations, aspiring to move into better positions at some later point.

Data on the economic impact of immigrants describe two populations. Those who entered in the postwar years moved easily into a porous labor market where both those with skills and the larger number with minimal training found opportunities. They generally settled in working- and lower-middle-class areas as first and second generations experiencing social discrimination but stable livelihoods. Forty years later, a change in policy brought a second wave from outside the EU, entering with skill sets in high demand in a rapidly changing economy. Coupled with migrants from within the EU, the post-2004 cohort easily filled a host of gaps in the workforce created by the declining birthrate. Studies on the impact of the second group have consistently found that, since their admission was predicated on labor needs, there was little or no negative effect on the employment or wages of native-born workers (Gougard et al., 2011; Manacorda et al., 2007). In fact, studies of recent residential patterns revealed that immigrants are more economically independent and less likely to live in public housing than native-born citizens. As in the United States, pressure on wages appeared in sectors where new arrivals competed with established immigrant groups.

Economic Issues in Immigration Debates

Unlike the 200-year-long American evolution of immigration policy, the British experience has been necessarily defined in a much shorter time frame. As recently as 1948, the British dramatically put out the welcome mat for millions of Commonwealth subjects; by 1962, they were ready to restrict the flow severely; and by 1980 they no longer considered citizenship an option for most applicants. For more than twenty years, the doors were effectively closed, and only a major change in government in 1997 led to a rationally based system of admissions. Between the first wave of immigrants drawn to an open labor market after World War II and the wave linked to global changes in the economy after 2005, the 50-year debate on immigration policy was dominated by racial arguments, conjoining economic issues with sociocultural fears and bias. Indeed, the mix of economic and cultural opposition to migrants was prominent in the Brexit vote of June 2016, conflating fears of migrants taking jobs from nationals with hostility to non-British cultures, and frustrating attempts to construct rational and strategic planning.

On the surface, some of the issues resembled those raised by American and European leaders over a much longer period. Waves of immigrants arrived, often gravitating toward specific industries, raising fear and hostility among locals who saw their own livelihoods threatened. In Britain, such concerns were magnified by the existence of a long-standing national working class and the absence of an immigration history in which newcomers complemented and adapted to local situations. The British were perennially concerned with capacity and linked immigration to demographic saturation and the limitations of the landmass. Labor organizations and parties, always the first to identify threats to workers, were at best wary of immigrants, frequently joined by conservative groups concerned with strains placed on education and social services.

Economic elements in the immigration debate are harder to define in Britain for three reasons. First, restrictions on immigration began relatively soon (1961) after the movement really began (1950–52) and continued to expand through the 1981 restrictions on admission and citizenship. In the postwar years, what was considered massive immigration from New Commonwealth nations totaled only 500,000 over the nine years before the first restrictive laws took effect. Unlike Germany, which admitted millions of foreign workers through the early 1970s, Britain accepted a much smaller number, and between 1965 and 1994 the population growth due to immigration was close to zero. Explaining patterns with relatively small numbers and little change in flows is necessarily a risky exercise.

Moreover, the immigrant labor population after the war could easily be seen as a replacement cohort for the casualties Britain had suffered. Military and civilian losses were more than 450,000, almost 1% of the total population, many of whom were working-age men. The need for able-bodied labor was enormous, and immigrants who had entered during the war to work in essential industries were indispensable to reconstruction. As a critical component of postwar development, they were difficult to analyze as an independent labor force.

Finally, net immigration was essentially zero for a substantial part of the 1945–2010 period. After 1994, it grew slowly and only reached 200,000 in 2004. Immigration laws passed after 2005 closely linked admission to vacancies in the labor market, encouraging those with skills or holding firm job offers and limiting others to gaps in employment in heavy industry and the service sectors. By 2007, a study by British economists clearly documented the net contributions of immigrants from EU members (measured as the ratio of revenue generation to required expenditures) as outpacing those of native workers by a significant margin, and the net contributions of those from outside the EU as virtually identical to those of native workers (Dustman & Frattini, 2014). By 2011, the contributions of immigrants from all sending nations exceeded those of Britons. As both replacement and growth factors, immigration, as regulated by policies adopted since 2005, appears to have contributed to a stable and often thriving British economy.

Despite that conclusion, concern and emotional debate over immigration remain prominent features of British politics. One reason is wariness about immigrants who do not arrive under the auspices of the reformed system, specifically refugees, asylum seekers, and those entering the country illegally. The former category includes 80,000 or more who arrived in 2001 and 2002, and 20–30,000 per year since then (Figure 3.1), and reflects the dramatic pressure exerted by those fleeing conflict in the Middle East in the last three years. Although numbers pale in comparison to the hundreds of thousands who sought asylum in Germany in the mid-1990s (and the millions since 2013), the post-2000 surges led to a series of policy measures that mandated stiff visa requirements, penalties on traffickers, and denial of benefits while asylum claims were being evaluated. Ongoing debates have failed to resolve key questions regarding British capacity to accommodate refugees and, by extension, immigrants more generally.

A second concern would be the number and status of undocumented immigrants. Variously estimated between 417,000 and 863,000 in 2007, and still a small percentage of the overall population, growth of this elusive group has inspired proposals similar to those passed in some American states, few of which have become national policy. At the same time, the government has moved to "regularize" a small percentage of illegals (about 15%), mostly long-term migrants who have established residence and employment. The debate is ongoing, intensified by the post-2013 refugee crisis in Europe, where 1.5 million entered in 2015.

Only a small number of those have reached Britain. In both his 2010 and 2015 election campaigns, Prime Minister David Cameron championed measures to reduce immigrant admissions from hundreds of thousands to thousands, cracking down on illegals, tightening access to benefits, increasing deportations of those without work. Despite documented economic contributions, politicians across the ideological spectrum, and much of the public, continue to believe that costs and labor competition are overbear-

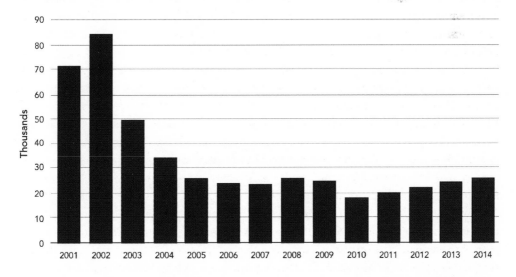

Figure 3.1. Asylum Applicants to the United Kingdom, 2001–2014. (*Source:* British Home Office, Annual Statistics, 2015)

ing. If basic economic data cannot explain steady opposition to immigration, we need to look for the reasons in other forces that shape immigration policies, especially political and social priorities in Britain where, as in the United States, economic issues are often interleaved with political sentiments to shape irrational and as well as rational debate.

Political Alignments and Immigration

The Setting for the Twenty-First Century Debate

In the United States, an important immigration watershed occurred relatively late (1965) in a history of immigration filled with waves of foreign arrivals. Well before then, immigrants had expanded the nation's diversity despite frequent resistance. With the comprehensive 1965 law, doors were opened to immigrants from across the globe, renewing old concerns that they would not assimilate. Even after 150 years in which immigrants consistently blended into the "melting pot" of society, doubts about newcomers from Africa, Asia, and Latin America persisted. The years since 1965 have seen both public hostility and acceptance, and calls for deportation coupled with forgiving legislation for those without documents, portending continued assimilation as well as controversy.

As noted earlier, a significant British comparison might be found in the time span in which immigration policies were developed—55–75 years in which political leaders had to deal with millions of potential immigrants while they simultaneously struggled to build a postwar economy and redefine relationships with dozens of former colonies. It is not surprising that immigration debates were hobbled by both fears and ignorance in such an environment.

A second comparison lies in British attitudes toward the outside world after two centuries of the Empire. Prominent in that history was the inevitable colonial sense of superiority, based in long-standing domestic traditions of nobility and strict class division, which were easily transferred to rationalization of dominance in the colonies. Since the British had little interest in religious or cultural conversions, the colonies were simply possessions, seen primarily as sources of resources rather than imperial states worthy of social and political obligation.

A critical corollary of this attitude was its racial element. To regard blacks and Asians as incapable of governing themselves meant that there was little reason to expand education, modernize agriculture, or introduce elements of Western culture in the colonies. It is hardly surprising that racial bias permeated postindependence discussions, particularly in the positions of British leaders who openly dismissed immigration into Britain as unimaginable for "coloured" people. Britain's experience of centuries of racial separation in the colonies and little diversity at home was too extensive simply to disappear with the arrival of postwar independence and migration movements. Immigrants who did settle in Britain experienced segregation and discrimination. Postwar riots in Brixton and Liverpool were identified with racial minorities and comparisons drawn to race-based incidents in the United States. If immigration of any kind was alien to Britain, immigration of nonwhites was inconceivable to both the elites and the public.

Political Institutions: The Primacy of Party Rule

Unlike the United States, British political parties compete in a parliamentary system where the winning majority and its leadership are expected to define and implement policy. Between 1945 and 1965, British governments opted to avoid major immigration legislation, focusing instead on narrower issues such as definitions of Commonwealth citizenship as they disengaged from colonies. After 1965, both major parties embraced restrictive policies. The Labour government under Harold Wilson put aside its ideological empathy for immigrant labor and passed the first clearly restrictive law in 1968. The successor Conservative government of Edward Heath followed suit in 1971 with a bill mandating permanent restrictions on New Commonwealth citizens from Africa, Asia, and the Caribbean. Three years of Labour rule from 1976 to 1979 brought no modifications to the 1971 Act, foreshadowing the policies that Margaret Thatcher would follow for eleven years as she enforcing increasingly harsh policies based on the Nationality Act, which passed in 1981. As restrictions were repeatedly affirmed by the courts, party consensus emerged to support 50 years of minimal permitted levels of immigration.

The change that finally occurred in British immigration policy was largely due to the enlargement of the European Union and its mandate supporting the free movement of citizens, which was initiated in 1985 and later expanded to include all members in 2004. Although Britain was lukewarm in its response to the expansion, it acquiesced to the admission of ten new member nations, leading to the movement by large numbers of Poles and other East Europeans into core EU states—Germany, Spain, France, and Britain—in response to economic growth and job opportunities there. Within six years, more than 500,000 Polish nationals had settled into jobs in Britain, and recruitment of workers from both new EU and non-EU members was increasing across Europe. Labour governments under Prime Minister Tony Blair took the opportunity to emphasize skills in growth areas, and passed a series of immigration reforms to accommodate those changes. Given the need for workers, especially in high tech and modern industries, the latest laws could just as easily have been authored by a Conservative opposition tailoring immigration policy to economic growth.

Although both major parties allowed pragmatic interests to override ideology, Conservatives have stayed closer to their roots on this issue. Restrictive laws passed on their watch were pursued with a passion based on their belief that immigrants undermine British culture. In opposition, Labour politicians were generally faithful to British unions but avoided similar support for workers from Commonwealth nations and rarely rebutted elitist, even racist, messages being codified into law. When the EU adopted rules of free movement of workers in 2004, Labour downplayed potentially adverse effects on British workers by interpreting the new system in terms focused on macroeconomic adjustments of the relationship between labor and capital.

How Great Britain Kept its Distance from EU Immigration Issues

1. Although the UK is a member of the European Union (with a plan to end membership by 2019), it is not a party to the Schengen Agreement, which mandates borderless travel rights to members. Britain can restrict entry according to its own rules.

2. The UK did not adopt the EURO as its currency, maintaining its own system of financial rules and security in international relations.

3. The UK limited the access of non-British residents to many domestic benefits, including jobless assistance, housing subsidies, disability.

4. Immigrants and noncitizens were required to satisfy British officials that they were "habitually resident" to be eligible for benefits.

5. British leaders engaged in continuous discussion of separate rules from other EU members while the country was in the Union, and have insisted on maintaining national control as they negotiate terms of separation and a new relationship with the EU.

6. Most analysts of the Brexit vote to leave the European Union believe that the highest priority for the post-withdrawal agreement is British authority to accept or deny immigrants, including those from the EU, even if that provision forces Britain to accept severe restrictions on access to European markets and financial services.

Despite strong evidence that immigration has been used primarily to fill gaps in the British workforce, Conservatives have consistently resisted immigration from New Commonwealth and other African, Asian, and Caribbean nations. After Conservative MP Enoch Powell raised the temperature of discourse with images of "rivers of blood" during the 1968 riots, the party reinforced negative public sentiment in passing the highly restrictive British Nationality Act of 1981. Margaret Thatcher used her long tenure in power to push her position that immigrants were incapable of assimilation. Publicly, she defined her stance as the obvious response to British needs, often arguing that current rates that admittted 45–50,000 immigrants annually would be equivalent to adding two new towns per year, a graphic if distorted view of how immigrants settle, and one that ignores the fact that a large percentage of those immigrants were making up for declining numbers in the British population.

Conservatives have successfully focused on those immigrants most likely to be resented by citizens; in the 1970s and 1980s, they highlighted rioters and unemployed youth. In the years since the 2005 reforms, the targeted groups have been refugees and undocumented immigrants, as Conservatives have continued to argue that the nation has insufficient capacity to accommodate them. Some targets reflected political hot issues. When mixed-nationality couples were denied reentry into Britain after trips abroad, Britain was rebuked by regional and international human rights commissions. Even as the nation saw some recovery from the 2008 economic recession, voters provided unanticipated support for the UK Independence Party, which had been organized around opposition to all immigration as well as to British membership in the European

Union. Frequently embarrassed by its extremist fringe and prone to clumsy statements (UKIP leader Nigel Farage publicly admitted that Vladimir Putin was his most admired statesman), the party has posed a growing threat to both major parties' ability to promote rational immigration policies.

Following UKIP's strong showing in local elections in May 2013 and a 13% share of the national vote in 2015, Conservative prime minister David Cameron proposed tougher immigration laws, with heavy fines for companies hiring illegal workers, residency checks, and increased deportations. Labor proposals to legalize long-term undocumented workers and their families predictably failed to gain support. Although Britain ultimately developed an admission system that incorporated travel and work rights of citizens of EU member states, and clear eligibility rules for applicants from outside the EU, resistance has persisted. Most anti-immigration leaders focus on those in the country illegally and refugees seeking admission, but undercurrents of fear of any large foreign presence are obvious in party platforms and the provocative positions taken by leaders. Faced with even small-scale incidents during the refugee crisis of 2013 and beyond, the government has struggled to find palatable responses—the case of a single refugee who managed to cross into Britain through the tunnel from France is a prime example (see box below). Support for the UKIP position in the Brexit vote indicates that anti-immigration sentiment remains a disruptive force, pushing both parties' positions to the right and challenging the system in place. Opposition parties everywhere tend to focus on the failures of policies held by the majority, but in Britain their party programs are far more likely to become law with a change of government.

Britain's Immigration Dilemma: What to Do with a Refugee Who Walked through the Tunnel from France?

On August 4, 2015, 40-year-old Sudanese refugee Abdul Rahman Haroun eluded French tunnel guards in Calais and walked 31 miles on the narrow edge of the structure to reach Britain. In flip-flops, after 11 hours of dangerous passage. 15 migrants had previously died trying to follow this route.

The British were initially unsure how to handle his unauthorized entrance, but arrested Haroun and charged him with causing an obstruction in the tunnel. He remained in custody until January 18, 2016, when he was released on bail. In the meantime, he was granted asylum on December 24.

Reactions to his plight, and the asylum decision, were divided. Most Labour Party members hailed the outcome; Conservatives voiced concern that it would encourage more attempts to enter the country illegally.

In December 2015, Haroun was granted asylum status, allowing him to remain in Britain.

Thousands of migrants—as many as 2,000 per night—have tried to hitch rides or hide in vehicles passing through the tunnel; more than 8,000 were arrested in the first half of 2015. The French refugee camps in Calais have been overcrowded with frustrated refugees for months; in February 2016, the government announced plans to drastically reduce the number and size of those camps and redistribute refugees to other centers.

Institutions beyond Parties: Government Administration and Interest Groups

In Britain, government agencies charged with implementing laws often assume a certain level of ownership of policy and groups they oversee. In this case the Home Office—the cabinet-level department responsible for homeland security in general and immigration in particular—has earned a reputation for strict control. Virtually all of the legislation passed since 1962 has delegated the authority to interpret regulations and make decisions on individual cases to that department. Unlike their counterparts in the United States and Europe, both the executive and judiciary have most commonly deferred to Home Office decisions without review by either branch. As a result, potential immigrants with cases pending for residence, family reunion, even deportation, confront an agency with a consistent history of denying applications. Indeed, the agency has defined its mission as primarily regulation and oversight rather than facilitation or resolution of immigration cases. The distinction is important, as the Home Office is the first—and often the last—step for any immigrant seeking residence or assistance with employment, housing, language instruction, or race relations.

An array of groups that support the rights of immigrants has developed over the last three decades. After 1981, as localities struggled to create programs to ease racial tensions in their communities, a number of independent and quasi-governmental commissions were formed to monitor progress in facilitating education and employment services. The independent, publicly funded Commission for Racial Equality serves both enforcement functions and a promotional role; the British Institute of Human Rights assesses compliance with covenants of the European Commission on Human Rights; and web-based organizations such as the Migrants' Rights Network and 50.50 Inclusive Democracy work to mobilize lobbying efforts when particular cases or new legislation are being considered. Unite, the largest union in Britain, most recently asked members to oppose moves made by UKIP to garner support for its anti-immigration platform. Local church groups associated with the central offices of the Archbishop in Westminster have joined human rights groups to support the rights of mixed-nationality couples to live without restrictions. Appeals that cite contradictions between British policies and EU standards have won the support of coalitions of church, human rights, and union groups, particularly since the opening of borders to EU members after 2004.

The influence wielded by interest groups and rulings from European commissions may be most evident in the improvement in British responses to the reality of multiracial communities and problems encountered in housing, employment, and education. For a long time, governments were slow to institute proactive policies in the face of public hostility and their own lack of experience in dealing with minorities. In 1965, the Labour government passed the first Race Relations Act outlawing discrimination, and successor governments have at least voiced support for protective laws. Despite such support, the Commission for Racial Equality, established in 1975 with substantial powers, was understaffed and underfunded; both supporters and opponents were critical of its record in facilitating equal treatment for minorities. National policies supporting multicultural programs stalled as governments focused on reducing numbers of immigrants and left matters of social and economic integration to often indifferent localities. In 1997, the newly elected Labour government finally recognized the reality of multiculturalism officially, but toned down new proposals when criticized by both ends of the political spectrum. Conservatives and many moderates objected to any policies that hinted at reverse discrimination, and staunch liberals opposed what they saw as attempts to stereotype and segregate minorities, so that most proposals were tabled indefinitely.

In the aftermath of the September 11, 2001, attacks in the United States, Conservatives renewed their arguments that multiculturalism implicitly fostered terrorist activities. National concern with Britain's substantial Muslim minority (over 2.95 million in 2014) increased after the 2005 attack on the London rail system, shifting the focus from immigrants in general to Muslims. Since then, debate has moved away from original divisions over state support for religious schools to direct concerns with anti-British education and potentially provocative religious practices—for example, the wearing of head scarves by Muslim women. With the return of a Conservative-led coalition in 2010, Prime Minister Cameron boldly equated multicultural efforts made by prior administrations with encouragement of minority isolation and threats to the greater good. With that declaration, he proposed returning most policy authority back to localities, entrusting major issues of racial and ethnic relations to community boards and citizens.

However prominent international commissions, church organizations, and political lobbies might have appeared in press coverage, the major players in immigration debates are still party leaders and the agencies that implement their policies. The most virulent interest groups have moved to form new parties, mostly recently the UKIP. Founded in 1993 to oppose alliance with Europe, it broadened its agenda to focus on public hostility to immigration. Others, such as the British National Party, have appeared to inspire opposition throughout the postwar period. As strong voices in the immigration wars, they have demonstrated the power of public opinion, the final political element to be considered.

Public Opinion and British Policy

The taxing experience of dismantling the Empire almost certainly shaped public ideas about accepting immigrants, many from former colonies, into Britain. Overall opinion has ranged from unenthusiastic to unequivocally hostile for more than 70 years. Once migrants have been identified in general questions they tend to get blamed for a host of social and economic ills: pressures on council (public) housing, unemployment, the high costs of social services, slums, crime in urban centers. Even after immigration numbers were sharply reduced in 1965 and 1971, citizens continued to believe that too many had been admitted. Table 3.2 illustrates the historical pattern. In addition, 1964–1979 data from the British Election Studies reveal that more than 80% of the general population believed that there were too many immigrants in Britain. Percentages were still high in 1979, when Margaret Thatcher's Conservative Party made immigration a major

Table 3.2. Agreement that Too Many Immigrants Have Been Admitted to the UK, 1964–2011

% Agreeing that "too many" have been admitted (*Source:* British Election Study Data)	
1964	85
1966	8
1970	89
1979	87

% Agreeing that Immigration admissions had gone "too far" (*Source:* LPSOS-MORI)	
1983	88
1987	87

% Agreeing that "too many" have been admitted (*Source:* Transatlantic Trends)	
1989	62
1994	63
1997	61
1999	56
2000	65
2001	55
2007	67
2009	55
2010	60
2011	58

Sources: British Election Studies, 1964–1979; LPSOS-Mori, 1983,1987; German Marshall Fund, *Transatlantic Trends*, 1989–2011.

campaign issue. In 1983 and 1987, the studies used a slightly different question, to which almost 80% agreed that the government had "gone too far" in admitting immigrants. Between 1989 and 2011, an independent survey found much lower percentages (56% to 66%) agreeing that there were too many immigrants in the country, still a clear critical majority long after the numbers had been reduced and only episodically increased to meet national economic needs.

High levels of negative sentiment pervade opinion, but the animosity underlying the opinion has been most evident in the rhetoric of nation's political leaders. Openly racist rationales for immigration restrictions legitimized claims of inferiority; fear of primitive violence was stoked by Enoch Powell in the 1960s; strong opposition and harsh language by Prime Minister Thatcher and her home secretaries during the 1980s kept immigration at minimal levels for more than ten years. More recently, Conservatives have cast Poles seeking jobs in Britain as economic and security threats, and images of workers streaming in from sluggish economies in southern Europe as well as the Middle East were used by the UKIP in elections and the Brexit vote to claim that the nation would be held hostage by outsiders. Official political discourse was fierce and alarmist, reminiscent of sentiment in the riot-stricken 1980s.

Table 3.3. British Assessment of the Proper Level of Immigration, 1995–2011

% Agreeing that the # of immigrants should:	1995	2003	2008	2001	1995–2011 Change
. . . increase a lot/little	4	5	4	3	−1
. . . remain the same	27	16	17	18	−9
. . . reduce a little	24	23	24	24	0
. . . reduce a lot	39	49	55	51	+12

Source: British Election Studies, 1995–2011.

Other data portray a continuously hostile, or at least wary, public. Table 3.3 taps the public's views about government policy, specifically what level of immigration should be pursued. Since 1995, the percentage believing that the number of immigrants should be significantly reduced moved from 39% to a high of 55% in 2008 and a somewhat lower 51% in 2011—a point at which the economy was recovering from three years of recession. When combined with those favoring a small reduction in immigrants, the majority position rises to 75%, but in either case represents a net increase over the figures in 1995. In 2006, almost half thought that immigration was not good for the country, and fully three-fourths believed that immigration was either a very big or fairly big problem in Britain (Table 3.4). In 2009–10, the middle of the latest recession, 60% of those born in Britain favored a large reduction in immigration. Even among the foreign-born, almost 90% favored either maintaining the current number (42%) or reducing it (48%). Despite government reports that unemployment rates among immigrants were no higher than those of Britons, willingness to link immigration to the nation's economic woes was widespread.

Table 3.4. British Assessments of Aspects of Immigration, 2006

How much of a Problem is Immigration in Britain?	
None	4%
Not big	18%
Fairly big	38%
Very big	38%
Don't Know	2%

Agreement with the statement "Immigration is good for Britain"	
Agree	34%
Disagree	45%

Compared to other European and American Opinion, Percent of British Ranking Immigration in the Top Three Topics Causing Worry:	
British Ranking Immigration as a Worrying Topic	46%
Americans	33%
French	13%
Germans	8%

Source: British Election Studies, 2006; Eurobarometer 60, 2006.

Table 3.5. Attitudes toward Immigrants in Europe and the U.S.

	% Agreeing With Statement			
	U.S.	Britain	Germany	France
Immigrants in our country want to be distinct from our society	51	52	66	45
Immigrants are a burden on our country	41	37	29	52

Source: Pew Research Center, European Survey May 5, 2014, reported in "A Fragile Rebound for the EU on the Eve of European Parliamentary Elections"; U.S. Survey September 28, 2015, reported in "Modern Immigration Wave Brings 59 Million to U.S, Driving Growth and Change through 2061."

With the perspective of more than one nation in hand, we can begin to build comparisons with data from the United States and other European nations. Surveys conducted by the Pew Research Center in 2014 and 2015 asked respondents to answer two related questions: whether immigrants wanted to be distinct from British society, and whether immigrants were a burden on the country because they take jobs and benefits (Table 3.5). Interestingly, British sentiments were more positive, albeit it by a small margin, than those in the United States, and much more positive than those in France. The outlying French opinion appeared before the string of terrorist attacks began, suggesting that hostility ran deeper there. Only Germany displayed stronger confidence in the contributions made by immigrants, exhibiting, remarkably, higher opinions than Americans.

A final comparison is presented in Table 3.6, which includes data on foreigners as a percentage of total population, percentage of foreigners from outside the EU, and percentage believing there are too many immigrants in their countries. Important differences separate Britain, France, and Germany. Despite having by far the lowest percentages of both EU and other foreigners, British respondents are as likely to complain that there are too many of them. British tolerance of foreigners is, at least by this measure, related less to actual levels of immigration than to other factors.

Table 3.6. Concentrations of Foreign Residents and Public Opinion on Immigrant Levels, 1988–1992

Nation	Foreign Population as % of Total	Non-EU Foreigners as % of Total	% of Public believing too many immigrants in nation
France	6.4	3.9	45
West Germany	8.2	5.3	47
Britain	3.3	2.2	45

Source: Eurobarometer Surveys 30,35,37, 1989–1992.

The Role of Immigration in the Brexit Vote

Most analysts have concluded that hostility to immigrants played an outsized role in the campaign and result of the June 23, 2016, vote calling for Britain's exit from the European Union. Resistance to the EU's policies on economic issues has been a chronic theme in UKIP and some Conservative appeals, but had never aroused enough support to shape policy, much less force withdrawal from the Union. Prime Minister Cameron thought an early referendum would reject that option and allow his government to deal with EU issues without constant calls for ending membership. As the voting date neared, however, UKIP increased its focus on immigration, endorsing major ads portraying hordes of migrants challenging borders, with the caption "Breaking Point," and claiming that a Stay vote was "one for uncontrolled immigration." Labour's rejection of the Leave position was muted, and a YouGov poll found that fully 45% of its respondents agreed that they voted Leave in hope of reducing immigration. Despite the support of the prime minister, most members of parliament, and strong majorities in urban centers and Scotland, the vote to remain failed by a convincing vote (51.9 to 48.1%). Claiming that his mission had been achieved, UKIP leader Nigel Farange resigned, the prime minister stepped down, and the leading Conservative champion in favor of leaving the EU, Boris Johnson, withdrew from consideration as prime minister, leaving Home Secretary Theresa May with the difficult task of negotiating the terms of withdrawal with EU leaders.

Continued access to European markets is a major determinant of British economic health, but the EU policy supporting free movement of people as well as goods and services within the Union would not allow British restrictions, a key if not prime expectation of the Leave vote. Britain stands to lose not only a major source of labor, in the persons of workers unwilling to apply for immigrant status and work without EU protections, but also the freedom of British citizens to work on the continent. In the aftermath of the vote, instances of violence against foreigners increased, raising concerns about the safety of immigrants in Britain. Whatever the eventual terms of leaving, immigration will take new forms, most likely those of reduction and restriction.

Some aspects of those changes appeared before the Brexit vote. Seeking to mollify critics, the Cameron government proposed to tighten restrictions on immigrants, including those from EU member states. It also promised to restrict benefits for migrants from Europe and deport those without proper housing—a veiled reference to the possibility that Roma, or Gypsies, might try to settle in Britain as they had in France. Cameron's pledges foreshadowed but did not win over the sentiment that resulted in the Leave vote. His pronouncements also illustrated the increasing power parties of the Right have to force both government and opposition into more restrictive positions. Labour and the Liberal Party accused the government of an "ugly tone" on immigration, but otherwise posed a lackluster alternative to voters. In the longer term, the pragmatic immigration system introduced hardly a decade ago will be challenged, as sentiment linking immigration to economic and cultural difficulties continues to be a powerful force.

Great Britain: Reluctant Host Revisited

The discussion of immigration in Britain reveals how different its experience has been from that of the United States. The United States was from its inception a port of permanent call, a door more often than not open to a wide variety of ethnicities and religions through which immigrants could make and remake its culture. Britain's national identity was established before it set out to conquer distant lands, solidify its position as the world's strongest power, and become the world's trade center—all celebrating the culture that made it possible. It is hardly surprising that the British experience with immigration would take paths unlike that of the United States.

We noted earlier that geography has historically played a vital role in defining both engagement with other nations and the perceptions of their cultures. For the United States, that meant isolation from foreign conflicts and a land mass so large that a wide range of settlers could bring different identities while developing the rich natural resources open to them. Britain's insular status served to protect the nation from attack as it developed an economy needing resources and the power to seek them abroad; at the same time, it could discourage immigration, facilitating a history in which its Anglo-Saxon traditions would deepen. Movement into the island nation was minimal, reinforcing the reality that Britain would protect its homogeneous, homegrown population.

In its quest to build self-sufficiency and prosperity, Britain served both royal and nationalist egos as it developed trading posts and harvested the raw materials available on distant continents. Those ventures drew it into relationships with peoples of Africa and Asia, defining both Britain's economic position and its attitudes toward those suppliers. The exploit-and-trade business was most lucrative when Britain's overseas partners were poor and subservient, giving rise to a relationship model in which superiority was an essential component. Whereas American isolation, abundant space, and ample resources facilitated continuous immigration for over 200 years, Britain's insular status served as a prime rationale for solidifying the homeland population without immigrants and establishing an empire to supply its needs, as well as to establish worldwide power.

The preference for an English-only populace was also buttressed by the fact that however worldly Britain would become, its size would prescribe limits on population growth. Even with emigration regularly reducing the number of citizens residing there, the United Kingdom has long been densely populated relative to European nations. In the twenty-first century, that feature continues to influence public perceptions of the need to restrict growth even as the native birthrate has declined to a level below that needed to replace current generations, and an increase in immigration since 2000 has provided the revenues to support an aging population. Although geographic isolation and size have facilitated the perception of a homogeneous, independent population, globalization has necessitated increased engagement with the outside world. Ironically, geographic reality has become a compelling case for increased immigration.

It is tempting to assume that history has created a changed environment with updated attitudes toward population mix and growth. Reviewing the role of geography in immigration issues, however, reminds us that ages-old perceptions are not so easily modified, even when basic facts (population density, native birth rates) are undisputed. All nations revel in the glories of their history, embellishing high points and creating a past worthy of guiding contemporary culture. Just as the United States has made the immigrant tradition a centerpiece of its current identity, Britain has been heavily shaped by its imperial past. The enormity of British expansion and control was unparalleled, and its persistence over time testified to remarkable English influence. Opinion data revealing chronic negative views by Britons of outsiders are the best evidence of how important that period continues to be to UK citizens.

The seventy years since the end of World War II have produced critical changes in immigration politics. Dozens of former colonies achieved independence, often resulting in substantial negative interactions with the British. In frequently truncated periods of transition to self-rule, Britain gave up the role of patron, often leaving abruptly and offering little in the way of financial assistance. Conflicts ensued in many of the new states, some hostile to their own minorities, who would look to Britain for refuge. Commonwealth law, never anticipating independent nations seeking favorable immigration status, toyed with generous admission but ultimately closed doors. A public fearful of immigration from former colonies easily trumped any sentiment of obligation.

[handwritten margin note: postarwil lead to independen for Brit. colonies & weakend relationsly]

In many ways, the Empire inevitably retarded understanding in the postwar world. Contempt for New Commonwealth residents was prominent in the stances political leaders took, often invoking racist claims abandoned or at least muted in other Western nations. Leaders of both parties attributed urban riots to racial minorities. Several prime ministers explicitly insisted that nonwhites could never fit into British society; candidates and party leaders continued to oppose immigration as unnecessary and a threat to national culture, all of which undoubtedly contributed to the "Leave" vote in 2016. Although Labour governments have taken positive steps to encourage skills-based immigration, Conservatives and right-wing groups have maintained a consistent opposition, diminishing Labour's traditional role.

History has played a key role in maintaining a hostile environment for immigrants. Even as the public view of immigration as a bad thing moderated over the years, mainstream as well as minor parties have been able to resurrect negative sentiments in response to modest shifts in the economy or singular episodes of immigrant transgressions. Most observers of the UK Independence Party have concluded that even without the voting support necessary to win elections, the party and the fear that it fosters make it difficult for competing parties to change their own views and policies on immigration. Rightist movements have found a comfortable home within the comforting narrative of an imperial past.

Because immigration was so strictly limited between 1968 and 2000 that no one could realistically argue that foreigners were flooding the British market, economic factors before 2004 played more of an episodic than constant role in debates on the issue. When real gaps in the workforce appeared, there was little hesitation to import workers. During the war, thousands were recruited from the Caribbean colonies; when postwar reconstruction demanded additional labor, Britain brought in large numbers from Poland and they, like those from the Caribbean, eventually settled into permanent residence. An underperforming economy was used by Conservatives to discourage immigration for an extended period after 1973, and only when the economy heated up, in a period of declining national birth rates, did the need for additional labor arise again. As in earlier times, the Labour government initiated entry-friendly policies based on skills, and the rate of immigration grew steadily to meet those needs. Even during the years of the 2008–12 recession, employment among nonnationals remained stable.

The question facing the Conservative coalition government of David Cameron was how to continue a policy of selective immigration in the face of challenges raised by UKIP and his party's own right wing. Linking immigration reductions to withdrawal from the European Union stoked nationalist sentiments in the public, and the government faced a revived version of Enoch Powell's "rivers of blood" warning—particularly from those predicting uncontrolled invasions by Syrian refugees and East European Roma living in shantytowns and threatening local residents. As citizens of EU nations, Roma could in fact claim unrestricted movement, though no evidence suggests that Britain would be their destination of choice. Cameron's rhetoric was probably heated up by popular sentiment to include irrational proposals, such as limiting annual entries to hundreds each year, even though such a cutback would leave thousands of jobs unfilled for lack of qualified applicants. In the end, his compromises were insufficient to persuade a majority of voters to choose to remain in the EU, and he was unable to devise policies to address public discontent.

The dilemma—in which current reality is challenged by those wedded to the memory of earlier times—has given birth to a new era in Britain's history without membership in the dominant European Union, with its enormous economic stature and its equally enormous immigration and refugee challenges. Ironically, Britain will need both, as it strives to interact as an outsider with markets as well as labor needs. In the face of population decline and growing gaps in its working-age component, immigration policies will have to be developed that can attract foreigners no longer free to come and go with all the protections enjoyed within the EU. Whether current governments can craft workable adjustments will be determined by the tenacity of the opposition and the mettle of leadership confronting the challenge. If history is any guide, economics will trump ideological purity, even if the political costs are high.

Finally, it is increasingly evident that the alignment and strength of political forces are crucial in determining immigration policy in Britain, just as they have proven to be in the United States. Some comparisons are obvious. Despite strong evidence in both nations that immigrants accept those jobs that nationals reject, large segments of the public and strident political leaders believe that they either take jobs from nationals or end up on welfare rolls. Despite evidence suggesting that the native birthrate in both countries—and much more so in Britain—is too low to sustain their economies, the same public and same political leaders continue to promise a robust economy driven by native workers. And, despite evidence that immigrants admitted on the basis of their skills are better educated and not likely to utilize public services, a substantial segment of the public sees them as a net drain on the economy. Both American and British publics tend to hear and fear the worst of the immigration scenarios presented to them.

In both nations, the resolve of more conservative political parties appears stronger than that of their liberal counterparts. Since 1965, British Conservatives, and increasingly the UK Independence Party, have been the voice of alarm and persistent complaint that immigrants are alien to the native culture, just as Republicans in the United States have presented the almost certain nonwhite majority as a security threat, which should be confronted by strict immigration controls. British Labourites and American Democrats have tempered their advocacy for immigrants in the face of opposition from constituents. Liberal parties in both nations have initiated favorable legislation, which has been blocked by majorities in their legislatures. In both, opponents in large organizations have portrayed immigration in terms of its dangers; in both, groups supporting immigration and immigrant rights have tended to be less well funded and often more loosely organized. In such environments, it is hardly surprising that attempts to expand immigration programs have consistently been stalled or rejected outright. In both nations, political stalemate has resulted, with parties on both sides of the political center bickering over legislative details or weakening those laws that manage to get passed. Both Britain and the United States present case studies of how political leaders manage to simultaneously take strong stands and distance themselves from legislative action.

Where the comparison falters is in the easy rise of a far-Right party in Britain. Although fringe parties and third-party candidates have been common in American elections, their staying power has been weak and their ability to influence policy almost nonexistent. British Conservatives have generally been able to marginalize the fringe as well, as it did with the British Nationalist Party. A new arena, however, has opened up in European Union elections based on proportional representation (as opposed to the district-based constituencies in the British and American systems), where the odds are better for minor parties. The UKIP has utilized that advantage to legitimate its place in British politics and broaden the reach of its opposition to all things European. In that sense, the far Right has assumed a position similar to those occupied by the National Front in France and similar rightist parties in Italy and the Netherlands, presenting a greater threat to moderate policies in Britain than ruling parties have faced in earlier times.

At the same time, the very different situations with respect to undocumented immigrants need to be reemphasized. Although British leaders often claim that a massive underground network of illegal workers and families exists in the UK, the actual numbers are small in both absolute and comparative terms. Entering and working in Britain, with its ocean border, strict controls at all ports, and monitored work permits, is far more difficult than on the continent or in the United States. Estimates of the undocumented in the United States in 2016 amounted to more than 11 million, even with record departures registered during the 2008–12 economic recession. Given both the porousness of two long borders and an inadequate system for tracking foreigners entering the country, an understandable focus on undocumented immigrants surrounds *why didn't Bomba do this?*

all policy discussions in the United States. Despite the claims of some in Britain, the undocumented are still a minor issue.

The apparent paradox is that, even in the face of ineffective border controls, public opinion in the United States has consistently favored regularizing the status of the undocumented and implementing realistic admission standards. By comparison, in a nation with fewer immigrants than Germany or France and an economy needing additional qualified labor, British opinion has continued to reflect the belief that immigration levels are too high and undocumented workers prime candidates for deportation. A logical explanation would be that even when economic conditions support increases in immigration, opposition to foreigners who differ ethnically or racially from the host population is sufficiently strong to obstruct supportive legislation. As a result, national debates in both nations have been mired in deep divisions, which prevent virtually any real action. Whether those patterns are shared in Germany and France remains a question whose answer might guide more general conclusions.

For Further Reading

Andrew Geddes. *The Politics of Migration and Immigration in Europe*. Thousand Oaks, CA: Sage Publications, 2003.

Randall Hansen. *Citizenship and Immigration in Post-War Britain*. Oxford: Oxford University Press, 2000.

Kathleen Paul. *Whitewashing Britain: Race and Citizenship in the Postwar Era*. Ithaca: Cornell University Press, 1997.

4

Germany

Denial, Acceptance, Recruitment of Immigrants

Where Great Britain stumbled into the necessity of dealing with immigration as a postcolonial issue, Germany confronted it in response to economic imperatives. In the aftermath of World War II, governments struggling with the effects of defeat and devastation embarked on what would become the world's largest experiment with temporary workers, with literally no positive immigration experience to guide them. The naiveté of many policies, the size of the immigrant labor force, and the transition from ad hoc to regular policies make this a fascinating example of multiculturalism by default. More than fifty years after initiating recruitment of foreign labor, lingering doubts about immigration have been replaced by the current challenge of dealing with refugees from Africa and the Middle East. With millions of dislocated persons entering Europe by both sea and land routes, European Union members have resisted calls to accept larger numbers but have been unable to agree on a constructive common policy. As the EU's strongest economy, Germany has assumed an outsized role, boldly calling for all to absorb what will be millions of refugees as positive additions to individual nations and the greater European Union. How that role plays out will shape both Germany's own future and that of the Union.

German Geography as Changing Borders and Multiple Neighbors

Unlike the more isolated United States and Great Britain, Germany sits in the center of a European continent whose boundaries and national allegiances have shifted with the fates of royalty, war, ethnic division, and reunification over the last two centuries. The German state now includes borders and a land area that has only a 25-year history. It is once again the most populous nation in Europe, the second largest in area, and by most definitions the most powerful in the region.

Germany's natural strengths lie partly in its resources. A land mass that comprises large areas of arable land and timber supports significant agricultural and logging sectors, as well as mining opportunities provided by reserves of iron ore, coal, copper, nickel, and natural gas. With a North Sea coastline of 1,484 miles, Germany boasts a small but robust fishing industry. Its urban centers, notably those in the western sector and rebuilt with American postwar aid, are hubs for industrial giants in pharmaceuticals and electronics as well as modern technology and finance.

The population of Germany stood at 80 million in 2016, but the growth rate has shifted to a negative trend (–0.19%) in the last three years, even with free movement of workers and families from EU member nations. The most recent census reports that the population count is almost 1.5 million lower than ten years earlier, with projections that by 2060 the number could drop by another 19% (*New York Times*, August 14, 2013). The pattern is similar across Europe, especially in the east, where a pattern of few or no children being born to working-age people became even more pronounced in the recession of 2008. Germany has had the lowest birthrate in Europe for more than 40 years. That deficit has created a graying population that has shifted the worker-to-retiree ratio from 4:1 to 3:1, and a continuous decline is projected for the next fifty years.

The replacement pattern in the United States, with increasing numbers of younger residents due to higher birth rates among immigrants, has not yet been replicated in Germany. Almost fifty years after the first groups were actively recruited, the foreign-born and those with foreign-born parents constituted only 8.5% of the population, although the proportion is much higher in the under-40 cohort. Turks are the largest single ethnic group at 2.4% of the total population; 6.1% are Greeks, Italians, Poles, Russians, Spaniards, Serbo-Croatians, and others. The majority reside and work in cities in the former West Germany. After reunification of West and East Germany in 1990, population density declined as the Eastern sector brought down the overall figure. Still, in 2016 it was the second highest in continental Europe (behind the size-related anomaly of Luxembourg), at 591 residents per square mile. In the east, only Berlin records density at a level comparable to major metropolitan areas in the west (Frankfurt, Hamburg, Munich).

With reunification came several changes that impacted immigration policy. Before 1990, German borders on all but the East German front and with Czechoslovakia abutted European Union member states—Denmark, France, Belgium, Luxembourg, the Netherlands, Austria, and neutral Switzerland. Although there were occasional disagreements with neighboring countries about border issues, disputes were mild and the flow of foreigners effectively controlled. Borders on the east were strictly monitored by East German forces trained to prevent crossings into the West, and the small number who emigrated successfully rarely travelled the East German route.

The precipitous fall of the Berlin Wall and the Soviet satellite governments of Eastern Europe found the West German government unprepared for the unrestricted arrival of easterners, and even more unprepared for the subsequent unification of two significantly different economies and political cultures. The new government spent more than 100 billion dollars annually for the next 20 years to support infrastructure and industrial projects in the East, utilizing large numbers of foreign workers in areas with scant experience with non-Germans. As important, reunification drastically altered the eastern border, formerly the tightly controlled division between East and West Germany, to the loosely patrolled expanse with Poland which opened an unsecured route for potential immigrants from Russia and Asia. In the years immediately following unification, Germany's economy struggled to integrate a much less prosperous eastern sector and simultaneously deal with new immigrants who used that area as a point of entry.

Defining critical geographical factors in a nation undergoing such major shifts is necessarily difficult. Still, three important features stand out. One was the position Germany has historically occupied, surrounded by past and potential rivals with traditions as deep as its own. In Germany, as elsewhere in Europe, strong national pride and wariness of foreigners have persisted through changing political climates, and we should expect to see that play out in immigration issues. Second, as a nation with substantial natural resources and industrial development, Germany is an obvious destination for immigrants seeking work and improved living standards. Finally, expansion of the European Union has in reality opened the borders of all member states, Germany included, to both new members and those who use them as transit routes. In the context of the flight of millions of migrants from the Middle East and Africa, the need for responsive German and European immigration policies has become all the more intense.

German Immigration History as Twentieth-Century Development

Early Experience with Nationalism and Noncitizens

If modern British history was defined by centuries of isolation and imperial rule, Germany's was shaped more recently, after emerging as an independent nation, by serial conflicts with neighbors over territory and borders. A German Confederation evolved into nationhood only with mid-nineteenth-century industrialization and the growth of urban centers. By 1871, the Prussian Empire had established national boundaries and introduced the first social welfare system in Europe. Robust industrial growth and the development of a large military force required importation of foreign labor, and the government moderated its hostility toward its neighbors by encouraging Poles to enter, initially as temporary labor but eventually as a permanent workforce. As social historian Ralf Dahrendorf has argued, however, Germany's view of Polish and other neighboring citizens was undoubtedly colored by hatred and distrust rooted in years of border conflicts (1967). The government reinforced negative attitudes by limiting access to services and prohibiting instruction and use of native languages, even by foreigners Germany had never considered to be permanent residents. Recognition of the critical need for foreign labor was grudging, accompanied by hostile public opinion and demeaning official policies.

By 1890, German industrial production, fueled by proximate natural resources, an increasingly urban population, and the availability of foreign labor, surpassed that of Great Britain. Expanding military forces set the stage for colonial ventures. Recognizing the cost of challenging Britain or France in areas already colonized, the Kaiser moved selectively to secure territories in Africa and the Pacific to increase German power and access to resources. Still, a constant military concern was border security and threats from France and Russia. When war broke out in 1914, Germany declared war on Serbia's ally Russia, convinced that its military power would overcome any forces arrayed against it. German forces did initially prevail, forcing a Russia weakened by internal revolution into defeat, but on the Western Front they could not compete with fresh American troops, and Germany surrendered in November 1918. The treaty ending the war returned conquered territories and stripped Germany of its colonial possessions. Saddled with large reparations obligations and punitive dismantling of industry, Germany's diminished economy declined, foreign workers returned to their homelands, and Germany was once again a nation with virtually no immigrants.

The period after 1918 saw the humiliation of a nation crippled by the harsh terms of the Versailles Treaty and the worldwide depression that followed. By 1932, popular support for the defiant National Socialist (Nazi) Party led to a 13-year consolidation of totalitarian rule characterized by foreign aggression and internal war on its own minorities, most notably Jews and gypsies. The Nazi government made extensive use of forced labor in the territories it occupied, making it clear that the only role for foreigners was to support a repressive regime. In defeat, blame and invective were commonly used to demonize outsiders, presenting the new West German government with monumental tasks of moderating public attitudes and establishing productive relations with former enemies. In that unstable environment, millions of Germans left the country even as millions of refugees from Central and East Europe flowed into the area that would be rebuilt as West Germany. The new government was thus challenged by massive war damage, a defeated and often bitter populace, major emigration and immigration, and the need to build a credible political system. Any idea of creating an environment friendly to immigrants was necessarily a low priority

The Postwar Boom and the Need for Immigrant Labor

The agreement ending the war included the loss of both occupied territory and part of what had been prewar Germany. The Allies divided Germany into two sectors, each of which soon became an independent nation. Berlin, the former capital and largest German city, was located in the East but divided into four sectors, each controlled by one of the four major victorious powers—an arrangement that inevitably led to tension and ultimately the isolation of the Western sectors within an increasingly hostile East Germany. In the early postwar years, chaos and conflicting policies plagued the divided nations. The Soviets imposed harsh conditions in the East, establishing a puppet government and dismantling entire industries for removal to the USSR. In the West, the three Western allies quickly recognized the futility of engaging the East and opted instead for a coordinated commitment to rebuild the West German economic and political systems. By 1948, American funds were supporting both reconstruction and economic investment, facilitating the new government's plans to create a viable postwar nation.

As important as the physical and ideological divisions created by the treaties were their human resettlement provisions. The two sectors created in 1945 were required to accept responsibility for Germans living in areas conquered by the Reich, including some 12 million who would return from East Prussia, Silesia, Poland, Hungary, Yugoslavia, Romania, and the Sudetenland. Large numbers seeking to avoid the severe conditions in the East moved through the Soviet-controlled sector to West Germany. Although the numbers were daunting, they were part of even larger changes occasioned by the War. German casualties included 5.5 to 7 million soldiers and civilians as well as more than six million Jews and other minorities lost to systematic extermination. In addition, an estimated 11 million people left Germany: prisoners of war, forced laborers, others leaving for economic or emotional reasons. Remarkably, the initial flow of displaced Germans returning to the Western sector filled much of the enormous shortage of working-age adults (Reimann & Reimann, 1979). Aided by $1.4 billion in U.S. aid, West German companies were able to modernize industries and recast them into global businesses, and the government agreed to a currency reform to establish Germany as a financially credible global economy. The success of those steps fueled a decade of reconstruction, growth, and prosperity aptly described as the *Wirtschafts-wunder* (economic miracle). The economy grew with the active participation of West Germans, East Germans seeking opportunities in the West, and other East Europeans drawn by jobs and the promise of a prosperous future.

All of that changed in 1961. Embarrassed by the continuous exodus of workers to West Germany, the Soviet-backed government of East Germany constructed an impenetrable wall between the eastern and western sectors of Berlin in 1961 and fortified the longer border between the two nations. In addition to the crisis created by the closing of borders, those actions cut off West Germany's access to kindred workers, forcing the still-growing economy to identify new sources of labor. Fortunately for the businesses needing workers, a model had been developed in the late 1950s to allow Italians to work in West Germany, and that served as a template for recruitment of foreigners from Turkey, North Africa, and Southern Europe. Bilateral agreements provided work-defined, temporary permits for foreign workers moving to West Germany between 1961 and 1973. German firms worked with foreign governments to set up recruitment centers in selected nations and qualified workers were granted two-year residence and work permits linked to specific businesses. Both government and business initially assumed that rotation would be efficient and smooth; those at the end of their two-year permit would be seamlessly replaced by others taking over their jobs. In reality, businesses soon realized that continuity and experience were valuable assets and argued for longer terms of work, and German governments agreed to waive the mandatory return to home countries. In a nation with no real history or expectation of permanent immigration, the consequences of renewed permits would be staggering. The number of foreign workers grew from 329,000 in 1960 to 2,350,000 in 1974—or from 1.5% of all workers in 1960 to over 11% in 1974 (Table 4.1). As Ray Rist observed in one of the first studies of guestworkers in Germany, those numbers were all the more striking because workers in 1974 had been in the country during years of recession (1967 and 1973) and were almost certainly well integrated into the economy (Rist, 1978). And, within a foreign population that reached 4,127,400 in 1974, large numbers of workers had brought or

Table 4.1. Foreigners in Germany, 1951–1974

Year	Total Population	Employed Foreign Workers	Foreign Population
1951	50,241,400		485,763 (0.99%)
1955	52,383,000		484,819 (0.92%)
1960–61	56,173,000	329,356 (01.5%)	686,160 (01.22%)
1968	60,184,000	1,089,804 (05.2%)	2,318,100 (03.96%)
1974	62,054,000	2,350,000 (11.2%)	4,127,400 (06.65%)

Source: OECD, SOPEMI (Continuous Reporting System on Migration), 1976.

started families. Even if they were not socially integrated, they had made their German homes permanent in all senses except official recognition.

The recession sparked by the oil crisis of 1973 raised enough concern among German leaders to justify a ban on recruitment, ending the 12-year flow of new workers. At the same time, the ban motivated thousands of guestworkers living in Germany to send for family members before further restrictions were imposed. The overall number of foreigners in the country remained stable, even increasing as children were born and families settled into lives in Germany. Immigration thus became an issue more by default than systematic planning.

Attempts to Define Policies Relating to Foreigners after 1975

Although by 1975 it was clear to many that temporary workers were in Germany to stay, it was apparently not so evident to those in political power. The 1965 Aliens Act, which defined the status of foreigners living in Germany, was based on the assumption that foreign workers would serve the needs of both Germany (a labor force serving a growing economy) and the workers' home countries (relief from unemployment pressures, transfers to families, eventual return of skilled nationals). The locus of decisions was clearly Germany, which retained implicit and explicit rights to terminate foreign employment. German leaders also assumed that without steady work, most if not all foreigners would choose to return home even if they had been in Germany for years. The Aliens Act included no provisions for family unification, consistent with the expectation that most workers would be single men, eager to spend two years earning market-rate wages and acquiring skills that would allow them to build lives in their native countries. No mention was made of potential German citizenship.

At best, such assumptions were naive, ignoring the likelihood that recruitment enticements (high wages, comfortable living conditions, union protection) would also be enticements to stay. The government consistently claimed that Germany was "not a nation of immigration" and that foreign workers were appropriately seen as guests who would at some point leave. As late as 1985, when a generation of foreigners born in Germany was already a presence in communities and public schools, the Interior Ministry issued statements rejecting the possibility of either minority status or permanent residence for foreign families. The position was rationalized by conflicting claims—that West Germany had reached its absorptive capacity at 4.4 million foreigners, and that the inability of foreigners to integrate (rather than be absorbed) justified restrictive policies (Esser & Korte, 1985). Even as political leaders insisted that Germany need not plan for an immigrant minority, extensive rights and benefits included in their contracts guaranteed them substantial security unlikely to be matched in their homelands. Virtually all in leadership positions endorsed a status quo, a system that accommodated the needs of business and the concerns of labor unions but anticipated no permanent foreign population.

The best evidence of the reluctance of both conservative and liberal governments to redefine policies was the unwillingness of either to at least modify unworkable terms in the 1965 Aliens Act. That law required all noncitizens to have residence permits, renewable for periods of two to five years or made permanent if the applicant could demonstrate having become part of the "economic and social life" of West Germany. Work permits, granted separately, implied economic security, and completion of education or language programs were accepted as proof of social integration. By 1985, 85% of the work permits were "unrestricted," signifying at least five years of steady work experience, marriage to German citizens, or status as a political refugee. Spouses and children were generally granted work permits (only 5% were denied in 1985). Overall, restrictive provisions of the 1965 law were rarely applied twenty years later. Even then, the Interior Ministry maintained that while the government was committed to the integration of foreigners who had been in the country for a long time, it would also limit new applications and assist foreigners desiring to leave.

The work permit guaranteed substantial benefits. Labor unions insisted that guest-workers receive the same wages and benefits as nationals to ensure that foreigners would not undercut local standards. That meant that foreign workers were entitled to health insurance, retirement contributions, family support payments, and unemployment assistance. In 1975, the government initiated programs in language and vocational training to supplement state efforts. The larger problem of educating the children of foreign workers was more difficult to resolve, since education is by law a state responsibility. Despite reports as late as 1981 that 25% of foreign children were not attending school regularly, the federal government did not intervene. Indeed, at the same time that European commissions were recommending expanded educational efforts, the West German government sponsored an Assisted Return program (in 1983), offering workers cash plus accrued insurance and retirement contributions if they left Germany. The program attracted just over 14,000 takers in 1983 and 1984, but illustrated the government's continuing reluctance to revisit its positions on permanent settlement.

ie number of non-German residents continued to grow, official insistence
...gners were not immigrants sounded ever more like willful denial of reality.
Twenty-five years after guestworkers were first recruited to meet the need for labor,
the government continued to resist proposals to expand citizenship options. As late as
1986, the Interior Department's official position was that "[n]aturalization should not
be an instrument for the promotion of integration, but rather should stand at the end
of a successful integration process. The Federal Republic does not intend to facilitate
naturalization." (*The Record*, 1986) That position echoed naturalization rules introduced
in 1977, when, in an attempt to define the rights of foreigners in the country after the
1973 recruitment ban, the government emphasized the discretion of the state in implementing naturalization rules that all but ruled out foreign workers. The rules proved
highly effective, keeping the numbers of new citizens at fewer than 10,000 annually, far
lower than elsewhere in Europe.

The 1986 declaration reaffirmed official reluctance to update the 1965 law and
subsequent rules. The 1983 repatriation program encouraged foreigners to leave. It was
followed in the same year by a draft proposal to place severe restrictions on the rights of
guestworker families to visit workers legally in the country, an idea so widely opposed
that the ruling Christian Democratic Party tabled it indefinitely. In 1988, a new draft
reiterated the principle that Germany was "not a nation of immigration," and claimed
that since early guestworker programs had been one-time measures, all immigration
from non–European Union states should be outlawed as dangerous to German culture.
That draft prompted objections from both opposition parties and much of the CDU
itself. Such failures further highlighted the absence of policies to accommodate a growing long-term foreign population. That gap became even more unworkable as the 1989
forces of change united West Germany with its long-suffering East German neighbor
and dramatically opened the door to an influx of migrants from a shattered Soviet Bloc.

Special Immigration Cases: Ethnic Germans, Asylum Seekers, and Undocumented Workers

As noted earlier, the World War II settlement included the right of return for ethnic
Germans who lived outside the redrawn boundaries of West Germany, terms that were
affirmed in the new Constitution of 1949. In the years before the erection of the Berlin
Wall in 1961, more than 15 million people in this category made their way to West
Germany, first as expellees and later seeking jobs in a welcoming environment, most
of them settling easily into a recovering German society. The Wall became a 30-year
barrier to entry from the East but also allowed a respite from the obligation to accommodate ethnic and other refugees from the East. Not surprisingly, the 1989 collapse of
East European governments and the destruction of the wall revealed massive pent-up
demand for entry. The events of that time were historic by any definition, but were
especially so for Easterners asserting their right to return to the united Germany after
1990. Some idea of the new pressure is found in the number who took advantage of
loosened restrictions. As early as 1987, 78,500 crossed into Germany, and the numbers

in the next three years (202,000, 377,000, and 397,000) made the prospect of absorbing ethnic Germans sobering, even alarming, to governments after 1990 (Figure 4.1). *Asylum seekers low until wall went down*

Asylum seekers were a second challenge to the new German government. Reflecting the desire of the occupying powers to require Germany to recognize and respond to political oppression, the German Constitution (its Basic Law, or *Grundgesetz*), included a provision granting all persons able to demonstrate political persecution the right to asylum. That open invitation initially attracted relatively few applicants; between 1953 and 1968 the average number was 4,400 per year. As conditions in Eastern Europe worsened in the 1980s, the numbers increased, and in 1990 reached 302,600. Since Germany offered the most applicant-friendly rules in Europe, it was widely known as a way to avoid immigration restrictions. The largest number of asylum seekers were from nations that had provided the most guestworkers (Turkey and Yugoslavia), but after 1980 they came increasingly from the Middle East and South Asia. A long and complicated review process resulted in delays during which those awaiting decisions were by law housed and supported. When the Berlin Wall fell, numbers that were already alarmingly high soared, ultimately leading to major constitutional changes to restrict the flow.

A final group requiring attention was undocumented workers. Like other industrialized states, Germany had experienced some influx of illegal immigrants in the postwar

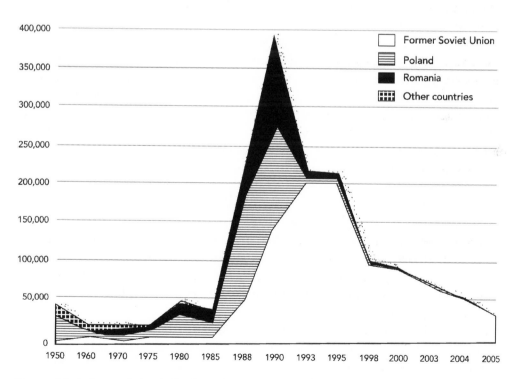

Figure 4.1. Inflows of *Aussiedler* into Germany, 1950–2005, by Country of Origin. (*Source:* German Federal Office of Administration, reproduced in Federal Office for Political Education, *Focus Migration: Germany*, May 2007)

boom but the overall numbers were low—estimated at 600,000 annually across the nine members of what was then the European Economic Community—due to the relative ease of legal admission. After that route was closed off in 1973, the number of illegal entries increased to more than 2 million in 1976, but the lack of concentration in any one country allowed governments to pay little attention to them. Germany never targeted them, preferring to quietly tolerate their presence in an economy quite able to absorb their presence.

Paying Attention to Foreigners after 1990

Even though the increasing permanence of foreigners with ambiguous status had not inspired any government action for more than thirty years, the fall of the Berlin Wall and the prospect of virtually wide-open borders to the east finally brought the issue into bold relief. The most immediate pressure was to deal with the removal of barriers between East and West Germany. During the summer of 1989, antigovernment protests in East Germany and neighboring nations forced East German president Erich Honecker to resign, leading to a cessation of East German challenges to border crossers, followed by the dramatic destruction of the Wall by protesters in a giddy display of liberation. Taken by surprise, West German leaders faced the daunting task of crafting a union that had not been seen as remotely possible for almost fifty years. In October 1990, less than a year after the Wall came down, reunification was declared and a common German government celebrated.

The tasks were enormous and the costs would prove to be even greater (averaging 100 billion Euros annually for twenty years). At a more human level, the process of socializing East Germans into both a competitive economy and a participatory democracy taxed the patience of Germans on both sides of the recent divide. In that context, the need for a change in policy toward foreigners was necessarily part of a much larger set of issues, but the urgency of the whole enterprise finally motivated leaders to address long-avoided questions of citizenship, working conditions, and future immigration in the unified nation.

West Germany had defined outsiders as belonging to discrete groups (ethnic Germans, asylum seekers, citizens of European Union members, non-EU residents), and the new government built on those categorizations by devising separate laws for each. After years of attempting to discourage the return of ethnic Germans, the 1990 *Aussiedler Rezeption Gesetz* (Return of Ethnic Germans Law) instituted an extensive application process, which had to be initiated outside the country. The 1992 legislation set a quota of 225,000; in 1996, a language requirement was added; in 2000, the quota was reduced to 100,000; in 2004, all right of return was slated to end in 2009, closing down a long-term source of immigrants.

West Germany's liberal asylum provisions were also revised to limit what had become unsustainable numbers (which peaked at almost 440,000 in 1992). Pressured by anti-immigrant forces in the newly unified nation, the centrist Christian Democratic government of Helmut Kohl moved to amend the permissive Article 16 of the Constitution. In 1993, two changes were made, one authorizing the return of asylum seekers to those countries that had allowed passage to Germany, and the other streamlining the review process to eliminate appeals, which had created backlogs and huge costs of supporting applicants awaiting decisions. With the new provisions, the only viable routes for asylum seekers would be by air or sea. The impact of the 1993 amendment was immediate. Five years later, the number of applicants had returned to pre-1989 levels, and by 2005 it had fallen to under 30,000 annually (Figure 4.2). The pace was remarkable, as Germany swiftly set strict limits on foreigners who had had special access to residence and citizenship for 45 years.

As the government finally addressed those issues, however, it found its reforms confounded by major changes in EU rules governing population movement among members. *free movement* Starting in 1985, five European Union nations (Belgium, the Netherlands, Luxembourg, France, and West Germany) had initiated what was known as the Schengen Agreement, to eliminate national borders by 1990. The plan was initially not embraced by other EU members, but in 1997 all fifteen signed the Amsterdam Treaty, which updated the basic terms of the European Union and incorporated the agreement's free movement for citizens of member states. As the EU expanded in 2004 and 2007, full right of movement

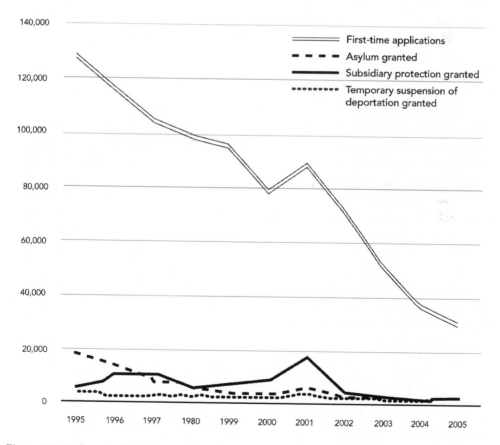

Figure 4.2. Asylum Applications and Decisions Taken, 1995–2005. (*Source:* German Federal Ministry for Migration and Refugees, reproduced in Federal Office for Political Education, *Focus Migration Germany,* May 2007)

was delayed until January 2014 for citizens of new members. At that point, restrictions were removed for the most recently admitted nations—Bulgaria and Romania—effectively opening borders for more than 500 million people living in 28 member states.

The flow of migrants within the EU followed patterns based mostly on the strength of national economies. For 18 of 28 member nations, the net gain or loss of population from migration between 1997 and 2014 has been fewer than 500,000 residents. Three nations experienced net gains of more than one million—Germany (2.2), Spain (1.6), and France (1.4). Two nations had a net loss of roughly 500,000 (Italy and Bulgaria), and three lost more than one million—Portugal (1.1), Poland (1.6), and Romania (2.5). In most instances, the numbers gained generally offset losses, due to declining national birth rates. In Germany, for example, the percentages of residents born outside the nation are roughly 4% (from EU nations) and 8% (from outside the EU), but the overall population for the combined East and West has remained stable over forty years, as a robust economy and smaller supply of national workers in the West attracted immigrants from less-prosperous areas of Europe. That dynamic has been similar elsewhere on the continent and in Britain.

Naturalization to Citizenship in Germany

Until 1990, German naturalization laws were based on the 1913 Nationality Law, which delegated all decisions to government authorities. 1977 Naturalization Guidelines required knowledge of the Federal Government's political system, spoken and written German fluency, and at least 10 years' residence. The regulations were prefaced by the statement that Germany was not a country of immigration, and dictated that personal wishes and economic interests must not be considered. States were allowed to add evidence of assimilation: Bavaria for example required knowledge of the state's anthem (Geddes, 2003).

Not surprisingly, naturalization rates of foreigners were among the lowest in Europe, averaging less than 0.5% of the foreign population per year. By 1990, 70% of the foreign population had lived in Germany for 10 years; more than 1.5 million had been born in Germany.

After 1990. Reforms partially reduced the obstacles to naturalization: by authorizing citizenship for those with 15 years of residence and reducing the waiting period for second and third generations to eight years, allowing second- and third-generation foreigners who had returned home to reenter and abolishing the waiting period for spouses of foreigners to enter.

Still, naturalization rates were low, inspiring five years of reform proposals.

The 2000 Reforms made significant changes: shortening the waiting period to eight years, allowing spouses and children to be naturalized in four years, and limiting conditions to knowledge of German and a clean criminal record.

After almost 40 years of restrictions, foreigners living in Germany were able to seek citizenship without the long and arduous process which often ended in denial.

Between 1980 and 2000, Germany was severely challenged by new and unresolved immigration issues involving: noncitizen guestworkers recruited in earlier years; the uneven but significant return of ethnic Germans; an unworkable constitutional mandate to accommodate all asylum seekers; the abrupt reunification with East Germany and its underemployed population; EU citizens free to live and work in Germany. It is hardly surprising that reform efforts focused more on particularly pressing issues rather than on more comprehensive immigration policy. That task was finally begun in 2000. Following the lead of other nations, Germany adopted a reformed Citizenship Law, which created a skills/educational basis for residence and work visas. It was in many ways similar to programs that had recruited temporary workers forty years earlier, authorizing residence for up to five years and facilitating the admission of more than 20,000 technology specialists in its first round. A year later, a special commission recommended a broader definition of national needs based on demographic shifts, officially acknowledging for the first time that Germany was an immigration nation and proposing an unlimited residence permit under which non-EU workers could plan permanent moves. The 2000 law included admissions provisions for individuals able to invest 1 million Euros in German projects, language instruction and startup support for the nonwealthy, and hardship grants for refugees.

The 2000 Immigration Law defining legal entry in economic terms lent credibility to processes of naturalization spelled out in earlier legislation but rarely used in an environment that had discouraged foreigners from pursuing citizenship. The 1977 discussion had taken place four years after the end of the admission of virtually all foreigners and stressed restrictions; applicants had to demonstrate that they were "furthering the public interest"; requests for citizenship could be denied if lifestyles were too different from those of Germans. The official considering the case had sole discretion over the final decision, and the number of successful applications was perennially low.

The historic shifts emerging in 1990 changed all that and led to the adoption of less onerous citizenship rules. A 15-year residence requirement was established for original immigrants (eight years for second and third-generation applicants) and the conditions of assimilation were removed. After 1990, children born on German soil to foreign parents were automatically granted German citizenship and required to choose either that or the citizenship of their parents (if the parents were not by then German citizens) at some point between ages 18 and 23. Dual citizenship was authorized and, unlike earlier laws, the 2000 act supported family reunification. In the optimistic atmosphere of *Die Wende* (The Change, the unofficial label for the reunification period), long-term non-German residents finally gained clarity of status.

German History as a Saga of Aggressive Expansion and Rebirth as Peaceful Economic Power

Any comparison of German immigration history with that of other nations quickly confronts the reality of huge differences. Nineteenth-century Germany engaged in competition with neighbors for territory and control, extended boundaries into the Near

East, shifted alliances to deal with potential aggression, and built economic strength with the use of forced labor. It sought opportunities for colonial conquests long after others had laid claim to territories in Africa and Asia, and sided with the weaker combatants in World War I, alienating nations with similar cultures and economies. Its embrace of National Socialism solidified a pattern of aggression including contempt for non-Germans and an unlikely role as host to diverse populations.

At the same time, some of the themes prominent in the histories of the United States and Britain could be seen in more extreme versions in Germany. Fear and distrust of different cultures ran deep in America and Britain, as well as Germany; new arrivals were relegated to less-desirable neighborhoods and jobs everywhere. In all three countries, local governments vacillated between encouraging schools to instruct foreign children in their native languages and insisting that all students learn and use the language of the host nation. Racism toward nonwhites was common socially and supported legally. In all three, debates on immigration were filled with claims that capacities had been reached. And, over time, all produced restrictive laws and immigration systems, often avoiding or postponing difficult issues.

The most important comparison might be derived from the images attached to immigration over time and in each place. Despite occasional lapses, the United States has long applauded its immigrant heritage and the pluralist society it established. In contrast, Britain consciously cultivated a role as controller of others rather than host, and Germany alternated conflicts with neighbors with campaigns to ban foreigners from the homeland. When population movement emerged as a major international force after World War II, German and British policies rejected any role for themselves as immigration nations until the turn of the twenty-first century. How influential those histories have been in guiding policy will be the question addressed in the next sections.

The Economics of Immigration in Germany

For the last 110 years, the German economy has been impacted by relations with its neighbors—hostility and war for the first 40 years, and recovery within the context of an increasingly united Europe in the last 70. Unlike both the United States and Britain, Germany moved from domination of foreign citizens to humiliation by future allies, to massive recruitment of labor from nations despised in earlier times. It is hardly surprising that economic needs would inspire changing, often conflicting policies as they were created construct a new and stable order in the aftermath of World War II.

As noted earlier, the German Reichs in the nineteenth and twentieth centuries were rooted in the lore of a strong nation fortified against its neighbors and admitting foreigners only when labor was needed. The tension inevitable when nations admit to the need but not the desirability of foreigners was especially strong in Germany. Immigrants were prohibited from using their native languages yet never embraced as permanent members of the culture. Two wars in first half of the twentieth century instilled the belief that foreigners were enemies on all fronts, anathema to the concept of a superior German *Volk*. By the time a compelling need for foreign labor reappeared in the early 1960s, the government needed to realign its citizens' orientation toward outsiders while drawing on scant experience with either immigrants or a society that would welcome them. It is that context which framed economic policy, and its political consequences, after 1961.

The Early Postwar Economic Impact of Foreign Labor

Faced with the task of constructing both a new economy and an open political system, postwar West German leadership quickly adopted the mandate of the occupying powers to build its economy with a capitalist base and foreign monitoring. More than one billion dollars from the Marshall Plan provided funds for infrastructure and the modernization of businesses to compete in emerging markets. Major population movement from former German territories provided much-needed labor during the first years of reconstruction, but shortages began to appear as the economy moved into overdrive. Industrial production more than doubled between 1950 and 1957, and gross national product increased by 10% annually. As the most vibrant postwar economy in Europe, West Germany was allowed to join the North Atlantic Treaty Organization (NATO) in 1955, and became one of the founding members of the European Economic Community (the EEC, forerunner of the larger European Union) in 1958. With efficient production and globalization demanded by Marshall Plan overseers, West Germany moved from devastation to growth in a remarkably short time.

What the Marshall Plan funds and guidelines could not provide was a reliable source of labor to sustain growth. By 1960, the flow from the East was slowing as East Germany moved to retain its own workforce and finally closed off that route with the construction of the Berlin Wall and tightening of the longer border in 1961. By then the economic importance of imported labor had become clear. Studies examining cost-benefit ratios in a net migration of three million people from East to West between 1945 and 1961 documented economic gains for West Germany ranging from 22.5 to 36 billion Deutsche Marks. The workforce lured from the less promising climate in the East was well educated, often with professional experience, and easily assimilated as it filled major gaps with working-age, German-speaking war survivors.

When the Wall and tighter overall security on the border forced West Germany to expand its sources of foreign labor to include Southern Europe, North Africa, and Turkey, fears that the economic benefits would disappear were allayed by the almost seamless absorption of those workers into the booming economy. Despite their educational and language deficits, new workers settled into jobs in heavy industry, construction, and basic services, lived in low-cost housing, and rarely utilized government services available to them as members of Germany's labor unions. A 1976 analysis factored in a comprehensive set of costs borne by West Germany as well as those expended and saved by home countries, and concluded that net benefits of imported labor had increased to over 6 billion DM in the ten years after 1961 (Blitz, 1976).

To be sure, the full employment enjoyed by German as well as foreign workers was not the only force fueling the economic boom between 1960 and 1973. An undervalued German currency facilitated a robust increase in exports, and capital stock grew at a fast pace as well; currency revaluation in the early 1970s worked to normalize trade balances as well as employment levels. But the availability of foreign workers undoubtedly played a critical role in guaranteeing a constant labor supply in a system that was able to prosper while delaying the structural adjustments which would slow the economy down after 1973 (Giersch, Paque, & Schmieding, 1992).

Economic crisis and recession in 1973 were expected to produce major shifts in a West German economy no longer needing new labor. Some changes did take place, especially in industries approaching the limit of their natural resources (coal mining) or becoming uncompetitive with other nations (steel). Unemployment, hardly visible in the twenty years prior to 1973, crept up from 2.5% in 1974 to 5.3% in 1975 before falling in the following year. Among foreigners remaining in Germany, unemployment rates were higher than those of native workers between 1974 and 1976, reaching a high of 7.4% in 1975. Still, government leaders who had consistently dealt with foreign labor as a temporary phenomenon resisted offering cash incentives for foreign workers to return to their homelands, although they did engage in discussions with Turkey and other sending nations about facilitating employment in their home countries for those who chose to leave Germany.

Germany and Switzerland were the only European nations to experience a reduction in the number of foreign residents after 1973, and even there the declines were less than expected. The number of employed foreign workers fell from 2,595,000 in 1973 to 1,932,600 in 1976, or from 11.9% of the workforce to 9.7%. Official reports noted that these declines had little effect on overall patterns of employment. One issued by the Organization for Economic Cooperation and Development (OECD) in 1976 found that even as major industrial nations banned recruitment in 1973 the only real changes were in the demographic makeup of foreign populations after that date. Only Britain pursued policies actively discouraging family unification; Germany attempted to restrict residence permits in densely populated urban centers, but ran up against official government policy, which insisted it did not to wish "to make the coming of families of the foreign workers to Germany more difficult" (quoted in Rist, 1978, p. 81). Despite demands from Conservative leaders for repatriation and restrictive residence permits, German governments were unwilling to adopt harsh family unification policies. As a result, the foreign population gradually shifted from consisting predominantly of single or unaccompanied males to families. Between 1973 and 1974, Germany recorded an increase in foreigners in the population due to the birth of children to foreign parents, a pattern that would continue for the next 40 years.

Predictions that in times of tight employment Germans would exercise their right to preferred hiring and take jobs filled by foreigners proved incorrect. One reason was that by 1973, when unemployment rates rose, the prospect of working in occupations at the bottom of the economic ladder had become unacceptable to a generation of Germans used to the mobility afforded them by the boom economy. Unemployment benefits were generous, encouraging native workers to wait out a recession that proved to be relatively short. That pattern facilitated continued employment for foreigners, who by then were clearly essential to basic heavy industry and the service economies. Like immigrants elsewhere, foreign workers in Germany began their new lives in the trenches of least desirable jobs, a start that despite its lack of commitment to permanence or citizenship, was sufficient incentive to stay, raise families, and eventually build better lives.

1973–1990 Economic Roles for Immigrants

By the mid-1970s it was clear that the fundamental tenet of guestworker policies—that foreign workers recruited into sectors with labor shortages would rotate out or leave when economic conditions no longer demanded their presence—was unsound. Foreigners were more likely to bring family members to Germany than join them in the homeland, and those with relatives already in the country would remain. The Socialist government in power between 1974 and 1982 was able to avoid any major changes as the recession eased and employment prospects improved for foreigners as well as citizens. That stance was aided by increasingly persuasive evidence that foreigners were vital cogs in a system able to weather economic downturns.

As noted earlier, the CDU government that assumed power in 1982 did produce proposals to reduce the foreigner population. An Assisted Return program offered cash and accumulated pension contributions, but relatively small numbers opted to take advantage of it (fewer than 30,000 over a four-year period). Even less successful were calls to deport children who had overstayed their visits and stricter plans to limit immigration in the future. Both were withdrawn as studies reported that even with more foreigners taking advantage of socioeconomic welfare programs, their spending, taxes, and pension contributions produced net gains for the economy. In addition, analyses continued to show that immigrant workers had no negative effects on the wages of others. Given the choice between pursuing anti-immigrant policies widely derided as too harsh or quietly accepting foreigners as economic contributors with restricted rights, the Conservative Kohl governments consistently opted for the latter.

The Collapse of Soviet Eastern Europe, German Unification, and EU Expansion after 1990

By far the biggest challenge to the German economy after 1945 came with the disintegration of Soviet influence in Eastern Europe, when the removal of the barriers to free movement between East and West opened up unparalleled opportunities for immigration. Coming on the heels of the 1985 Schengen Agreement, which had started to abolish border checks among Germany, France, Belgium, Luxembourg, and the Netherlands, the 1989–90 collapse of the East created a larger, effectively borderless economic environment. The strength of the German economy promised the country a major role in translating those changes into a larger and even more robust EU superpower.

As noted earlier, the Kohl government had recognized the need to address the asylum issue even before the borders changed in the early 1990s. The Basic Law was amended to allow restrictions comparable to those imposed by other European nations, and that change led to an immediate drop in the number of applications after 1993 and reduced pressure to accommodate refugees. But the magnitude of that economic issue was minor in comparison to the massive needs for infrastructure improvements and rejuvenation of the economy in an Eastern sector that lagged behind the West by all measures of economic health. Polls conducted in Germany after the initial euphoria of reunification revealed serious concerns about the costs of rebuilding the East and creating parity in standards of living, and early cautious cost estimates were soon replaced by recognition that actual expenditures would amount to hundreds of billions of Euros, figures that effectively put off any debate about the costs and benefits of foreign labor.

Still, the issue of regularizing the status of long-term foreign residents demanded attention, especially in the context of the extensive unemployment caused by the displacement of nonproductive labor in the East. The Socialist government that followed the long period of CDU rule drew upon both ideology and basic economic evidence to craft new laws. Between 2000 and 2005, the SPD introduced the right of citizenship to children born in Germany, created a permanent residence/work permit to facilitate the entry of immigrants with technological skills, and finally passed a comprehensive law embracing both reasonable paths to citizenship and admission of immigrants in areas with shortages of qualified nationals. Data on employment and contributions to the economy continued to demonstrate net positive effects. One widely cited study concluded that between 1988 and 1998, immigrants had been responsible for the creation of 85,000 new jobs, effectively raising the gross domestic product (GDP) by 1.3% (Loeffelholz & Kopp, 1998). Others noted some exceptions to that rule, notably within lower levels of occupation, during times of economic stagnation or decline. Overall patterns, however, indicated that immigrant effects on wages were insignificant when the economy was strong. In 1995, the Institute for Economic Research in Essen reported that the Gross National Product (GNP) in 1992 was almost 60% higher than it would have been without immigrants, and the number of new jobs more than offset any initial strains in the labor market. In 2003, almost 60% of immigrants were employed in the tertiary sector—positions in the least desirable jobs. Other analyses indicated that assimilated immigrants made fewer demands on services, and the degree of assimilation increased with years spent in Germany. The extra costs incurred by the use of state services decreased steadily after 1973 and mostly disappeared by 1994. The positive impact on the nation's economic health offset the rare and relatively small effects on the wages of native workers, even in the unskilled job sectors dominated by foreign labor (Gieseck et al., 1995).

The strongest evidence of positive effects on the economy in Germany have been identified in sectors for which specialized training is necessary (technology in particular), and in the areas of retail and food service. The latter was in evidence from the early days of recruitment of guestworkers, as ethnic restaurants, groceries, and small retail businesses catering to Greek and Turkish populations flourished. Loeffelholz reported in 1994 that 28% of all restaurant owners registered in Germany in 1992 were foreign, and 20% of all self-employed foreigners operated small retail stores. As young foreigners living in Germany moved in increasing numbers into areas requiring professional certification, the number of those starting their own companies grew as well, adding to evidence that immigrant entrepreneurs were positive economic agents.

By the time control of government shifted to the conservative CDU/CSU in 2005, the challenge of Germany's population demographics was apparent to anyone examining longer-term prospects for economic growth. Like Britain, Germany faced and continues to project an aging population. With one of the consistently lowest birth rates (1.4 in the early 1970s, and below the replacement rate ever since), Germany has arguably the most unfavorable labor demographics in Europe. Without new immigration, the number of people in the 20–65 age bracket in 2013 will shrink from 50 to 33 million by 2060, and the Labor Department has issued warnings of severe labor shortages persisting into the next generation and longer. Before the migrant surges of 2014 and beyond, there was no evidence of likely change despite the fact that the federal government was spending more than 265 billion Euros annually on subsidies designed to encourage larger families in a nation where home-based motherhood is widely respected but less frequently encountered. Legislation raising the age of retirement and new family-friendly work subsidies have attracted unanticipated support from both major parties, as the size of the working-age population remains a persistent omen threatening national prosperity.

In the years following the breakup of the former Soviet Union and its Eastern bloc, the German government struggled with what many feared was an uncontrollable surge in immigrants, representing asylum seekers, the newly opened border with East Germany, and EU expansion to 28 nations, among other factors. Asylum seekers were restricted by the constitutional change in 1993; otherwise, population movement was governed only by the perceived and real marketplace for labor. Still, German governments continued to acknowledge the need for a welcoming, proactive immigration policy, and no labor glut emerged. Even with the effects of the 2008 recession still evident in most of Europe, and with Germany providing the largest share of financial aid to struggling EU economies, net immigration in 2013 was up 13% from previous years (chapter 1, Figure 1.4). For the first time since 1995, population increased by 369,000, consisting mostly of EU arrivals from Eastern and Southern Europe.

Whereas much of the population shift in Germany after 1990 reflected the enormous changes taking place on the continent, more recent patterns have resulted from the increased globalization of the German economy. A 2013 study reported that 30,000 Chinese students were attending German universities with the promise of employment after graduation, most commonly in high-tech industries. A full 43% of new immigrants in the 20–65 age group had technical degrees or master craftsman certification required in international industries. Only 25% of 2012 entrants were unskilled or semiskilled, down from 40% in 2000 (*Deutsche Welt*, May 26, 2013).

Following years of open borders and the active recruitment of labor, 2012 marked the first net increase in population in Germany, but even with a net figure of 250,000 immigrants per year the population has been projected to decline by as much as 14 to 18 million people by 2050. Some of that decrease will reflect uneven immigration levels, but the main contributor to the decline is a falling fertility rate among the foreign-born. That rate, still higher than that of native Germans, is below the 2.1 children per woman required to replace the current population. Unlike those nations whose immigrants come largely from countries with high birth rates, Germany cannot count on immigrants to spur population growth.

By 2012, there was little debate over the role of immigrants in sustaining Germany's economic health. The Merkel government, reelected in 2013, quietly supported progressive immigration policies, including programs to recruit highly educated workers from within and outside the EU and the introduction of the Blue Card (granting renewable residence rights) and its extension to non-EU applicants who had offers to work in Germany. Business leaders fully understood that globalization required the flexibility to adjust the workforce. In a hard-hitting review of Germany's shortsighted economic policies, a June 2013 piece in the popular weekly *Der Speigel* argued for the elimination of entrenched traditions that reduced competitiveness and productivity, including generous vacation leave, short workweeks, early retirement, extensive family leaves, and short school hours. Pointing to a pattern in which families were limiting the number of children in order to secure their own prosperity, it also called for extended childcare services and higher subsidies to encourage larger German families. But the emphasis in its review was on the importance of welcoming immigrants into both the workplace and society, cracking down on hostility, and overhauling schools in immigrant neighborhoods.

Lingering Questions in the Economic Discussion

The questions that linger in the economic debate are less about the need for foreign workers than how to manage their entry and employment. Five are prominent. First is the lingering concern that foreigners will compete with Germans for jobs, especially in middle and professional levels of work. In earlier times, immigrants were largely unskilled or semiskilled workers whose presence facilitated the mobility of Germans. Since 2000, immigrants have been more likely to enter bringing skills and education, and having been recruited to fill jobs at higher levels. Critics fear that despite providing increased support for German scientific and professional training, highly educated immigrants will dominate important industries. Data on unemployment and immigration since the 2001 push to recruit highly trained foreigners began, however, suggest otherwise. Unemployment increased only when immigration levels remained constant or decreased—the common pattern until 2010, when recovery from the recession opened up positions in all sectors. In fact, Germany's attempts to lure scientists and professionals have been cautious compared to other nations, posing little to no threat to domestic employment. Still, the fear of a turnaround in that pattern persists. When sluggish economies in other European Union nations rebound, that fear is, illogically, transferred to the possibility that the presence of non-westerners in those nations will make it harder for Germany to compete in Europe. Despite evidence that the need for highly trained workers is only likely to grow, concerns about foreign competition persist.

A related issue is the economic wisdom of supporting a working class dominated by the foreign-born. However uneasy Germans were when guestworkers were mostly single males from southern Europe and Turkey, they probably understood that workers contributed more to state revenues through higher productivity, consumption, and taxes than they siphoned off in services. As the demographic portrait changed to include family members, the image of minimally employed workers with families became one of economic dependency. Although competition for low-level jobs has always been minimized by protection for German nationals in union contracts in Germany, the potential threat of a dependent working class looms large as a factor in public resistance to immigrants with families.

Third, the ultimate question of capacity lies always at or just below the surface of other economic or social concerns. As one of the most densely populated European states, Germany has a natural tendency to think that limiting growth is essential. Political leaders of all parties have supported limits on immigration even as they acknowledge the existence of a low national birth rate and labor shortages. In a nation where population demographics make shrinkage more ominous than growth, "economic saturation" claims persist, often encouraged by political leaders.

Fourth, there is no doubt that Germany's economy is inextricably linked to the economies of European Union nations. As the strongest economic power in the EU, Germany has played a key role in all issues—expansion and recession, aid for distressed economies, common policies in agriculture, financial bailouts, refugee admissions, and immigrant rights. Some of those who are concerned about the financial onus Germany has borne since 2008 argue that it should pursue its own economic agendas rather than buy into costly EU policies and guidelines.

Finally, the seemingly unlimited numbers of refugees seeking new lives in Germany present unprecedented economic as well as sociopolitical challenges. Given the strength of the economy, continuing documented labor shortages, and ongoing support by the government, the likelihood that the majority of refugees will find work and eventually contribute economically is high, especially since many relocating from Syria are well educated. Initial costs are almost certain to decrease and be recouped. As in other nations, the most daunting questions deal less with economic absorption than with cultural and political integration, to which we turn next.

(compare w/
U.S.
1) public opinion dominates actual data

Political Alignments and Immigration

Few nations have experienced as many changes in their political context as Germany has since 1945. Emerging from defeat in World War II, two forcibly separated German nation-states necessarily allied with the two principal antagonists of a half-century of Cold War conflict. They adopted competing political systems, with one multiparty democracy in the west facing off against a totalitarian East Germany that enjoyed no competitive elections and severely limited personal freedoms for its citizens. West Germany embraced a capitalism fueled in part by foreign labor, while the East adopted a state-run economy with no need for additional workers. When the 1989 breakdown of Soviet control of satellite states in Eastern Europe led to the unification of the two Germanys, the rigid ruling structures of the eastern sector were abandoned and joined with West German political institutions. To understand the political context in which immigration issues were addressed in those years, the discussion must separate the periods preceding and following the events of 1990.

Germany before 1990

"Guest" definition of foreigners despite welcoming / NEED for their labor

While gradual shifts defined political discourse in most Western nations during the postwar period, the West German context was reshaped by the rapid and drastic overhaul of its political system after 1945. Under allied monitoring, denazification programs exposed and prosecuted those responsible for the brutality of the Nazi period, and stressed the importance of democratic values and institutions. Economic aid was provided for projects that embraced free market principles. Most importantly, the new Constitution of the Federal Republic of Germany (Basic Law), adopted in 1949, created a political system similar to those of Britain, France, and the United States, although it was unprecedented in Germany. Its structure included a parliamentary government buttressed by guarantees of individual rights and a judicial branch to resolve disputes, all designed to promote healthy party competition and marginalize radical groups.

The spectacular postwar economic recovery served to legitimate the governments that oversaw it and, by extension, the system in which they operated. Throughout the initial period of growth (1949–1973), governments led first by the moderate-to-right Christian Democratic Union, then by a grand coalition of the CDU with the left-of-center Social Democrats, and later by the Socialists by themselves, all benefited from a prosperity made possible in part by foreign labor. Both major parties endorsed the recruitment of foreigners with their policies if not their wholehearted support. Even after an economic slowdown and the end of official recruitment in 1973, more than four million noncitizens remained as a visible presence in German workplaces and communities, continuing to fill important economic roles.

Despite their continuing role in the national economy, foreigners posed challenges to the obviously effective political system. Seeking to shield Germany from long-term obligations, political leaders from all parties repeatedly defined imported labor as "guests" who would not stay permanently. While these workers enjoyed wages and benefits comparable to those of Germans, they lived mostly in poor areas, spoke little or no German, and were often depicted as dangerous or disreputable. Political leaders avoided consideration of permanent integration for almost 30 years, while a generation of foreigners born in Germany reached political maturity. The EEC and its successor EU were silent on citizenship policies. Public opinion was consistently guarded well into the 1980s, continuing to express the belief that foreigners should be sent home if jobs were tight. Since by then most foreigners were long-term residents, the public clearly embraced a collective denial of the reality of an immigrant presence. As indicated earlier in this chapter, the context of the immigration issue during the 40-year period before 1990 was thus one of official avoidance coupled with an uneasy public tolerance of those immigrants already in the country.

The German Democratic Republic (East Germany), by contrast, experienced no pressure to import labor after 1945. Full employment discouraged potential immigrants, and the continuous absence of foreigners enabled a culture of discrimination against the few who lived in wary communities. Unification in 1990 necessarily incorporated the EU requirement that there be no restrictions on movement and employment, but for at least ten years the slowly rebuilding economy presented little attraction to outsiders. The eastern sector did experience a wrenching shift from secure employment to a more competitive work environment as the two economies merged, but the long period in which the eastern economy struggled meant that immigration was not initially an urgent issue.

[margin note: no immig. content in E. Germ]

The Post-1990 Context

Any illusions that immigration would remain under the political radar abruptly disappeared with the dramatic changes sparked by events in 1989. Although the first waves of newcomers from the east were German, they were soon followed by others from Eastern Europe, Russia, and beyond. The euphoria of unification was short-lived as the challenges of accommodating workers from the east, absorbing an outdated East German economy, and dealing with dramatic increases in the numbers of asylum seekers became evident. Germany, so long content to let immigration issues simmer on the back burner of the national agenda, suddenly found the issue too urgent to avoid.

[margin note: contrast to U.S.]

Government action was remarkably prompt and comprehensive. Laws tightening asylum provisions in the constitution passed without serious opposition in 1992 and 1993, reducing the number of applicants to more manageable levels. The government committed billions of Euros annually to rebuild infrastructure in the eastern sector, followed by even larger amounts to increase wages in modernized or new factories and industries. The process proved to take much longer to accomplish than originally projected and caused considerable resentment over living standards, but the united Germany still managed to remain the strongest economic power in Europe.

Despite influxes from the East and increased EU access to German employment, labor shortages reappeared in the late 1990s. Prodded by EU commissions to rationalize the status of foreign residents, the SPD government under Gerhard Schroeder passed legislation that finally recognized the rights of long-term resident foreigners to permanent residency and citizenship. Those measures, however, did little to ease shortages, and both Socialist and Christian Democratic governments enacted policies that would, for the first time since 1972, encourage immigration in a rationalized system geared to labor force needs. After 40 years of temporizing labor policies, Germany overhauled its immigration system in the short space of ten years.

The current political debate is thus a product of fifty years of contrasting experiences, moving from pragmatic and restrictive, to restrictive, to aggressively pragmatic approaches to immigration. The public has reacted with a mix of hostility and acceptance. The need for additional population has offered a seemingly easy path for policymakers, but one which, we will see, is littered with political obstacles.

Partisan Politics and Immigration Policy

Like Britain, Germany defines its politics largely in partisan terms. One major party—the centrist/conservative Christian Democratic Union and its Bavarian affiliate Christian Social Union (CSU)—has often formed a coalition government with the smaller, business-oriented Free Democratic Party; the more liberal Socialist Party (SPD) usually partners with the environmentally focused Green Party. Since 1949, the CDU/CSU has been in power for twice as many years as the SPD, reflecting the moderate-to-conservative leanings of the electorate. The two major parties coalesced in 1966–69 and 2005–09 in grand coalitions, but have more typically joined with minor parties to govern.

The most striking feature of party immigration politics has been a consistently low level of confrontation. During long periods of CDU/CSU control (1949–1966, 1982–1998, 2005–present), the party and its leadership have dealt with immigration as a simple answer to labor needs in a healthy economy. A CDU government negotiated the initial agreements bringing workers from Southern Europe, North Africa, and Turkey, agreeing to basic employment benefits for foreigners to placate labor unions and quietly tolerating the presence of undocumented workers. Their pragmatic orientation allowed them to define limited terms of residency while undoubtedly knowing they would eventually extend them to satisfy business preferences for longer and renewable permits, which would facilitate continuity in their industries.

The CDU's policies appeared to be brilliantly conceived, providing a workforce that required little accommodation and could be terminated if economic conditions changed. Given the obvious economic advantages of a labor supply with few obligations, the SPD could hardly oppose the programs. They well understood the need for additional labor to sustain growth, and their insistence on fair wages and benefits allowed them to lay claim to the worker protections already included in the CDU policies. To argue for greater benefits for foreign workers would have offended their union base; to argue for more security or longer work permits would have aroused resistance to permanent commitments. Rather than engage in futile opposition, the SPD bought into the government's guestworker proposals, effectively creating bipartisan policy.

Following the cues of major parties, the smaller Free Democratic Party agreed quickly to the temporary worker model which, in fact was closer to its own philosophy than that of the CDU. Free Democrats were openly and rather narrowly committed to the interests of business—the primary beneficiary of a steady supply of labor with minimal investment. The only party to the left of the SPD has been the Greens, who, until the mid-1980s, focused almost entirely on environmental, international peace, and animal rights issues. Thus, for at least 25 years the parties were in remarkable agreement on issues concerning the foreign-born. All agreed that recruiting temporary workers was desirable; all bought into the limits placed on them—including political activity— that effectively prevented them from becoming their own advocates; all agreed to halt recruitment in 1973; and all avoided advocacy roles until the Greens finally made that part of their broader agenda in the mid-1980s.

The apparent grand nonpartisanship did have some cracks. Friction between ideologues and pragmatists existed within each party, as more philosophical conservatives in the CDU, CSU, and FDP were opposed to the presence of so many foreigners in a society proud of its homogeneous culture. More ardent liberals pressed for assurances of equal treatment and easier paths to citizenship. Confronted with disagreements, the parties made modest compromises to forestall opposition, and the issue was rarely worthy of major coverage.

More remarkable than the long initial period of party consensus was the continuation of that pattern into the late 1980s. By then, the permanence of the foreigners' presence was obvious. They had arrived a generation earlier, found and kept work, and raised children ready to enter the labor force. Since Chancellor Kohl was a key figure in creating the Schengen Agreements dismantling EU borders, the conservative coalition had to know that change was on the horizon throughout Europe. Still, his government committed a series of blunders by floating proposals to add restrictions to foreigners, and Kohl was heavily criticized for both the proposals and intemperate statements from his ministers. But the SPD opposition, perhaps sensing that public opinion was still not disposed to full acceptance of foreigners as immigrants, did not seize the opportunity to challenge long-standing policies, the Greens remained focused on other issues, and the resolution of immigrants' status remained unaddressed for another 20 years.

Lack of enthusiasm for radical parties was clear throughout this period. The ultra-Right National Democratic Party (NPD), founded in 1964 and successful in withstanding challenges to its right to compete, was most visible in Bavaria where a resurgent nationalism continued to attract support. Consistently considered marginal by most Germans, the NPD has been the face of German anti-Semitism, ethnically based hatred, and a nationalist agenda, but has never been victorious in the electoral arena. It has never attracted enough votes (5% is the threshold for seats in parliament) to participate in national politics, but has also never stimulated enough outrage to mobilize widespread opposition. Incidents of violence against foreigners have been linked to rightist groups—most recently the Pegida organization—but the NPD has not chosen to ally itself with those acts in its quest for electoral support. Until the emergence of the AfD (Alternative for Deutschland) in 2013, initially a party focused on opposition to the EU, extremist parties have been consistently ignored or rejected by German voters.

Signs of support for right-wing groups have increased. In Dortmund, a former hub for the steel and coal industries, neo-Nazi leaders have blamed the large immigrant minority (about 33% there) and particularly the recently arrived Romanian Roma for high unemployment and crime rates. Although they still have not managed to win seats in the national parliament, right-wing extremists have captured one seat on the local city council, adding to their one seat in the European Parliament and two in state legislatures. The Alternative for Germany has been more successful, winning more votes than the CDU in elections in Chancellor Angela Merkel's home state of Mecklenburg/Vorpommern in 2016. Before the migrant crisis such strength would have been unimaginable in a nation enjoying both leadership in the EU and a prosperous national economy. Fear that Germany has overextended its capacity for welcome has fueled renewed claims that refugees will not integrate into the host society. That challenge, standing as it does in stark contrast to the success Germany has had in building a prosperous system with the participation of millions of immigrants, demands attention and policies far more extensive in scope and detail than those which sufficed in the earlier periods.

The Critical Role of Political Leadership

The previous chapter noted the significance of strong rhetoric by prominent British political leaders from the early stages of immigration to the present—Enoch Powell serving as mouthpiece for the most hostile British opinions; cabinet ministers routinely insisting that blacks could never assimilate; Margaret Thatcher maintaining that Britain lacked the capacity to absorb outsiders. Whatever their personal views, German political leaders have been conspicuously reserved in their public positions, especially when foreign workers were seen as temporary solutions to labor gaps. Even during the 1973 recession, when the majority of foreigners opted to remain in Germany rather than leave, leaders of all the major parties moved to accommodate their presence until the economy improved.

The absence of anti-immigrant rhetoric in the positions articulated by German political leaders reflected convenience and immediate-term pragmatism, if not willful denial. Millions of foreign workers had rounded out the labor force and leaders assumed that they were content, even grateful, to continue to do so. As the national birthrate remained low, the need to replenish the working-age population was constant, putting leaders in the permanent position of identifying foreign labor in positive terms. Opposing the foreign workers' presence would have invited economic crises impacting all, a reality that leadership used when arguing that those workers still took jobs shunned by Germans and thus facilitated both mobility and prosperity. At the same time, German prime ministers from Adenauer to Kohl were hardly effusive in their support for foreign workers and their families. They generally spoke only through their ministers, who maintained that guestworkers were contributors to the economy but not prospective citizens. As cold as the sentiment was, it allowed leaders to rationalize a stance reassuring to Germans and, at least for the short term, acceptable to the noncitizen population.

A second likely contributor to the low profile displayed by immigration issues was the risk harsh rhetoric might entail. Even 60 years after the end of World War II, Germans understood the burden of their nation's legacy of violent persecution and the need it imposed upon them as a people to protect minorities with humanitarian principles. Consistent with that commitment has been the careful avoidance of public language or policy that articulates excessive restrictions or negative characterizations of the nation's foreign minorities. The resulting avoidance of discussions about foreigners by leadership was conspicuous for more than fifty years, until a Socialist government finally articulated support for birthrights and naturalization of foreigners within Germany in 1997 and enacted a skills-oriented admission system which actually lauded the contributions of immigrants.

Defining political leadership in terms of long-term issue avoidance might seem odd, since leadership, by definition, assumes proactive behavior. Critics in Germany consistently chastised governments for not including immigration on their agenda and ignoring the anomalous position of long-term residents. Governments took few positions (the SPD) or drew up proposals so convoluted they were never considered (the CDU). The only positive interpretation of such a pattern suggests that German leadership consciously kept the issue off center stage to construct a period in which the presence of productive immigrants could be, gradually, appreciated, and later embraced, by the public. Whether that acceptance could have been achieved sooner is a question without answer, but one still asked by many.

Other Actors: State Agencies, Interest Groups, and Extremist Influence

Given the paucity of national debate on immigration prior to 2000, it is not surprising that the activity levels of nonparty agencies were low. Part of the reason lies in the differing levels of responsibility for services relevant to foreigners that have been allocated within the federal system. Most important decisions over entry and work permits are made at the federal level, but in Germany power over education and social services are delegated to the *Länder*, or states. At both levels, German administrative offices operate in a culture of bureaucratic authority known for its comprehensiveness and efficiency. Decisions carry a weight of finality, which translates into a power of implementation similar to that in Britain. The level of interaction between national and lower levels is not high, and the existence of two authoritative government agencies may have tended to discourage interest groups that might, if they were willing to organize and assume a more visible presence, want to demand more resources.

That tendency is exacerbated by the extensive control which state agencies have over two areas central to immigrant life: education at all levels, and housing. In the early periods, state variations in curriculum and programs for non-Germans were common. The model in Bavaria, for example, assumed that children would return to their homelands, and provided instruction in their native languages, effectively segregating them from German children. In contrast, foreign children in Berlin were consciously integrated into classes with instruction in German. Only later, when it was evident that foreign children were not leaving after a year or two, was a common language curriculum adopted across the ten states. Even later, federal funds were supplied to make up for deficiencies in language instruction, supporting intensive classes in German for both long-term residents and new arrivals. Similarly, initiatives to identify housing and welfare services were left to state agencies for years before federal programs were initiated.

Groups lobbying for better treatment of foreigners have been more visible in response to anti-immigrant incidents. Despite much smaller numbers of foreigners in the eastern sector, acts of violence have been more frequent there. A long history of state-tolerated hostility toward non-Germans combined with serious unemployment after 1990 to create volatile conditions and a spate of incidents. Arsonists set fire to a home of a Turkish family in 1993; neo-Nazis killed a Turkish worker in Dresden; in 2006 a Turkish member of the Berlin Assembly was stabbed. In the charged environment of the 2014–16 refugee crisis anti-immigrant violence, including arson attacks in Dusseldorf, hate speech, and overt harassment of refugees increased dramatically. A coalition of church groups has demanded more protection for immigrants; local groups formed at least temporarily to provide assistance in areas where foreign residents were concentrated. Political leaders across the board have condemned violence and promised a larger police presence, and local industries have provided additional security to deter aggression. Unlike other nations, Germany has seen few prominent pro-immigrant or even immigrant-based organizations that might become permanent lobbyists for government action. Before citizenship rules were eased and larger numbers of foreigners sought naturalization, migrants had good reason to fear that political activism could jeopardize their residency and work status, mirroring the pattern observed in other nations where both legal and undocumented immigrants resist mobilization efforts. It is, ironically, commonplace for immigrants representing significant percentages of the population in all of the nations studied here to be reluctant to organize on their own behalf. Pluralism apparently works better for established groups than those new to that environment.

Even with dramatic changes in citizenship access and leadership commitment to assist immigrants after 2000, public fears of foreign influence on the German culture have at times been inflamed by extremist descriptions of immigrants. A prominent example was the 2010 appearance of Thilo Sarrazin's, *Deutschland schafft sich ab* (*Germany Doing Away with Itself*). Sarrazin argued that immigrants were predominantly lower class and less intelligent than Germans, collectively watering down the culture and degrading society with ethnic traits described in crude and demeaning terms. Jews were also derided as genetically inferior, raising the specter of Nazi ideology under the umbrella of non-German threats to German civilization. Reaction to the book was overwhelmingly negative. Sarrazin was forced to resign his position as director of the Central Bank and banned from the SPD; political leaders from all major parties disavowed his claims, and students organized boycotts of the book. Membership in the National Democratic Party declined to a new low of 6,000 members in 2013. That reflected a consistent pattern of public rejection of extremists of all stripes since 1949, even as a minority shared their fears about foreigners.

Resistance and potentially strong opposition to foreigners remains, however, susceptible to claims that immigrants represent both economic and security threats. A 2013 report from the Office for Protection of the Constitution noted a 10% increase in membership of Islamist groups in Germany, to a new total of 42,550. Sensitive to criticism that terrorists in the 2001 attacks in the United States had been based in Germany, governments have monitored residents from the Middle East, and public concerns about religious differences and nonnative customs have increased, highlighted by sporadic but increasing numbers of incidents in recent years.

Since 2013, all plans for rational immigration have taken a back seat to the need to deal with the refugee crisis, which brought more than a million refugees to Germany in 2015 and smaller but still unprecedented numbers in other EU nations. Chancellor Merkel has been steadfast in urging Europe to admit those arriving in Greece and Italy

The Two Faces of Germany in the Refugee Crisis

As the most populous and most economically powerful EU nation, Germany has become the destination of choice for more than a million refugees since 2013. How has the nation greeted the deluge entering the country?

The German Willkommen. From the onset of massive numbers entering Europe, Chancellor Angela Merkel has been resolute in her commitment to open doors to new lives in Germany. At least initially, citizens followed her lead: hundreds of volunteers greeted travel-worn families in Munich's main railroad station; communities retrofitted buildings into temporary shelters; residents offered housing and assistance; local governments set up settlement offices. Vowing not to repeat German policies that had discouraged earlier groups from assimilating or becoming citizens, the chancellor championed paths to assimilation into the fabric of Germany society. Merkel has asked other EU members to follow the German example by absorbing large numbers of refugees.

The Resistance. Since immigrants were identified as troublemakers during holiday celebrations in Cologne, public sentiment and conservative leaders have voiced opposition to Merkel's welcoming policies. The Bavaria affiliate of Merkel's own party has threatened to sue the government for taking in refugees who could have been sent back to "safe countries" through which they travelled. More ominously, a sharp increase in violence against immigrants was recorded in 2015—more than 220 incidents, including arson attacks on migrants' homes or shelters. The anti-immigrant PEGIDA group has increased its opposition, including demonstrations and campaigns against candidates supporting Merkel's inclusive policies.

A Change in German Politics? Resistance to Merkel's policies is similar to that of a growing anti-immigrant sentiment in the EU. With upcoming elections in Germany, the specter of a nationalist surge is one that will concern observers throughout the EU and beyond.

and to assist them in asylum applications, but sheer volume and the evidence that some radical extremists are posing as refugees have created opposition across the continent and stalemate in the EU. In Germany, violent incidents at a New Year's celebration in Cologne, individual attacks in small towns, and the much larger attack in Berlin's Christmas market in 2016, have increased fears that many of the immigrants welcomed since 2014 represent major security threats. However willing Germany has been to accept refugees, its policies will necessarily be intricately connected with the resolve of fellow EU members and their commitment to common policies.

European Union Policies as Influences on German Immigration

The EU has faced a number of difficult issues as it has sought to expand its core responsibilities, but the magnitude of the challenge presented by the refugee crisis to the 500 million people living in the 28 EU states is unparalleled. Although EU agreements do not yet govern immigration admissions, four have had significant impact on Germany as well as other members: (1) the Schengen Agreement of 1985 and its successor the Amsterdam Treaty of 1997, effectively eliminating internal borders; (2) rules governing movement and consideration of asylum seekers; (3) the 2011 Directives establishing common rights for EU citizens in all states, and (4) the Long-term Directives, which defined rights of movement for all legal non-EU workers.

These signature agreements clarified essential components of immigration in the EU. A 2008 pact began with the explicit statement that Europe could not admit all wishing to migrate there. It focused on the growing problem of asylum seekers entering EU nations even then (through Greece, Bulgaria, Romania, Hungary, Slovakia, Latvia, Lithuania, Finland, and Poland), by granting interior nations the right to return undocumented migrants to the nations that had admitted them only to facilitate travel to other European states. Two other agreements established the authority of the EU to enforce standards of treatment of noncitizens. Specifically, the Single Point Directive detailed protections which all non-European workers would enjoy in member states, including basic legal rights and social benefits available to nationals. To remove any ambiguity about the right of movement within the EU, the Long-Term Residence Directive required all states to agree that all non-Europeans would be free to move across members' borders without restriction after completing five years' residence in any one. Even if common admission policies have not yet been established, EU agreements have provided comprehensive and progressive rules covering noncitizens currently in the Union.

Despite having spearheaded early border agreements, supporting membership for Eastern European nations, and affirming the directives on the rights of immigrants, Germany has voiced some resistance to their consequences. In 2013, Interior Minister Hans-Peter Friedrich was outspoken in his opposition to the free movement of Romanians and Bulgarians when they attained full EU membership in 2014. A host of conservative political leaders labeled the movement of workers from Eastern Europe "poverty migration" and "welfare migration." Unlike more extreme demands made by far-Right parties in Britain and France, conservatives in Germany (before the rise of the AfD party) proposed narrower changes allowing any member to refuse additional immigrants. Since 2015, the AfD has assumed the mantle of strident opposition by its growing strength in state elections, a sign that German politics may be becoming more similar to politics in other EU nations.

Since 1960, overt opposition in Germany to immigrants has been limited mostly to outlier politicians and has not been endorsed by either major party. But both leadership and public opinion have become more concerned with security issues originating in the Middle East, dwarfing reservations about the impact of unskilled East Europeans. EU rules on the status of people legally entering and residing in member nations have been endorsed, but initial acceptance of more general international rules mandating assistance to refugees has evolved into policies that effectively limit new admissions as German leaders have watched fellow members (Italy, Greece, Bulgaria) overwhelmed by the numbers arriving at their borders. As late as 2012, the number of applicants for asylum in EU nations numbered fewer than 200,000, including large groups from Russia, Georgia, Serbia, and Kosovo. By 2016 more than eight million refugees had fled nations battered by war, famine, and poverty (Afghanistan, Syria, Iraq, and several African nations) and utilized established sea and land routes to Europe. More than four million from Syria alone sought relocation and asylum, and the worldwide total exceeded all historical examples. The number of refugees attempting Mediterranean crossings (increasing from 59,000 in 2007 to almost 500,000 in 2015) made the crisis acute, finally bringing EU leaders together to discuss rescue programs and make plans to deter smuggling.

The initial responses by EU nations were minimal (only pledging to accept 12,000 refugees; Germany agreeing to 10,000 and 18 members refusing to accept any). Germany accepted 77,000 refugees in 2012, and Italy 12,000, but arrivals in Italy and Greece foreshadowed more conflict than cooperative response. When EU leaders finally proposed proportionate acceptance of 125,000 refugees across the Union and a naval offensive against traffickers, Britain, Hungary, and others opposed any mandatory program; governments were adamant in refusing to make refugees a part of employment-based immigration; and talks were suspended while politicians tried to develop alternative plans. Individual nations opted to close borders, blocking routes to countries in northern Europe where even relatively welcoming governments reintroduced border checks. Absent common policies, the EU floundered while its members constructed inconsistent policies with only vague hopes for containing the flow from Turkey through stronger controls along its coast. A 2015 agreement to channel 2 billion Euros to Turkey to house refugees who had been turned back after reaching Greece drastically reduced new entrants, but provided no real solution to the problem of the millions already in the EU. More ominous, by mid-2016 unstable conditions in Turkey threatened to stall or undo the Turkish commitment and reopen sea routes to hundreds of thousands of migrants still attempting to reach Europe.

Public Opinion and Immigration Options

Little in Germany's history of relations with foreigners would suggest a public supportive of significant and permanent immigration. Although the 1949 Constitution embraced tolerance and generous provisions for refugees, the laws that recruited millions of workers after 1961 were restrictive and accommodated foreigners only for limited periods.

As noted earlier, even as businesses applauded the work ethic and contributions of guestworkers, political leaders resisted any notion of permanent residence or citizenship for more than 30 years. In 1980, CDU candidates opposing more tolerant SPD proposals actively stoked public apprehension of the growing permanence of the non-German population. That fear was reflected in opinion polls, with majorities agreeing that there were too many foreigners in the country (Hoskin, 1991). On the other hand, some surveys documented some change in that pattern. The National Social Surveys conducted in 1980 and 1984 included questions about specific areas of concern, and found that a generally negative orientation was tempered when particular policies or activities were mentioned (Table 4.2). Respondents were asked to note their agreement or disagreement with four statements: that foreigners should adjust their lifestyles in Germany; that they should be sent home when jobs were tight; that they should not be allowed to engage

Table 4.2. Attitudes toward Foreign Workers in Germany, 1980–1984

Statement:	Agree Totally/ Mostly/Some		Not Sure/ No Opinion		Disagree Totally/ Mostly/Some	
Guestworkers Should:	1980	1984	1980	1984	1980	1984
Adjust lifestyles	66	56	14	15	21	24
Be sent home if jobs are tight	53	41	14	16	34	42
Not be allowed political activity	57	47	13	12	37	40
Marry only in their groups	46	34	14	13	42	52

N = 2955 (1980), 2995 (1984)

Full Text: 1. Guestworkers should adjust their lifestyles to the German lifestyle.
2. When jobs are tight, guestworkers should be sent home.
3. Guestworkers should be forbidden all political activities.
4. Guestworkers should choose their spouses from among their own people.

Source: German Allbus Surveys, 1980, 1984.

in political activity; and that they should marry only within their own groups. Negative judgments about how foreigners should be treated and were expected to behave actually declined over the four-year period covered in the two surveys. Even the increase in those agreeing that foreigners should adjust their lifestyles in Germany was seen as a positive opinion, reflecting a view that foreigners would increasingly blend into the host society.

A 1991 study focused on the correlates of more sympathetic views toward foreigners and found that positive orientations were associated with a more liberal ideology and a preference for the Socialist or Green parties. It also revealed that those with closer social contact with foreigners as colleagues or neighbors were more inclined to welcome them. Even stronger predictors, however, were age, education, and a generally less materialist outlook held by the generation growing up after the difficult postwar years and benefiting from expanded access to university education. Though still a minority of the population, that group was far more likely to support more progressive immigration and naturalization policies (Hoskin, 1991). Such patterns suggest that changing demographics might ultimately result in more liberal immigration policies, as wary older generations are replaced by those with fewer fears and greater sympathy for non-Germans.

Still, most data collected during this period documented strong reservations among the public in general. The 1986 Election Study posed five questions about foreigners in Germany (Table 4.3). On three of the five, majorities expressed negative opinions, favoring reductions in the number of foreign workers (while agreeing that they were

Table 4.3. Selected Attitudes toward Foreign Workers in Germany, 1986

Does the German economy still need foreign workers or not?	
Still needs them	61%
Does not need them	39%
Should the number of foreign workers in the Federal Republic be reduced or left as is?	
Should be reduced	70%
Should be left as is	30%
Foreigners persecuted in their homelands have a right to asylum in Germany. Do you find this good or not good?	
Good	67%
Not good	33%
Are asylum seekers mostly those politically persecuted or mostly those with economic reasons for wanting to enter Germany?	
Mostly political	23%
Mostly economic	77%
Should asylum be made more difficult?	
Should be made more difficult	80%
Should not be more difficult	20%

Source: Germany National Election Study, 1986.

still needed in Germany), questioning the motives of asylum seekers, and supporting stricter requirements for their admission. The desire to reduce the number of foreigners persisted, mirroring positions taken by the Kohl government throughout the 1980s.

As noted earlier, the disruptions occasioned by the breakup of Soviet-backed regimes in Eastern Europe and the unanticipated unification with East Germany quickly captured center stage for both government and public after 1990. But the simultaneous problem of huge increases in the numbers of asylum seekers served as a catalyst for major changes in hopelessly inadequate policies, and led to dramatic reductions in the number of acceptable refugees by 1993. In the process, however, closing the doors to millions by extraordinary constitutional revision reinforced public opposition to additional immigrants.

Those fears appeared in public opinion surveys conducted in the post-1990 period. The percentage of Germans opposing dual citizenship rose (from 47% opposing in 1993 to 64% in 1999). Even as a majority saw immigration as a low priority, 62% believed that immigrants were not well integrated into the society and that Muslims did not accept German values (Abali, 2009). Between 1998 and 2008, the percentage of Germans who believed that immigrants should adhere to German values increased from an already high 89% to more than 97%. Where greater contact with immigrant minorities had been linked in earlier studies to greater tolerance, in 2008 such contact correlated with belief that the cultures were in fact different and unlikely to integrate successfully.

By 2008, the onset of worldwide recession once again raised concerns that immigrants were a source of social instability. Surveys by the Allenbach Institut für Demoskopie found that majorities believed that immigrants caused social and academic problems in schools and were a drain on social support services. Although the percentage of those believing that there were "too many immigrants" in the country declined markedly (from 79% in the mid-1980s to 53% in 2008), negative characterizations that now focused on Muslims as being hostile to women, fanatical, violent, and vengeful were voiced by strong majorities.

As Germany emerged from the recession with its economy intact, negative views of immigrants clashed with arguments from business leaders that greater numbers of foreign workers were essential across all sectors of the economy. Immigration analyst Ulrich Kober concluded that "Germany underestimates the importance of its 'welcoming culture' and overestimates its appeal as a country of immigration," and urged greater government action to promote immigrant-friendly policies (*Die Welt*, December 12, 2013). Faced with an official push to support foreign workers and intense competition for skilled immigrants from the United States and other EU nations, the public was strongly urged to be more receptive. By 2011, the Gatestone Institute reported that percentages of people who thought that there were too many immigrants and that they placed too much pressure on public services had reached their lowest postwar levels (53% and 58%, respectively). Although Germans continued to believe that Muslims resisted integration and that a ban on wearing the Muslim veil was appropriate, a 2012 EMNID survey found much higher public appreciation of foreign labor. Seventy

Similar to U.S. public opinions foreigners negative when economy bad & positive when econ. good

percent believed that immigrants facilitated investment in Germany, 62% agreed that immigrants ease the effects of an aging population, and one-half accepted immigrants as an effective response to labor shortages. Still, two-thirds continued to believe that immigrants were responsible for crime, caused trouble in the schools, and put pressure on social security resources. And with the refugee crisis came renewed opposition. Between February 2015 and January 2016, the percentage of respondents in a YouGov poll who believed that the number of asylum seekers was already too high rose from 45 to 62, while those thinking Germany could accept more dropped from 27 to 18, mirroring negative sentiment across the EU.

Overall, public opinion toward immigrants in Germany's 70-year experience since 1945 has been inconsistent: naive and resistant to reality, fearful, especially during migration crises, but also pragmatic and occasionally even solicitous. A mostly consistent record of economic growth coincided with seismic national changes, in governmental structure, in economic and political union with 27 European neighbors and the assumption of a leadership role in that union, in reunification with a painfully underdeveloped East Germany. For a historically nationalistic culture, defining a positive relationship with immigrants would have been a challenge under any circumstances. In that context, the portrait of a German electorate that reflects both pragmatic beliefs that more human capital is necessary in a globalized world and concerns that the change will include people whom citizens would prefer not to face is hardly surprising. That portrait is not so different from the ones observed in Britain and the United States, where immigration has necessitated both shifts in labor forces and accommodation of new minorities.

Germany as the Evolving Immigration Nation

It is worth restating that unlike the United States, and more like postwar Britain, Germany's orientation to immigration developed within a relatively short period of tumultuous change. As a postwar creation of allied traditions imposed upon a defeated society developing its own plan for dealing with economic immigrants, Germany stands as a class of one. We should anticipate that even as some parallels among basic influences exist, experiences should be expected to differ, perhaps significantly.

An important element in understanding contemporary German immigration politics is the presence of tensions and conflict between nations in its history. Kingdoms, empires, and nations with whom Germany fought for centuries have become allies in the world's largest economic union. Even as it retains its national borders and the heritage of an older culture, Germany has linked its present and future to that of 27 fellow EU members, forcing old rivalries to be recast as necessary partnerships in prosperity. The driving force of nationalism has had to be modified to be a source of pride rather than isolation and exclusion. Revising a nation's sense of itself would be difficult for any culture; for Germany, it has meant reinvention, of political institutions, foreign relations, and attitudes toward people with widely varying traditions.

Germany has reinvented itself throught history from exclusionary to global

To a remarkable extent, reinvention has been successful. Confronted by the epic failure of Nazi Germany, postwar leadership accepted dictates to build a government from scratch, adopting democratic principles and practices new to both leaders and the public. It rebuilt infrastructure and industry, lending much-needed credibility to the parties and leaders who managed the task. The halo effect of these achievements allowed postwar governments to focus on building a permanent democracy.

The importance of the legitimacy earned by economic reconstruction became apparent when Germany began recruitment of foreign workers in 1961. Bolstering the economy with foreigners only 20 years after the war could have revived friction and discrimination, but both Conservative and Socialist governments built in protections for what was projected to be a temporary work force. Even with such assurances, public adjustment to living and working with non-Germans was tentative, and political leaders avoided any overt planning for a permanent non-German population. But in temporizing the foreign presence, governments inadvertently made it possible for generations of Germans to witness the productive roles foreigners were playing in their only partially adopted state. When the government finally proposed overhauling the immigration system, opposition was muted and the process remarkably short—especially in comparison to the often torturous pace of immigration-related legislation in the United States. At the functional level of adapting policy to circumstance, postwar German governments managed a significant if belated transition to an environment in which foreigners would be an important presence.

A strong economic rationale for recruiting a foreign presence in the workforce was central to their acceptance. The need for working-age adults to supplement an insufficient German workforce has been constant for the last 50 years, even with the removal of EU borders and periods of recession. As the economy has evolved, labor needs have grown to include highly trained professionals as well as lower-tier workers, and the profile of immigrants has become more like that of Germany itself. Absent a severe economic downturn, immigrants will continue to be instrumental to German prosperity.

That said, the tension between geohistorical past and multicultural present has persisted, even before the refugee crises beginning in 2013. Public opinion, encouraged by relentlessly skeptical political leaders, continues to harbor doubts about foreigners, so that even those who concede the need to supplement the national workforce believe that doing so brings liabilities: for instance, needy children in schools, families straining social services, questionable political loyalties, reluctance to embrace German values, and increasingly, threats to security. Although they rarely make the point explicitly, many think that foreigners should be all but invisible, contributing labor but not displaying cultural differences, even those as benign as headscarves. Not surprisingly, even the children of the foreign-born have been reluctant to engage in political activity, affirming a marginal status and lack of advocacy for beneficial policies.

The German response to the deluge of refugees has been the boldest expression of openness to immigrants in not only its own history, but also in Europe more generally. The Merkel government ardently championed the case for a broad EU policy in which all members would accept proportionate numbers of refugees, and demonstrated its own commitment by taking in more than a million in 2015. That stance, however, has been followed by criticism from opposition parties, a startling growth in support for the far-Right Alternative for Germany, and unsettling setbacks for Merkel's party in state elections—including major losses in Berlin and Merkel's home state of Mecklenburg-Vorpommern in September 2016. Four months later Bjorn Hoche, representing the far-Right flank of the AfD, denounced German atonement for Nazi atrocities and called for a stronger commitment to a German national identity which rejects incorporation of foreigners. The December attack in Berlin by a rejected Tunisian asylum seeker added to national concerns that immigrants pose real security threats. That weakness has been intensified by the inability of the EU to gather support from a number of its members, assuring still greater opposition in Eastern Europe and leading to the dramatic British vote to leave the Union. Unrest in border towns and refugee camps, increasingly desperate calls from Italy and Greece for relief in rescuing those seeking entry by sea, and border closings in several states have indicated that a European solution is not imminent. The UN has issued requests for resettlement of much larger numbers in temporary camps in Mediterranean nations. The stalemate in the EU threatens to undermine its authority with a return to nationalist policies that shun cooperation on important issues.

The possibility that tolerance for immigration has reached its limit in Europe makes it tempting to see public disapproval as an unsettling sign of overt hostility in the less tranquil times that have engulfed the region. The ongoing refugee crisis is a test of just that hypothesis. The numbers and plight of refugees in 2015 defy easy comparisons to American experiences with desperate migrants from dissimilar cultures, where new ethnics have historically raised concerns that any concentration of minorities would produce violence-ridden ghettos and threats to stability. But the similarities do exist, demonstrating that second generations have gradually moved into the circles of the majority and both nationals and immigrants have accepted that natural social mix. A similar, though less pronounced pattern has been observed in Britain, suggesting that the public can be both guarded and accepting of ultimate immigrant integration. Whether such adaptation and assimilation will occur in the current environment remains an unanswered question.

For Further Reading

Joel S. Fetzer. *Public Attitudes toward Immigrants in the United States, France, and Germany.* Cambridge: Cambridge University Press, 2000.

Joel S. Fetzer and J. Christopher Soper. *Muslims and the State in Britain, France, and Germany.* Cambridge: Cambridge University Press, 2005.

Christian Joppke. *Immigration and the Nation-State: the United States, Germany, and Great Britain.* Oxford: Oxford University Press, 1999.

Ray C. Rist. *Guestworkers in Germany.* New York: Praeger, 1978.

5

France

Haven or Hell for Foreigners?

However disruptive immigration issues have been in the United States, Britain, and Germany, recent incidents in France have demonstrated new dimensions of volatility and national concern. Since 1980, it has been the site of protests in immigrant communities, forced removal of European gypsies, violence toward Jews, legal restrictions on Muslim schoolgirls wearing headscarves, assassinations of newspaper staff publishing cartoons mocking the Muslim prophet, and mass killings in Paris and Nice. Despite a long-established secular tradition in which all religions are tolerated and protected, hostility toward minorities has raised the specter of marginalization and even persecution in the name of national security. How those traditions and events converged, and how governments have dealt with them as the immigrant population has grown, round out the comparison of Western nations.

French Geography and Its Limits

With 210,200 square miles of territory, France is the largest nation in the European Union, and its 66,736,000 million inhabitants (2016) make it the second most populous (behind Germany's 80,681,129). With extensive ocean borders to the north, west, and south, it has had more natural isolation from neighbors than other European states and is relatively rich in natural resources. Arable land provides ample agricultural capability, still farmed in relatively small plots as owners have resisted larger cooperatives or mass production. Minerals and timber are also abundant. A commercial and industrial base in machinery, chemicals, metals, textiles, and transportation manufacturing, as well as agriculture and tourism, have accounted for steady production since the beginning of industrialization, facilitating historically stable economies for a slowly growing population.

Demographically, the nation includes relatively few highly urbanized centers, coupled with smaller towns and rural areas in the west and north. When industrialization took place in Europe in the mid-nineteenth century, France did not experience the rapid urbanization undergone by its neighbors, as proud local traditions slowed migration to cities. As importantly, the national birth rate remained level even when the economy was growing and major losses in World War I (1.4 million war deaths) kept population figures flat. This long history of modest or no growth resulted in a much lower population density compared to Britain or Germany: the 2016 figure was 306 residents per square mile, or half that of either neighbor.

In the early years of the twenty-first century, France, like its neighbors, began to feel the full force of an aging population. With a national birth rate below 2.0 in 2013, France experienced its lowest population growth in a decade. Even with the second highest fertility rate in the EU (behind Ireland), France faces an occupational demographic outlook with fewer workers than youth and retirees. That situation has been alleviated somewhat by the free movement of labor within the European Union, where in 2011, more than 2.1 million people born in other EU states resided in France (about the same number as in Britain and Spain, but one million fewer than in Germany) and supplemented the national work force. At the same time, resistance to increasing immigrant numbers hindered plans to bolster the workforce through proactive recruitment.

Despite ocean and mountain frontiers, French borders have been tested by conflicts with neighbors for more than 200 years, with alliances among monarchs expanding and reducing areas of control with some frequency. Even after the French Revolution ended monarchical rule in 1794, the imperial aspirations of Louis XVII, Napoleon, Napoleon III, and Louis Philippe (as well as those of neighboring rulers) kept France in a more or less continuous state of war. The borderland between France and southwestern Germany was a frequent battleground; Alsace-Lorraine alternated between German and French control several times before its current borders were set in 1945. Forty years later, the Schengen agreements began to dismantle the borders that France had struggled for years to protect from its neighbors, and the last remaining barrier, with Spain, fell a decade after that. France has been both victim and beneficiary of such border changes over time, but a prime mover in the new order.

French History and Its Frequently Open Door to Immigrants

As early as AD700, North African Muslims crossed the Mediterranean to settle in southern Europe. Although most settled in Spain, a sizeable community established residence in France. Later, movement into the country continued in relatively small numbers, increasing somewhat in the nineteenth and twentieth centuries as France acquired colonies in Africa and Asia and opened routes for modest immigration traffic. An appropriate beginning to this history is the French age of empire, whose forces would define the shape of the current immigration environment.

Early Experiences with Empire

As one of the early centralized monarchies in Europe, France dabbled in foreign exploration and conquest throughout the seventeenth and eighteenth centuries. What is commonly referred to as the first colonial empire was created by victories in North America, the Caribbean, and India, but the French presence there was short-lived as ambitious leaders turned their attention to European domination in the early nineteenth century. Napoleon initiated conflicts with varying enemy coalitions before being stymied in Russia in 1812. After recalculating his strategy, the exiled Napoleon returned to mount an unsuccessful effort against Britain and its refreshed allies in 1815. His wars were remarkable in that they almost conquered Europe, but even more so for their massive casualties (between four and six million over 12 years) signaling an inglorious end to the continental empire. Postwar treaties stripped France of its European territorial conquests, the Saar and Savoy regions in France, and its colony in St. Lucia, but allowed it to retain almost all of its other colonies.

Despite its defeat in Europe, France quickly returned to policies of expansion. In 1830, the government ventured into Algeria, followed by excursions into Morocco, Tunisia, and West Africa. After 1871, its forces expanded the empire in Southeast Asia, taking control over Vietnam, Cambodia, Laos, and enclaves in China. In the next 30 years it successfully colonized Tunisia and Central Africa, including Mauritania, Senegal, Mali, the Ivory Coast, Benin, Niger, Chad, and the Congo, and rounded out its possessions by conquering most of Polynesia. By 1900 it was world's second largest empire, embracing 110 million people and over 4.8 million square miles of territory. The treaty ending World War I added further territorial control over Syria, Lebanon, Togo, and Cameroon. Despite its disastrous beginning in the Napoleonic Wars, the French imperial century was impressive in both size and shape.

The French approach to colonial responsibility differed greatly from that of the British. Where the British sought to define colonial rule by commercial and military control without commitment to economic or political development, the French aspired to revolutionize at least some aspects of life within their possessions. That sense of mission undoubtedly reflected the prevalent revolutionary sentiment of the eighteenth and nineteenth centuries by bringing concepts of liberty and equality to the colonies. In 1789, the French National Assembly passed a law declaring that all residents in the colonies were French citizens enjoying all the rights assured in the new constitution. It also required territories to adopt the French language and governing structures, assuming that colonies would of course desire both citizenship and assimilation into a greater French culture. In Africa, that assumption translated into a mission to develop and refine what the French saw as primitive cultures. Little effort had been made to accomplish that goal during the ill-fated conflicts in Europe, but the 1848 revolution created new zeal for policies designed to spread French culture throughout the empire. In Senegal, a model system of four communes was actually set up, but was never replicated in other colonies.

Not everyone in France favored the missionary model. A significant element in elite circles rejected assimilation, preferring the British model of rule without extensive commitments, but a stronger faction insisted that a notion of equality could coexist with French views critical of local cultures. The ideal of assimilation was tempered by a more pragmatic first step of "association" based on the French structure of government, with only limited opportunities for French citizenship. By 1912, dual systems operated in all colonies, with access to quality education, medical care, and government employment effectively restricted to French nationals. Improvement of basic services and opportunities for colonial residents stalled, taxes were imposed to support the governing elite, and trade agreements favoring France mandated. Despite an original commitment to inclusion in the French nation, the systems that emerged were much closer to the British model of segregated external rule. By 1914, only 4,500 Algerians had been granted French citizenship; still fewer (2,500) were naturalized from all colonies in West Africa.

Unlike other European nations, France experienced a relatively high population influx in the 1920s and 1930s. Some of that was due to the return of French citizens who had been living in North Africa; some was due to the open door policy, which only France maintained between the wars, continuing measures initiated in World War I to fill gaps in the labor force created by the huge number of casualties. The reception during that 45-year period was generally warm, with the host government assisting in the construction of a mosque in Paris and facilitating residence permits and citizenship. North Africans and East Europeans settled permanently, creating what became prosperous ethnic neighborhoods in cities and their suburbs. That experience encouraged France to see a profitable future with its colonies, advantageous to the ruling power and at least acceptable to the public.

These hopes were dashed in World War II and its aftermath. Far from assuming a position of leadership in the interwar period, France watched from the sidelines as Germany reemerged as an industrial powerhouse and military giant in the hands of a political extremist. Other war-weary nations did the same as Hitler moved easily into Eastern Europe, realizing too late that he would extend aggression to all fronts. In 1940, German armed forces occupied Paris, creating a divided nation with German control in the north and a weakened French zone in the South, which surrendered in 1942. To complete the humiliation, German forces overran French territory in North Africa and their Japanese ally took over French colonies in Southeast Asia. French forces, which had persevered in World War I and expanded the empire after 1917, collapsed early in the second war, setting the stage for the end of the French empire after 1945.

The Postwar Breakup of Empire and the Defining Experience in Algeria

The defeat of Germany and Japan in 1945 allowed France, liberated by Allied forces in 1944, to join the victors in setting the terms of peace. A return to the prewar world at first appeared possible, as the allies granted a mandate over Syria, Lebanon, Togo, and Cameroon to France. But the desire for independence, which had simmered for years, erupted after colonial possessions worldwide witnessed defeat in France and devastation in Britain. Promises to reward loyalty with protection from attack had been broken by the war, and colonies everywhere responded with demands to end imperial rule.

Where Britain generally chose to hasten independence, France preferred to negotiate with colonies, ceding control but maintaining relations with eighteen nations in Africa. In two areas, however (Indochina and Algeria), the French opted to resist the movement for independence, with disastrous results in both. Heavy losses in Vietnam forced the French to withdraw its forces in 1954, and many believed the French would then see the advantages of a diplomatic resolution in Algeria. Instead, political leaders insisted that the presence of a large French community there demanded an aggressive French stance, leading to a long and costly war in North Africa. What followed was a seminal experience for both nations. The postwar French government saw a unique situation in Algeria, which, unlike other colonies (1) continued to send thousands of workers and families to established communities in France, and (2) included more than a million French citizens living within its borders. To French political leaders, Algeria was simply too much a part of France to give up.

France's relations with Algeria certainly suggested a bond that would not disappear with the war's end. The French had been prominent there for more than 120 years; in 1848, the French government declared that Algeria was no longer a colony, but rather an integral part of France. Three regionally defined departments were created, within which local officials, councils, and even mayors would be popularly elected; French residents lived in both seacoast cities and rural villages. A very early Algerian uprising in 1871 had been followed by a long period of peaceful coexistence, indicating a successful union of French and Algerian residents.

And traffic was heavy in both directions. As citizens of an "integral part of France," Algerians moved freely to and from France for more than one hundred years. Initially concentrated in Paris and southern port cities, they worked in all sectors there before extending their presence into the interior. Their numbers increased significantly during World War I, when more than 120,000 were brought to France to aid the war effort and another 172,000 joined the armed forces. The postwar economic recovery in France, coupled with a slump in North Africa, quickly drew additional numbers of Algerians to France, causing the French *colon* population to fear that large-scale emigration would deplete the supply of cheap labor within Algeria. They even pressured the government to tighten immigration rules, with the effect that opportunities granted to Algerians "integral to France" to move were restricted. In France, many sectors dependent on foreign labor suffered, as Algerians were thereby prevented from leaving Algeria. Although there was a certain symbiosis in the relationship, the bond claimed by the French was dictated more by a colonialist perspective than by common interests.

However firm the French believed their ties with Algeria to be, they badly miscalculated both the hostility in Algeria toward their presence and the zeal of the National Liberation Front (FLN), a powerful independence alliance. Resentment of the French was most visible in contempt toward imperious *colons*, but was exacerbated by the perception of the French as having performed in a cowardly manner in World War II. The FLN was an eclectic collection of Muslim fundamentalists, communists, local merchants, and assorted nationalist groups, making it exceptionally difficult to target. Its campaign of resistance began with attacks in areas popular with the French, before escalating to assassinations of French and French-Algerians. Densely populated neighborhoods favored the rebels, as locals shielded fighters and constructed maze-like escape routes. Military strategies devised by a succession of French generals were no match for attacks that, supplemented by rural forces, sabotaged troop movements and compromised transportation. The brutality was unlike anything the French had encountered, terrifying the local expatriate community and leading their protectors to engage in increasingly harsh tactics. By 1958, the costs of continuing the war had become staggering and the prospects for success and restoration of prewar relations dim, even under the leadership of highly respected President Charles de Gaulle.

The fledgling government of the French Fourth Republic had been ill-prepared for the military failures it could not prevent. French forces had abruptly left Indochina in 1954 and by 1956; 400,000 French troops in Algeria were losing to insurgents in yet another rebellious colony. That situation, coupled with the unsuccessful alliance with Britain to resist nationalization of the Suez Canal in Egypt in 1956, led to the fall of the government and a clear leadership vacuum. In 1958, France looked to de Gaulle, who moved to stabilize his nation with a new constitution that proclaimed the Fifth Republic. Initially, he supported continuation of the war in Algeria, but soon saw that France had lost enthusiasm for it and victory was unlikely. A 1961 referendum confirmed that view, and De Gaulle announced a French withdrawal and an independence agreement by 1962. Despite wide support for ending the war, nationalist strongholds in France and the *colons* still in Algeria were furious at what they saw as betrayal, factors that would reappear in immigration discussions then and in the years to follow.

After spending most of World War II as an occupied nation, France had engaged with its own colonies in Asia and Algeria in hopeless wars that dragged on for almost 16 years. The human consequences were enormous. More than a million lives were lost and unrest persisted for years after hostilities officially ended. More than 900,000 fearful European Algerians left North Africa for France. That exodus, continuing well into the 1980s, laid the basis for what became a continuous struggle to accommodate immigrants within a newly wary nation.

The Complex Legacy of Algeria in France

France's history with Algeria has left an indelible stamp on French Immigration:

1. Algeria moved from being France's most favored colony in the mid-19th century to being its worst adversary in the eight-year war for independence ending in 1962; more than 700,000 were killed;

2. Hundreds of thousands of French citizens lived in Algeria and almost as many Algerians in France; after 1962, neither country made efforts to deal with their conflicts of loyalty; Algerians remain the largest immigrant minority in France;

3. The award-winning film *The Battle of Algiers*, was banned in France;

4. In 1961, French police in Paris killed 200 people protesting the war in Algeria;

5. North African history received little coverage in French schools well into the 21st century.

Immigration During and after the Algerian War

The conflict in Algeria cast a shadow over the long history of immigration into France and hindered recruitment of labor. As a nation with a sluggish birthrate dating to the nineteenth century, France had a long history of encouraging migrants from neighboring Italy, Spain, and Portugal, as well as Poland. French immigration policy was expansive, with no preferential quotas or ethnic hierarchy and notoriously loose procedures; a government ordinance of November 1945 even separated residence permits from work permits, allowing immigrants to enter without the work visas required elsewhere in Europe. An Office for the Protection of Refugees and Stateless Persons was created in 1952 to facilitate those fleeing persecution and war, further demonstrating willingness to accept immigrants without real consideration of their contribution to the economy.

Like Germany, the French government particualrly needed to recruit foreign labor in the years after 1945. Agreements between the government and both European and non-European nations facilitated labor flows and guaranteed legal and social protections for migrants. Most immigration, however, was arranged by French businesses, bringing thousands of workers to fill gaps in the labor force without formal documents or processes. The French Ministry for Social Affairs tolerated such practices in deference to the growing needs of industry and pledged to facilitate immigration and naturalization after workers had settled in France. Laws governing citizenship were flexible; by 1965, 90% of immigrants had been legalized, often long after entry. As other European nations were also recruiting labor, France relied heavily on sources in North Africa. The proportion of Europeans living in France fell steadily after 1945 as the rate of entry from Algeria (part of France until 1962), Tunisia and Morocco (former protectorates), and Turkey increased dramatically. Unlike Britain, France welcomed migrants from former colonies, and by 1982 more than one million Muslims had joined the 1.5 million naturalized Muslims already in residence.

To be sure, the presence of a sizeable Muslim population in France caused considerable tension during the years of war with Algeria. Before his stance evolved to support independence, de Gaulle acknowledged that the Algerian migration to seek higher living standards in France would in all likelihood alter the essence of French society (Fetzer & Soper, 2005). Others feared that national security was at risk from religious zealots allowed into France. Most Muslins who chose to settle in France, however, showed little interest in political activity, practicing their religion unobtrusively in makeshift facilities dubbed by observers as "cellar Islam." Faced with persistent gaps in the labor force, governments opted to continue loose admission policies and benefited from the contributions of immigrants, who almost never posed a threat. Still, the memory of Algeria remained fresh to French citizens, who, it will be recalled, had not experienced high levels of immigration before. The prospect of immigrants entering the country who might well be Algerian sympathizers had to be unsettling after 1962, as the nation absorbed more than a million new workers and thousands of returning French and French Algerians. In the short term, labor needs trumped fears of troublesome immigrants, but the seeds of friction had undoubtedly been sown.

When the 1973 oil crisis led to economic recession throughout Europe, opposition to immigration surfaced and, like Germany, France halted new admissions. Although some foreigners returned to their homelands, the main effect of the ban, in France as elsewhere, was to motivate those staying to send for their families. Successive governments pushed restrictive laws, almost all of which were later struck down or failed to win enough support to enact. An attempt by the government to ban family unification was quickly overturned by the Council of State. Later, proposals by the government to deny entry to immigrants deemed unlikely to assimilate (Muslims and African blacks) were abandoned as violating colonial agreements and long-standing policies of unprioritized admissions. Rules that allowed police and other state agents to use race as the basis for questioning were also struck down. In 1977, the government offered foreigners cash payments (10,000 francs) to leave the country, but the few takers were mostly from Spain and Portugal. In 1978, the government raised the ante by proposing to deport hundreds of thousands of Muslims and their families, but the effort died for lack of legislative support. An effort to reduce the rights of ethnic North Africans by limiting the number who could claim French nationality by birth was made in 1993 but rejected by the Socialist government, which took power five years later.

Many if not most government initiatives prior to 1980 were restrictive. Later, however, political leaders moved to normalize immigrants' status and facilitate their integration. The first step, taken by the Socialist government of Francois Mitterand, was to regularize the status of immigrants whose naturalization had been delayed by the suspension of immigration in 1974. It also offered amnesty for immigrants who had entered France before 1981, and 123,000 legalized their status within months. Two years later the government introduced an automatically renewable ten-year residence and work permit, further securing immigrants' tenure in France. Such initiatives were red flags to a new right-wing political movement led by Jean-Marie Le Pen and his National Front Party (FN) which, as the national economy faltered in the 1980s, blamed immigrants for the slump. With an openly discriminatory platform and ties to neo-Nazi groups, the FN found support in local elections, especially in economically distressed suburbs and small towns. By 2002, the Front had gone national, and shocked all observers by outpolling the Socialist prime minister in the first round of the presidential election before losing to the Gaullist incumbent (Jacques Chirac) in the second round. Even in defeat, the anti-immigrant party became a major electoral player.

The strong showing by the National Front was undoubtedly aided by the economy's continued ill health in the years following the oil crisis of 1973. Recovery was slow everywhere but especially so in France, where growth was minimal, unemployment reached 7.8% in 1981 (from 2.3% in 1974), and industrial output continued to decline. The Socialist government moved to stimulate job growth with subsidies and intervention, but important demographic changes—increases in the number of women seeking work and in the number of retirees—were already challenging recovery. A sluggish GDP and persistently high rate of inflation, accompanied by labor protests, allowed conservative and rightist groups to target immigrants as economic villains.

Ethnic Unrest and the Changing Immigration Debate

One consequence of years of loose immigration policies was that little attention was paid to migrants' well-being. As immigrants settled in poor suburbs, strained urban ghettos, and created miserable shantytowns, the French appeared to accept lower living standards for foreigners as natural. In the mid-1990s, high unemployment rates and substandard conditions finally sparked protests and outbreaks of violence in several cities. An African group set off a bomb in a Paris train in 1995, killing seven and wounding 80 people, and reprisals against Muslims followed. Gang violence and an increase in crime rates were attributed to immigrants, and all major parties agreed that responsive measures were needed. Prodded by unrest, if not by poor conditions, the debate about the role of immigrants finally focused on their place in French society, a discussion missing in a long history of acceptance of foreigners as a permanent but quiet lower class.

French ideas about immigrant absorption are rooted in at least two strains of thought, both resembling American philosophical traditions more than those of France's European neighbors. The first was the philosophy prominent in the revolutions of 1789 and 1848 espousing the inalienable rights of all humans to liberty and equality. Those ideals persisted through territorial expansion, European wars, and changing economic conditions. The French version of colonial rule supported conquest as a kind of family enlargement, apparent in the treatment of Algeria as part of France governed with the same rights as those enjoyed within its own borders. Like the British, the French did not expect that colonial citizens would emigrate in large numbers. But they did embrace a more extensive mission, offering French schools and a cultural role model that could be replicated in some if not all colonies. When independence demands emerged, French decolonization moved to free its possessions from imperial rule, doing little or nothing to discourage reinstatement of local traditions. Although a few newly independent colonies maintained French or quasi-French institutions, there was generally little enthusiasm for independence as defined by their former rulers.

The second, related theme of French relations with foreigners (both immigrants and colonial citizens) was the belief that assimilation would be an obvious choice for immigrants simply because French culture was, quite simply, so attractive. One scholar summarizes that philosophy succinctly: "French nationhood is constituted by political unity, it is centrally expressed in the striving for cultural unity" (Brubaker, 1992, p. 1). Being part of France assumes embrace of its culture. The melting pot metaphor would thus be as natural in France as it had been In the United States; immigrants would arrive with cultural differences but quickly opt to shed old loyalties and become truly French. Interestingly, one variation was that of religion, which in the United States was often first seen as fostering a dangerous resistance to assimilation, even as suspicions about Protestant and Catholic loyalties waned with time. The French initially assumed that religious differences would not hinder assimilation; after thousands of North Africans served in French forces in World War I, the French supported Muslim practices without concern that schisms could develop. However naive they may have been, the

French believed that in choosing France as a permanent home, immigrants would be eager to redefine themselves as French first, and members of a religion or ethnic group only within the construct of French identity. In this conception, multiculturalism really referred only to the origins of people united under the national umbrella, not to distinct identities within the greater society.

In assuming that immigrants would assimilate, the French expected them to accept without hesitation the concept and reality of *Laïcité*, considered by most as fundamental to the definition of French democracy. That concept is, most simply, one of secularism, or the separation of church and state. It forbids religion from intruding in government matters and government from intruding in religious activity, but more importantly, it expects that a citizen's identity and first loyalty is to the nation rather than to a religion or religious leader. The conflict that that posed for devout Muslims was either not anticipated or considered minimal, a misconception which would later prove to be a major obstacle in dealing with immigrant issues.

By the mid-1970s, it was clear that large numbers of immigrants would remain in France with no intention of remaking their identities, including their religious loyalties. In 1975, France had almost as many foreign workers as more populous West Germany (1.9 million in France, 2.17 in West Germany), and more than three times as many as other European nations. In a pattern of settlement after the 1973 oil crisis similar to that in Britain and Germany, the number of new foreign workers declined dramatically but the number of family members accompanying them increased, making the total number of immigrants higher and their sojourn in France more permanent. The primary source of labor after 1975 shifted from Portugal to North Africa, such that by 2002 the number of immigrants from Africa, Asia, and the Middle East was almost three times the number from Europe. The number of asylum applications also soared. Between 1980 and 1987 it reached almost 180,000, increasing to more than 280,000 between 1988 and 1994, with the largest numbers from Africa and the Middle East.

The most prominent feature of French immigration after 1945 was the volume of immigrant arrivals made possible by lax entry, residence, and naturalization laws, leading to 30 years of recruitment of essential workers with little attention to integration or other consequences. The second wave, mostly family members joining working-age males after 1973, began to arouse fears that new immigrants would not assimilate, and for the first time France enacted restrictions on admission, rules for family unification, and even procedures for deportation. The third wave arrived in three distinct categories. The first, encouraged by EU as well as French leaders, began with the 1985 dissolution of borders among the five signatories to the Schengen Agreements (France, Germany, Belgium, Luxembourg, and the Netherlands), and its extension to all fifteen EU members except Britain and Ireland in 1995. In allowing free movement by European residents, EU members believed that labor supply would naturally move with demand to create stable national economies. As membership expanded to East European nations, workers moved to more promising economies in the West, but a second category of workers—from outside the EU—also arrived to participate in thriving underground economies, including that in France. Even as non-EU immigrants settled quickly into new jobs, they were viewed as unlikely to assimilate and thus were seen to constitute a threat to an increasingly outdated vision of a homogeneous French state. Still, the surge was driven almost completely by demand, supported and exploited by employers across all sectors of the economy, facilitated by welcoming ethnic communities, and tolerated by governments sensitive to the economic benefits of their presence. For much of the 1980–1990 decade, political leaders across Europe found ways to minimize nationalist concerns, ignoring restrictive policies and quite probably certain that if jobs became scarce, migrants would simply leave for whatever destination offered better prospects.

What caused those immigration systems to falter was the third post-1985 category, made up of the seemingly uncontrollable throngs of asylum seekers. The initial surge was hardly a surprise, given the collapse of the Soviet Union and the newly opened borders across Eastern Europe, but it still exceeded all expectations. France and other states responded by expanding restrictive legislation. In 1993, the government finally moved to revoke the citizenship rights granted natives of its former possessions. The law abolished the automatic citizenship previously granted to second-generation immigrants, forcing them to attest to a "manifestation of will" between the ages of sixteen and twenty-one, in order to become eligible for naturalization. It also ended the long-standing right of those born in a former colony to claim citizenship by the "right of the territory." The rules for granting political asylum were narrowed to facilitate negative judgments, and decision processes were streamlined to allow faster resolution. In 1997, the government, led by a Gaullist president and Socialist prime minister, initiated further changes, including an amnesty program legalizing the residence of almost 100,000 undocumented immigrants, a tightening of asylum and legal entry rules, and affirmation of the government's right to return illegal entrants to home nations. In 25 years, French policy thus evolved from a loose system of rules facilitating immigration to a set of laws essentially shutting out refugees and non-Europeans.

It should be noted that, unlike some nations with significant immigrant populations, France did assume some responsibility for their welfare, even as that "welfare" was officially defined in terms of integration and assimilation. Laissez-faire policies with little assistance for education were replaced in the early 1980s by laws increasing funding for schools in areas populated mostly by immigrants. Some housing standards were upgraded to alleviate conditions linked to unemployment, higher crime rates, and political protests. Still, the hostile posture of the National Front and its supporters continued to make immigrants a foil in battles over French economic and social problems, portending even more strident battles in the new century.

Accumulated and Unresolved Problems

As France sought ways to reconcile historic pride in its unified society with the realities of a diverse population, at least five problem areas intensified after 2000. First, the issue of sheer numbers came to dominate media and public discussions. Immigration levels hovered just above 100,000 per year in the mid-1990s, then grew steadily from 1997 to 2003 before leveling off at more than twice that number. The post-2002 annual rate of about 200,000 legal immigrants, of whom more than 40% were from North Africa, resulted in a 2010 total of just over 12 million resident immigrants or direct descendants of immigrants. The growth of the immigrant sector is especially visible when birth statistics are added: in 2010, 27% of newborns had at least one foreign-born parent. As is the case elsewhere in Europe, almost 40% live in greater metropolitan areas, most commonly in poor suburbs. The rate of naturalization is high, at about 150,000 per year, with North Africans accounting for the largest numbers. French law facilitates this by an updated law that provides automatic citizenship at age eighteen for children born on French soil to foreign parents. Naturalization of people from other EU countries is relatively infrequent (about 3%).

Even though the percentage of foreigners in France is smaller than in the United States or Germany, increases since 1997 and the likelihood of new refugees arriving from Africa and the Middle East have been perceived by many as an uncontrollable threat. Open borders with Spain and Italy have created greater Mediterranean access, borders with Italy and Germany have increased the specter of unplanned arrivals of East Europeans and the Roma. Not surprisingly, governments since 2000 have all pushed for tighter entry laws and higher deportation quotas.

Second, the persistence of ethnically defined areas with high unemployment rates has challenged strategies of increasing funds for education and job training. Suburbs of Paris and other major cities have experienced frequent unrest, violence, and confrontations with police. Three weeks of disturbances rocked the near-suburbs of Paris in 2005, highlighting the unrelenting despair rooted in minority unemployment. Increases in anti-Semitic violence increased as well, raising fears that Jews would leave a France they saw as unsafe. After the September 11, 2001, attacks on the American World Trade Center and Pentagon, Muslim areas were depicted as potential sources of terrorist activity, a fear stoked by the resurgent National Front. All combined to raise twin specters of immigrant terrorist attacks and anti-immigrant extremism.

Third, the seemingly minor issue of appropriate dress for Muslim girls described in chapter 1 escalated into a national debate made even more intense by efforts in some French towns to ban the full body–covering birkini in 2016. The initial incendiary incident occurred in 1989 in a small village, but led to disputes across France as schoolgirls and beachgoers claimed the right to observe the norms of their religion. Public leaders attempted to avoid or contain the issue by leaving decisions to local communities, leading to variations in interpretation which only escalated the problems. The inability of successive governments to agree on legislation about the veil abetted the crisis until 2004, and the belatedly passed law prohibiting the ostentatious display of all religious symbols was widely seen as aimed only at Muslims. Hostility has persisted; women have continued to wear the veil and birkini, and the bans have increased resentment among Muslims for the stigma they legitimized.

Fourth, governments have been criticized for their treatment of the Roma, transient groups from central and Eastern Europe who live in the tradition of gypsy communities wherever they settle. Such groups have a long history in Spain and other European nations, but concerns about their nonconformist ways have increased since Romania and Bulgaria were admitted to the EU in 2007 and granted free movement rights in 2014. In France, governments at both local and national levels have attempted to prevent them from setting up makeshift camps, citing criminal activity, unsanitary conditions, and disruptive children in schools. Since 2010, action against Roma has intensified, with police demolishing entire settlements and deporting their residents. Such solutions have been temporary at best, since EU borders, officially open since 2015, allow them to return at will. Moreover, actions against the Roma have led to condemnation by European Union Commissions on Human Rights. More than 10,000 gypsies have been evicted, and local and national surveys revealed widespread approval of the government's actions. The problem has hardly been resolved, since the French countryside is both a popular destination for new groups and a long-time home for many who settled earlier.

Finally, France faces the same dilemma as other European Union nations in the post-2000 world. As a member of the world's largest quasi-governmental unit, France acknowledges a need for common policies on issues such as immigration. With no real internal borders, all share responsibility over the vast area that is the EU, and rules governing transit, employment rights, and some labor conditions have already been developed. At the same time, most member states believe that basic questions of immigration—how many and who shall be allowed in, what internal laws define their rights and obligations—are the province of national governments even as they support some common approaches to asylum and illegal immigration. France has already accepted EU mandates (working conditions, political freedoms) and rulings (against the razing of housing and deportation of Roma) that run counter to public opinion and potentially weaken governments implementing EU rules. The refugee crisis arising in 2013 has already tested the resolve of EU decision making, and is sure to highlight friction among members.

Nowhere was the tension greater than in France in 2015, where radical Muslims associated with the Islamic State carried out attacks that killed 130 people and injured thousands in Paris, and in Nice in July 2016, where a Tunisian terrorist behind the wheel of a large truck took the lives of another 86 and wounded hundreds. Information that at least one of the assailants had entered Europe in the surge of refugees from the Mideast fueled demands for restricting the flow of immigrants. French president Hollande responded almost immediately to both attacks by reiterating his nation's commitment to welcome refugees, with the assertion that France would not be intimidated by foreign terrorists. He was joined by German chancellor Merkel, but others in the EU moved to reinstitute border checks and limit the entry of those from Syria and Iraq. As the EU considers policy options, the climate for agreement has worsened and the issue of massive population movement has been left unresolved.

Unresolved issues pose special challenges for French governments because security threats have become grim realities, and because basic immigration principles and policy remain unclear. Some of the pillars of French national traditions have been used to justify both inclusion of foreigners into the broad fabric of French society and exclusion based on nationalistic conceptions of the state. Nationality laws dating from the nineteenth century welcomed foreigners as recreated French citizens, yet both philosophers and politicians have insisted that all adhere to a prototype of French citizenship that is unique and necessarily difficult to achieve. Nominally, heady discussions of fundamental principles have often faulted foreigners for their insufficiently robust allegiance to a republican model generated in the eighteenth century, leading many to question how realistic traditional frameworks are for addressing twenty-first century needs.

Economics and Immigration in France

Postwar Immigration as the Beginning of a New Labor Force

France was one of the first European nations to import labor. After recruiting large numbers between the two world wars, post-1945 governments supplemented the national labor force with recruitment based on needs in business and industry. Three categories of entry were developed: temporary, with a one-year visa; ordinary foreign resident, with a three-year visa linked to specific work; and privileged resident, with a three-year visa renewable for ten years. All were officially required to have permits and were guaranteed the protections provided to nationals. Separate agreements were set up with Algeria, which was at that time considered part of France. No automatic permits were provided for family members, but workers could apply for naturalization after three years and then petition as citizens to bring relatives to France. An Office of National Immigration was established to facilitate entry and a Social Action Fund set up in 1958 to protect immigrant worker rights. Government approvals were technically required, but the cases of the vast majority of immigrants entering between 1946 and 1973 were handled by industries using processes, developed with government approval, to regularize immigrants' status after they settled in France.

The official and makeshift processes were ideal for meeting the variable needs of the labor market. Rules were flexible and the flow largely self-regulated by business and industry. For most of the period before 1974, the flow did fluctuate with market needs. Demand was heavy for the first five years, slowed between 1950 and 1955, then picked up after 1956. By 1968 100,000 workers were being admitted annually; by 1974, the immigrant percentage of the population had doubled, to 4% (Table 5.1). The French system of categorizing residents classified children born abroad as immigrants, but children born in France to immigrants were considered French, creating a structural undercounting of actual immigrant totals in official documents. (The German Research Institute on Migration, for example, lists two separate figures for France: foreign population as a percentage of total population—5.6% in 2005—and immigrant population as a percentage of total—8.1%—illustrating the difference in counting). Whatever count is used, the growth in numbers of immigrants during that period was significant.

Table 5.1. Immigrant Population in France, 1921–2013

Year	Immigrant Population (In millions)	% of Total population
1921	1.45	3.7
1931	2.74	6.6
1946	2.01	5.0
1954	2.32	5.4
1968	3.28	6.6
1975	3.89	7.4
1982	4.04	7.4
1990	4.17	7.4
1999	4.31	7.4
2005	4.93	8.1
2013	7.44	11.6

Source: National Institute for Statistics and Economic Studies (INSEE), 2006; UN Report, Trends in International Migrant Stock, 2013).

As long as immigrants were employed and the economy prospered, little attention was paid to their impact, since they provided manpower with no real negative consequences. By 1967, foreigners were improving their lot. Concentration in unskilled and lower ranks declined, and percentages in semiskilled, skilled, and white-collar occupations increased. They were still mostly concentrated in the industrial sector, in, automobile manufacturing, rubber, metals, and textiles and construction. In those sectors they clustered in the "hard labor" jobs. They still occupied the lower rungs of social status, but were well compensated for their work.

Restrictive Immigration and Redefinition of the Population

The 1973 oil crisis and the recession that followed brought real economic change. What had been a buoyant and expanding system quickly became one characterized by cutbacks and decreased output. Unemployment, which had stood at an abnormally low level of 2.3% in 1974, rose to 7.8% in 1981. Short-term measures passed by the centrist Giscard government failed to right the economy, which continued to struggle through six full years and a change in government. In 1980, the gross domestic product was up only 1.4%, and continued to expand at the almost stagnant level of 1.1% for the next four years. Unemployment figures remained stubbornly high, actually increasing through the Eastern European crises of 1989–1991 and peaking at 11% nationally in 1995 (Table 5.2). Even with relatively stable growth rates, the 1980–1990 decade was hugely disappointing to the French, whose postwar experiences had created widespread expectations of continuous prosperity. By the summer of 2016, the rate had fallen to

Table 5.2. French Unemployment Rates, 1980–2013

	1980	1984	1988	1995	2000	2004	2007	2011	2012	2013
Overall	6.3	8.5	8.8	11.0	10.1	10.1	9.9	10.4	10.3	10.9
Nationals				9.1	7.7	6.7	7.2	8.9	8.1	
Foreign				16.6	14.5		13.4	16.3	14.2	

Source: National Institute for Statistics and Economic Studies (INSEE), Annual Labor Force Surveys, 1980–2013.

9.9%, which was still higher than comparable figures in the United States and elsewhere in Europe (4.9 in the U.S. and Britain, 4.2 in Germany).

Despite the lengthy recession, immigrant numbers increased as foreign workers continued to request permission for family members to join them. That should have surprised no one, since the majority of foreign workers had lived in France for more than 20 years, and many had become citizens. Unemployment rates among them were higher than those of nationals, and many willingly moved to jobs in off-market sectors, including seasonal work (likely inflating the official unemployment statistics). Those sectors remained active, even expansive, easing the employment situation for thousands of immigrants. Nationally, the composition of the immigrant population continued to change in patterns consistent since 1990. Migration from European countries, which had historically outpaced that from outside Europe, was consistently lower than that from outside the EU (Table 5.3). According to Eurostat data, that pattern remained fairly constant through the 2008–14 period.

Not surprisingly, the profile of post-1975 admissions shifted. More than half of those who entered between 1974 and 2008 were family members, including parents and children. The resulting demographic challenged the calculus that had made immigrants

Table 5.3. Composition of Immigrant Population in France, 1975–2008

	1975	1990	1999	2008
Total Immigrants	3,400,000	3,600,000	3,300,000	3,600,000
FROM EU Nations	1,900,000	1,300,000	1,200,000	1,400,000
From Outside EU	1,600,000	2,300,000	2,100,000	2,100,000
% of Immigrants in the Labor Force	45	43	48	47

Source: National Institute for Statistics and Economic Studies (INSEE), Annual Labor Force Surveys, 1975–2009.

such an attractive labor source since 1945. Unlike the postwar era's unfettered, single male, the post-1974 immigrant added dependents in the midst of a recession. The rate of unemployment among foreigners—especially teenagers entering the workforce—began to register higher than that of nationals even as the percentage of immigrants in the labor force remained fairly constant. Government attempts to halt this pattern by limiting family unification were uniformly overturned by rulings of the French Council of State. In 1983, the normally sympathetic Socialist government went so far as to propose a policy of "repulsions" to stabilize the weakened economy. Both courts and the council rejected the policy as arbitrary, especially as most of those targeted had lived in France for most of their adult years.

Another change in the demographic profile of immigrants followed the breakup of Soviet control in Eastern Europe and the surge of workers into the West. Starting in 1985, border crossings from Hungary and Czechoslovakia began to increase, and the fall of the Berlin Wall in 1989 brought a deluge of asylum seekers into Germany and, in smaller numbers, France. That group often lacked language or job skills, highlighting the prospect of immigrants unable to work or, worse, needing economic assistance. The French rate of acceptance of asylum applications dropped precipitously after 1984 in an attempt to curb the flow of economically dependent immigrants into its still shaky economy (Table 5.4).

Elements in the Economic Debate: Employment, Contributions, Costs

Immigration debates in France have been confounded by contradictory claims, especially evident in critics' arguments that immigrants manage to both strain unemployment funds and take jobs nationals should have. Although discussions are often dominated by polemical social fears, the primary motivation for immigration has remained economic and the most fundamental issue employment, both of which can be empirically analyzed in terms of contributions to the economy and costs of supporting those without jobs. The largest group of immigrants continues to be long-term residents and their families,

Table 5.4. Asylum Seekers and Acceptance Rates in France, 1982–2011

Year	Applicants	Acceptance Rate %
1982	19,863	73.9
1984	22,350	65.3
1987	26,290	32.7
1990	61,422	15.4
1999	22,475	22.8
2009	47,686	22.0
2011	57,113	18.6

Source: French Office for Protection of Refugees and Displaced Persons (OFPRA), 2012

who moved to France in the 1945–1974 period. During the long period of economic stagnation after 1974, unemployment hit foreigners especially hard. Unemployment rose steadily from 1970 to 1994, dropped for six years then rose again except for a two-year decline between 2006 and 2008. The unemployment rate among immigrants has been almost twice as high as that of nationals over a 20-year period and consistently above 13% (Table 5.2). At the same time, the unemployment and migration rates are not correlated. High migration levels coexisted with low unemployment in 1970; unemployment levels have gone down as migration has increased in 2006. And, as the data in Table 5.3 reveal, the percentage of migrants in the workforce has remained remarkably stable at about 47% over time, including years when a relatively small percentage of immigrants had families living with them. A postrecession analysis by French economists at the University of Lorraine concluded that over time there has been no increase in unemployment due to immigration (Fromentin, 2013).

It is still the case that unemployment among migrants, especially those in younger age cohorts, has been persistently high. OECD data reveal that, contrary to patterns in Britain and the United States, more education has not clearly correlated with having a job in France. Higher education brought the rate down by only 36% in France, as opposed to 66% in Britain and 53% in the United States. Two conclusions may be drawn. The first is that highly educated immigrants have not competed successfully for jobs, suggesting that discrimination, as opposed to lack of qualifications, may have been a factor. Reflecting that concern, the 2006 Immigration and Integration bill passed by the Sarkozy government required that hiring companies review applications blind, with no knowledge of the ethnicity or race of the applicant. But a second conclusion is even more striking. Martin Schain has pointed out that while a university education is attained by almost as many immigrants as nationals in France, the high school dropout rate among migrants is alarmingly high (50%), drastically reducing the chances for any position (2012, pp. 17–18). Immigrants are much more likely to leave school than nationals, even as some of their schoolmates reach the university at a rate equivalent to French students. Unemployment will remain a stark prospect for immigrants as long as their performance in basic education lags behind that of their peers.

Most economic analyses include some measure of the contributions and costs of immigrants, but French studies have been few in number and overshadowed by gross statistics on unemployment. Prominent analyses include those that have emphasized costs to the state, such as the work of Jean-Paul Gourevitch (2008) estimating that the government spent approximately 72 billion Euros on essential services for immigrants in 2008. The bulk of this figure (52 billion) was for social costs, including health care, retirement benefits, and antipoverty programs, but excluded outlays for unemployment payments and family allowances. Another 13 billion Euros were estimated as lost revenue from tax evasion in the informal economy of illegal work, fraud, and counterfeiting. Security outlays were needed for manpower to deal with crime in immigrant areas; and 1.6 billion was included to cover educational costs for immigrant children. On the other side of the ledger were revenues gained from immigrant taxes and contributions to

National Insurance totaling 45.5 billion Euros. Gourevitch's analysis also included investments that France made in home nations, mostly former colonies, to reduce emigration by promoting development, and investments in integration programs in France. His conclusions included recommendations for strong governmental programs to increase immigrant employment and dedicated efforts to curb the immigrant-fueled informal economy and the surging pattern of petty crime in immigrant neighborhoods (2008).

Most economists argue that immigrants make far more contributions than those described above. The largest omission would be their role as consumers paying for services, purchasing homes, food, and clothing, and investing in family and other businesses. Those who operate small businesses create jobs, and many work in state agencies and the military. Even the lower-paid jobs can represent a form of added contribution, measured by the difference between what their labor is worth and what they are paid for it. Moreover, figures that suggest that retired immigrants take out more than working foreigners contribute are skewed by the fact that current retirees are those who were recruited by France in the '60s; the lengthy suspension of immigration by the government between 1974 and the mid-1990s created the current imbalance in contributions by cutting off the flow of workers who would have been replenishing pension funds. One of the official economic data sources used by the European Union, the OECD, concluded in 2013 that in general, immigrants contribute more than they cost across European nations. Germany and France were exceptions to that pattern, but the OECD attributed the French anomaly to the larger than normal retiree population (and absence of working-age immigrants in the period of analysis), high unemployment rates and generally lower wages among poorly educated immigrants, and the economic crises of 1974–1985 and the late 1980s (OECD, 2013). Given the unusual labor immigration history since 1974, standard models of costs and benefits are unlikely to fit the French case until previous demographic imbalances are replaced by the more normal distribution in the years after 1998.

The passage of time cannot, however, guarantee a solution to the strikingly high school dropout rate which inevitably leads to high support costs. Cohorts who have left school will continue to be a net drain on resources as poor candidates for jobs lacking opportunities to re-enroll in educational and training programs. That dilemma remains a challenge to political leadership, which has been slow to respond with government initiatives, a topic examined later.

Economic Immigration in Aging France

Like almost all of the EU nations, France has had cause to worry about changing population demographics and the difficulty in attracting labor sufficient to sustain its economy. The large number of retirees is one symptom of a system out of balance; another is the persistently sluggish national birth rate. Although that rate continues to be higher than most in Europe, it still hovers around the level needed for population stability, even with higher rates among immigrants, a pattern common to all European nations.

The French office in charge of critical statistics (INSEE) has projected that shortages in the workplace on the order of 750,000 positions will begin to appear after 2015 in two areas: the service sector, including jobs in health care and low-level industrial positions, and the technology sector. In Germany, a similar situation triggered planning for additional immigrants even before the refugee crisis unexpectedly provided more than a million in 2015. In contrast, both French analysts and French political leaders have focused on alternatives, including increasing retirement age (by up to eleven years) and contributions (by as much as 4.5%) to increase labor and reduce costs. Both would seriously abrogate long-held commitments to the workforce and almost certainly generate widespread opposition, even in the context of new concerns about foreign workers. A second proposal calls for motivating those not currently in the workplace—both the unemployed and those who have chosen not to work outside the home—to enter the labor force, even if that would require expensive retraining and improving school completion rates. Some proposals to increase the number of immigrants have also been made but remain tentative, given a lack of public enthusiasm for that option. The challenge thus persists, portending dangerous shortages in the near-term future.

Recurring Economic Issues

As in other European nations, the economic issues surrounding immigration are part of the national landscape and often difficult to separate from other issues. The recession brought on by the 1973 oil crisis affected all but allowed many to focus on costs related to immigrants; divisions within the French public might have produced hostility toward government, or others, if immigrants had not been available to blame for unemployment. Critical economic questions have deep roots in the basic debate about the consequences of an economy dependent in part on imported labor. The first question needs to be, Can the French accept—as they did in the postwar years—the presence of non-French workers who may not assimilate as completely as migrants in the past? Economic rationality would consider the question rhetorical, since the likelihood of nationals filling openings in areas critical to the economy is small and the possibility of mandating assimilation low. Maintaining an economy responsive to global shifts almost certainly requires cultural adaptations—some to address the historical preference for small-scale businesses, some to indicate an increased willingness to support education and training for foreigners, some to accept differences in the lifestyles of workers establishing new lives. Without some changes, the prosperity France seeks would appear to be unlikely.

Beyond the larger questions lie lingering challenges only partially addressed by makeshift policies in the last half-century. To retain a stable workforce, hiring and keeping productive workers requires investments in housing and education. The challenge also applies to refugees—especially in the post-2013 context—whose entry might have to be adopted as part of an overall EU plan but who have found scant support in their efforts to create new lives. Political leaders often exaggerate the number and influence of undocumented immigrants in the country, creating a scapegoat class but not the research needed to construct real options for dealing with them. Finally, the development of effective policy demands the objective analyses of costs and benefits of foreign labor, studies that have been hindered by French laws prohibiting accurate counting of ethnic minorities. As long as the claims that immigrants drain national resources go unrefuted, no government can provide policies to ensure a healthy economy without antagonizing a public opposed to the admission of a viable future workforce.

The Politics of Immigration

The Political Context

It is useful to recall that, like other European nations, France confronted a massive post-war challenge to rebuild its infrastructure and economy. Its colonies were demanding independence and its allies expected participation in building a multinational defense force and a collective economic union. Despite decades of close ties, its relationship with Algeria deteriorated precipitously, leading to an expensive and brutal war which drained precious resources in a losing cause. That conflict also brought realization of enormous cultural clashes with a population previously thought to be an eager junior partner in the French state.

Confrontations with colonial populations were a shock to long-standing popular images of colonials as aspiring French citizens. The French sense of identity, based in the republican roots of the Revolution, is rooted in a basic commitment to equality and loyalty to the culture—with all its fundamental social and political values—that safeguarded it. For the French, assimilation is the natural concluding stage of immigration, and for the hundred years after the Revolution immigrants had mostly done just that. Unlike the United States, which over time accepted the multiple identities that citizens maintained even as they became loyal Americans, or Britain and Germany, which did not encourage integration, France expected immigrants to adopt French identity. Even when that ideal was not embraced by the hundreds of thousands who arrived after World War II, it continued to guide French goals and policies. The French nation, to its citizens, deserves nothing less than the undivided loyalty of all who choose to reside there.

Pressured by reconstruction needs and the loss of colonies after the war, including the ill-fated attempt to retain control of Algeria, the short-lived Fourth Republic paid little attention to many major issues, including labor shortages. It implicitly delegated recruitment of labor to businesses, with the understanding that immigrants from whatever source could be officially processed later. Most immigrants arriving between 1950 and 1973 were admitted with few qualifications beyond their willingness to work in an economy eager to absorb them. The setting for the immigration debates for the next fifty years was thus the product of huge changes occasioned by the war and its aftermath, changes to which French governments, like governments elsewhere, responded with inconsistent laws, evasion of central immigration issues, and a polarized politics that made rational and gradual adjustment difficult or impossible.

National Government as the Locus of Immigration Policy

Historically, French immigration policy has been the preserve of the national government, in a highly centralized state in which highly centralized agencies have been charged with managing all aspects of this complex policy area. After the settlement of the Algerian War, that tradition was maintained by President de Gaulle and his successors. In that delegation system, no significant immigration legislation was passed by the National Assembly between 1945 and 1975, as administrative agencies pragmatically shifted rules as needed to keep labor sources active and businesses content. Broader issues of national planning were rarely raised, and no attempt was made to reconcile philosophical inconsistencies between the encouragement of diverse immigration and the preservation of a single national identity. The combination of pressing economic needs and bureaucratic handling of immigration issues served to delay any real debate, thereby facilitating a generalized acceptance of the necessity for immigrants with no real consideration of the longer-term consequences of their presence.

The admission and treatment of immigrants were functions of the labor market, tempered only by occasional initiatives designed to attract European workers whenever the number of Algerians exceeded implicit quotas. Agencies implemented decisions by means of *circulaires* detailing manpower needs, promoting integration measures and ethnic balance, and claiming success in rejecting undesirable immigrants. As early as 1968, the national Economic and Social Council differentiated between Europeans and non-Europeans, the latter described as temporary, and suggested that localities establish quotas. Parliamentary approval was not seen as required for small or large changes in policy. Between the 1974 suspension of immigration and the 1984 electoral success of the anti-immigrant National Front, mainstream parties struggled to find common ground for new policy, but ultimately defaulted to the ineffectual laws already in place, making only halfhearted attempts to entice immigrants to leave or to plan for their permanent residence.

Steps taken by the national government to promote immigrant integration were generally weak, especially as seen in the context of simultaneous restrictions on admissions and family reunion. In 1981, seven years after administrative policies suspended immigration and encouraged immigrants to return to their homelands, the leftist government changed course, lifting postwar restrictions on ethnic associations and providing funds to assist them. In addition, the tradition of delegating issues of urban poverty and disorder to localities was replaced by a centralized program establishing Zones of Educational Priority (ZEPs) defined largely by ethnic concentration and eligibility for national funds. Such efforts were still minimal, as all parties sought to identify noncontroversial ways to assist the increasingly permanent immigrant population.

Challenging National Control

Frustration with the failure of either major party to restart the economy grew steadily after 1974. Attempts by national leaders to tinker with immigration policies in the context of lagging employment and production created targets for opposition groups who claimed that the economy suffered from both immigrant competition for jobs and their higher rate of unemployment. Despite the flawed logic of that argument, anti-immigrant forces gained momentum, and divisions developed within the Socialist government over how to promote better conditions for immigrants in the face of strident opposition. By 1984, the National Front was able to translate popular resentment into a significant protest vote against the government, pushing the issue onto the national electoral stage for the first time.

The strength of the FN forced major parties to confront immigration and integration issues directly, and they were ill-prepared to do so. Other forces of the Right—the Rassemblement pour la Republique (RPR) and the centrist Union pour La democratie francaise (UDF)—sought to offer moderate policy options but found the public far more supportive of the FN's harsh positions. Socialists tried to defuse the FN's appeal by advocating restrictive as well as social integration measures, passing laws that introduced identification checks and limited family reunification. Three Socialist governments between 1988 and 1993 tightened regulations of immigrant rights, which set the stage for the so-called Pasqua laws (named after the incumbent French interior minister) increasing expulsions and granting local officials the power to withhold housing and marriage permits. Attempts by Socialist governments to find common ground with the RPR and UDF were undermined by constant pressure from the National Front, whose popular support was erratic in its national influence but continued unabated in local and national elections. By the early 1990s, most of the immigrants assailed by the FN had become French citizens, but the negative campaigns had sufficiently increased public opposition to make the distinction between naturalized citizen and foreigner irrelevant to the public. By dealing with immigration on an ad hoc basis for 40 years, by putting off major legislation, leaving immigrants' status and socioeconomic concerns unaddressed, mainstream parties had almost certainly facilitated the appeal of extreme groups. In the vacuum created by that inactivity, the FN was able to arouse public anger against any attempt to improve the situation of immigrant minorities, and both Socialists and parties of the Right were pushed to maintain or strengthen harsh policies imposed after 1974.

Although tumultuous political changes in the Soviet Bloc dominated national agendas between 1989 and 1995, EU expansion and immigration issues were still salient. Even as requests for asylum soared with the breakdown of Eastern borders in the mid-1980s, France played a central role in persuading members of the EU to join it and the other four original members in removing all internal border controls. Free movement of EU residents was thus guaranteed in 1995 and expanded with EU enlargement ten years later, assuring widespread access to jobs and residence in France.

The addition of Eastern European members, however, opened potential corridors of entry from the Middle East and beyond. Just as economists began to argue in 2001 that France would need foreign labor as business and industry expanded, the FN ramped up its attacks on immigration as diluting the French character with unemployable immigrants from dissimilar regions. Surprisingly, in this increasingly bitter political environment little actual change in policy occurred. Governments of the Right focused on tighter restrictions, but opposition from the Left worked to empower judicial boards, which tended to overturn them. Bowing to pressure from citizens and leaders to reaffirm national identity, all major parties rejected proposals for multiculturalism in public education or social programs as inappropriate in the French context, and in 2004 the government of Jacques Chirac finally took action on the long-simmering headscarf controversy by passing legislation that banned ostentatious religious symbols in public. At the same time, it also responded to European Union directives by adopting new antidiscrimination policies. Between 2003 and 2007, six superfluous or purely symbolic laws were passed, confirming that political calm—or stalemate—had returned to national politics, and attempts at comprehensive legislation came to a halt.

The Return of Immigration Politics to National Control

The inability of the political parties to develop clear immigration legislation undoubtedly facilitated moves to reassert national authority. Even before he assumed the presidency in 2007, Interior Minister Nicolas Sarkozy, acting in the style of French policymaking before 1985, issued a series of directives leading to passage of a comprehensive Immigration and Integration law in 2006. Many of its components incorporated measures endorsed by both the National Front and mainstream parties, for instance, increased deportation targets for undocumented immigrants (up to 25,000 annually) and new restrictions on family unification. It also included a provision requiring family members to learn French and demonstrate familiarity with French customs and laws, and increased the government's power to destroy the substandard housing found in Roma camps.

The law also introduced a system that for the first time linked new visas to skills in areas of demand in France, identifying—and thus limiting—those fields in which unskilled labor was needed. Although the *immigration choisie* (selective immigration) resembled policies developed by other EU members, the debate was paralyzed by demands from the Right for a policy of zero immigration. Finally, breaking with a peculiarly French tradition, the law authorized the inclusion of questions on race and ethnicity in the census in order to facilitate accurate data on minorities, only to have that provision struck down by the Constitutional Council in 2007. A companion Law of Equal Opportunities included measures to prevent discrimination, support education and retraining, and creation of an Office of Cohesion and Equality of Opportunity. In a real step away from previous laws, it required medium and large companies to use anonymous resumes when screening job applicants, pushing businesses not to reject qualified minorities. Even with some modification or opposition to its laws, the national government had reasserted its responsibility for immigration policy by 2007. It further strengthened its position in 2011, with the acceptance of three European Union directives: the "return directive," which set common standards for the expulsion of those in the country illegally; a standard for identifying and sanctioning employers who hired illegal immigrants; and a directive embracing a common Blue Card, by then a standard permit for skilled foreign workers with protections for residence and employment (Schain, 2012).

The role of President Sarkozy was critical, as he straddled disparate demands designed to achieve agreement on the proposals and overcome pressure to leave policy to the fate of public opinion. Fiercely opposed by the Socialists as shamelessly pandering the far Right, Sarkozy defended his approach as sympathetic to the difficulties which immigrants experienced—arguing, "It is not a mark of generosity to create ghettos at the gates of our big towns, where there is only hopelessness and, beyond that, crime" (*The Economist*, May 4, 2006). Ever the pragmatist, Sarkozy claimed sensitivity to rational immigration based on his own Hungarian heritage, and stressed his agreement with similar policies in most of France's EU neighbors.

Political Parties and the Special Role of the National Front

That political parties became important actors in a system dominated by the national administration is the best evidence of the extraordinary role played by the National Front and the prominence of the immigration issue. Since French confidence in national control over virtually all policy domains has survived 200 years of volatile as well as stable environments, it is even more remarkable that the government's failure to resolve immigration issues managed to lure voters into the political fray after 1980. As similar issues plague several EU member nations, it is important to assess the way in which immigration issues have shaped party politics, in France as elsewhere.

Several factors contributed to the success of mainstream French parties in controlling national agendas after 1958. The public welcomed the stability that mostly centrist parties brought, the economy was robust, and national leadership had ended the Algerian War and managed peaceful transitions from other colonial responsibilities. After years of prosperity, however, the 1973 recession raised fears that the government's openness to foreigners would hinder recovery. Mainstream parties that had supported immigration with little expectation of a need to change course were slow to respond. They agreed to suspend new admissions and placed limits on family unification, but stopped short of forcing repatriation or investing in retraining and integration programs. Until the 1984 elections, parties mostly continued to avoid immigration issues, hoping, as other nations did, that they would be resolved by market forces and disappear as the economy recovered. When immigration questions were discussed at all, they were cloaked in vague terms of integration, without specifying the necessary steps to achieve it.

Integration was hardly the calming response party leaders hoped it would be. Since Muslims were the most prominent immigrant group in France—constituting the largest Islamic community in Europe—they stood out as both a minority concentrated in poor areas and one whose faith made them unlikely candidates for rapid assimilation into the secular French culture. That situation was seized on by the previously obscure National Front. When it turned its focus to immigrants in 1983, it surprised everyone by winning almost 11% of the popular vote with a platform dominated by its promise to implement a zero-immigration standard. Its success enhanced the salience of immigration by framing it in terms of its potential to dilute French identity and the threat it presented to both the economy and the personal safety of French citizens. As the EU added Eastern European members in the early 1990s, the FN expanded its warnings to include unskilled workers and hordes of gypsies (Roma) from Bulgaria and Romania. Even as increasing numbers of immigrants acquired French citizenship, and loosened borders produced little increase in the number of workers from the East, the FN continued to attract support for its resistance to any and all foreigners.

But more important than its electoral role was the National Front's influence on both governing and opposition parties. Socialist as well as Gaullist parties hardened their positions. Under Socialist rule, the conservative interior minister Charles Pasqua tightened restrictions on families and students; center-right governments adopted many of the FN positions; public opinion continued to threaten the election of anyone sympathetic to immigrants. By presenting candidates for local as well as national office, the FN kept the issue alive, even as it rarely won seats. As noted earlier, a striking example of FN strength was the 2002 national presidential election, when Jean-Marie Le Pen came in second in the first round of voting. Although he was defeated in the second round, the vote shocked both major parties. In 2007, Le Pen was a distant fourth-place vote getter, but public campaigns continued to rail against acceptance of more immigrants who would take jobs from nationals (Le Pen's rallying cry was "Two million immigrants, two million unemployed"), and unrest continued in some of the poorest immigrant neighborhoods. Even though the FN failed to achieve major party status, more of its positions were embraced by its opponents. The head scarf ban was passed in 2004, and the French rejected the new European Union Constitution in 2005—a year in which riots broke out in Paris suburbs over laws making it easier to fire workers. In 2013, the FN's new leader (Le Pen's daughter Marine) continued to draw support, and in 2016 Nicholas Sarkozy returned as a candidate for president with the claim that nothing less than French identity was at stake. Rejecting the "stay as you are" multiculturalism favored by leftist parties, both Le Pen and Sarkozy appealed to voters with promises to root out dangerous immigrants. Sensing a turning point in French opinion, the FN upped its attack on the EU, demanding French withdrawal and new national policies on trade, currency, and immigration.

In this context, no party has sought to mobilize the immigrants themselves electorally. Because they have tended to settle in a small number of geographic areas, their potential influence upon the centralized system is limited, and even the Socialists have resisted nominating minorities. But beyond electoral structure, immigrant voting power is diminished by the fact that no party has become their firm advocate. That reluctance is perhaps based in the fear that opponents citing a strict interpretation of *laïcité* would claim that because minorities and majorities are equal in the republican state, a party identifying issues as ethnic would violate a powerful French principle of politics. Given the aversion to introducing ethnicity into a historically neutral political arena, the French public might well believe that their needs are better served by deemphasizing differences than by calling attention to them.

The role of the FN to this point has been greater than either the UKIP's in Britain or the AfD's in Germany. Despite its lack of real electoral success, it has exerted influence far beyond its support in numbers by forcing the major parties to embrace its position on its sole issue for an extended period of time. Centralized systems tend to facilitate such exaggerated power by allowing citizens to support extreme positions without having to grant them the power to govern. And, since party identification among voters is generally weaker in France than in other democracies, the FN has been able to attract voters with only loose party preferences. It has done so by focusing on an emotionally charged issue, calibrating the intensity of its campaigns to receptive audiences, and overstating the role of foreigners in the much larger national culture. It has also succeeded in undermining the major parties by highlighting their failure to deal decisively with the issue, even though it has defied resolution in all EU member states. Finally, the FN has made it difficult for governing parties to deal with immigration as a labor issue—the historical basis of population movement everywhere—by accusing them of ignoring immigration's greater purposes and danger. The FN has assumed the classic role of spoiler and sustained support for its positions far longer than most fringe parties. Even with a narrow focus on immigrants as scapegoats, the FN emerged as an arbiter of elections with a relatively small electoral base of the xenophobic and alienated, supplemented by those who are merely disgruntled. Given the continued salience of nationalist issues in France, its influence is likely to persist.

Interest Groups and Immigration

In the United States, immigrant groups, their supporters, and their detractors have all maintained high profiles and active campaigns as they face off at public events and utilize lobbyists to promote their interests. Activity has been much less visible in both Britain and Germany, where parties actually identify slots for group representation and hold much tighter reins on the policy process. France is closer to the European model, in which groups direct whatever pressure they can to major parties. In that context, Martin Schain's analysis of immigration in Britain and France concluded that there are "no groups of any significance that are advocating and working for the expansion of immigration in either country" (Schain, 2012, p. 32). Those invested in broadening immigration (mostly businesses) work with government agencies to secure visas for those qualified to fill openings. In France, that process was reactivated in the *immigration choisie* legislation passed in 2006, which, ironically, resurrected much of the recruitment system that existed prior to 1974. Still, businesses that have the most to gain from easier access to foreign labor have openly supported flexible policies through their national organization—the National Employers' Association. That group has offered only cautious endorsement of additional immigration, citing concerns about the failure of immigrants to integrate. Such reticence is unusual, especially in contrast to the German case, where the benefits of foreign labor are regularly extolled by business groups.

There have been some shifts toward greater group involvement in France. After immigration emerged as a major issue after 1980, the government rescinded a law that had prevented immigrants from forming associations, and the number of such organizations grew to more than 4,000 by 1990. Most were Islamic but others developed to promote French diversity or oppose racism in general, and most advocated for the right to be different. Even with legal recognition and access to program funding, however, few ventured into the controversial topic of multiculturalism, preferring campaigns for education and welfare programs to polemical political stands.

Some groups have sought only educative roles. Ethnic associations reacted strongly to an ill-conceived attempt by the National Assembly to praise the positive effects of colonialism, and the Representative Council of Black Organizations (CRAN) was formed as an umbrella group in 2004 to coordinate educational efforts. Those and other sympathetic groups—the Groupe d'information et de soutien des immigres (GISTI), Comite Inter-Mouvements Aupres des Evacues (COMADE), the Catholic Church—have rallied to support immigrant welfare and protest restrictive policies, but have tended to avoid electoral roles, preferring low-key activities. In 2007, a new Ministry of Immigration, Integration, National Identity, and Co-Development was created to promote integration in the aftermath of 2005 riots and renewed calls for deportations. The chief venues for discussion of immigration policy remain those controlled by the major and minor parties, and direct involvement of affected groups is limited mostly to community arenas. Immigration and pluralism have for the most part not been seriously linked or even seen as partners in the ongoing debate.

Public Opinion as the Hidden Definer of Policy

Before the 1973 oil crisis, France, like Germany, officially presented foreign workers as contributors to a thriving economy. The public appeared to accept the benefits of that labor force as long as the government managed logistics and the immigrants, like most of those who had entered in earlier times, ultimately adopted France as their identity as well as their home. Even after the 1974 ban, families were allowed to join immigrants already in residence with the assumption that they would integrate into a receptive society as its economy recovered. Governments of both major parties attempted to impose some limits on unification but mostly left situations to resolve themselves.

Absence of governmental action did not mean that the public was indifferent to immigrants, much less supportive of their presence. Surveys conducted between 1945 and 1980 revealed that while majorities accepted the presence of European immigrants, a steady 60 to 66% were not sympathetic to North Africans, consistently selecting the option that there were "too many in France." That sentiment predated the National Front but undoubtedly facilitated its emergence as champion of opposition as it gave voice to fears about breakdowns of public order, linked unemployment to high numbers of migrants, and forced such issues into the national electoral arena.

Between 1984 and 1997, hostility increased across changes of government, modest economic recovery, and responses to upheavals in the USSR and Eastern Europe. The gap between sympathy for Europeans and for North Africans increased, and by 1993 the French were the most negative respondents in a European survey measuring willingness to accept refugees and asylum seekers from the East. Those who believed that there were too many Arabs in France included solid majorities of centrists and Gaullists as well as supporters of the National Front. Respondents believed the government needed to take action to reduce the number of Arabs in the country even as they overwhelmingly agreed that immigrants worked in jobs rejected by nationals. A report prepared by the Commission of the European Communities in 1992 ranked twelve EU member states in terms of their hostility to immigrants, and found France ranking number 4 (Germany was number 2 and Britain 5). Although the timing of the survey on which the report was based coincided with the influx of huge numbers of asylum seekers in Germany and significant numbers in France, the hostility within all three nations was confirmed by other studies conducted in the 1989–2000 period.

Negative opinion persisted beyond the initial period of disruption in the Soviet Union and flight of people from satellite nations. A 1997 European Commission Eurobarometer survey found continued sentiment that there were too many immigrants across Germany, France, and Britain (Table 5.5), accentuated by a high incidence of self-described racism. There was also widespread inconsistency in opinions on what policies would be appropriate even in robust economic times. In 2000 Eurobarometer surveys (sponsored by the EU), French respondents were more likely to believe that asylum seekers should be accepted without restrictions (Table 5.6), but also supported restrictions on immigrants already in France. Remarkably, almost a quarter of the French (and German) respondents agreed with the statement that all immigrants should be sent home.

Table 5.5. Views of the Number of Foreigners in France, Germany, and Britain, 1997

Nation	Too Many	A Lot but Not Too Many	Not Too Many
France	46	40	7
Germany	52	39	4
Britain	42	40	12

Source: Eurobarometer 47, 1997.

Table 5.6. Sentiment toward Asylum Seekers in France, Germany, and Britain, 2000

	Accept	Accept w/ reservations	Don't Accept
France	26	55	14
Germany	17	66	12
Britain	12	55	23

Source: Eurobarometer 53, 2000.

Public opinion was indeed volatile during this period. A number of studies confirmed that fear—about jobs, public safety, costs of welfare programs—was consistently higher than actual experience with asylum seekers. Perceptions of threat were based on reports from news outlets, political leaders, or neighbors, but not on firsthand observations. At base, respondents were concerned about an amorphous threat to French culture, and directed whatever hostility they might feel toward the specter of alienated and disloyal foreigners disrupting French lives.

More recent surveys suggest that hostility is difficult to overcome. A 2010 *Financial Times/* Harris Poll survey found negative views among respondents in the United States, Britain, Germany, and France. A majority in Britain and near-majorities in the other three countries believed that immigrants make life worse in their nation. Only Germany recorded major disagreement with a statement that immigrants have a negative effect on the economy, indicating the persistence of a pattern of blaming immigrants for economic problems in three of the four nations. A report by the National Consultative Council on Human Rights (CNDH) confirmed that negative views were still held by large segments of the French population in 2013. Although only 16% claimed to be concerned about immigration, significant majorities believed the headscarf issue was still a problem for French society (80%), and that the Roma live mainly by trafficking and theft (78%). Sixty percent felt that "certain behaviors can sometimes justify racist reactions," and more than one-third admitted to being "a little" or "quite" racist (CNCDH, 2014). The Roma have emerged as easy scapegoats, perceived as alien immigrants unwilling to adapt their lives to the French culture.

Lack of consistency is often observed in the public's preferred policies for addressing immigration issues. A study conducted by the European Commission in 2000 asked respondents what level of decision making should be responsible for immigrants and asylum seekers (Table 5.7). The nationalistic French led other European nations in believing that both regular immigration and asylum issues should be dealt with by EU authorities. Given the support the National Front garnered by insisting that France control its own borders, the support of French citizens for cooperative policy is at least puzzling. Interestingly, when members of the European Parliament were asked about the need for a common EU policy on immigration, the French MEPs were similarly inclined, far more supportive of a single policy than their German and British counter-

Table 5.7. Public Preference on Who Should Make Policy on Immigration and Asylum

Nation	Immigration Issues		Asylum Issues	
	EU	Nations	EU	Nations
France	53	44	55	41
Germany	40	56	43	54
Britain	32	65	35	61

Source: Eurobarometer 48, 2002.

parts. Between 1993 and 2004, the French support approached unanimity (95%); British enthusiasm for unity fell by 13 percentage points. The French support for supranational control of an intensely debated national issue is at the very least remarkable.

Ironically, as negative views of Muslim immigrants were growing among the French public, Muslims themselves were positive in their views on permanent settlement. Most believed that progress toward integration was being made and perceived democracy to be working well. Their views about interaction with non-Muslims were liberal, with only 15% disapproving of marriage by a son to a non-Muslim, and 32%—about the same as French respondents—disapproving of the marriage of a daughter outside her faith. Local examples support the claim that Muslims and French non-Muslims do live together comfortably. A *New York Times* report featured the northeastern city of Roubaix, where the two populations have lived without incident for decades, celebrating Muslim religious holidays despite a poor economy and 22% unemployment rate (August 5, 2013). In a 2006 Pew Research Center survey, 72% of French Muslims claimed there was no conflict between being a devout Muslim and living in modern society, a much higher optimism rate than reported by either German (57%) or British Muslims (49%). Muslim elites also favored France as a place supportive of the integration of Muslims (reported in Schain, p. 20). Significant numbers of immigrants have succeeded in blending in with the culture of their adopted home, despite obvious conflicts about religious norms and security.

European publics have historically exhibited wariness, even hostility, toward the third world, and despite a reputation for welcoming immigrants, contemporary France is no exception. The low salience which the public accorded immigration issues in the postwar period might well have indicated that like their political leaders, they expected that such issues would eventually resolve themselves. Over long periods, French respondents reported that they did not find immigrants personally disturbing even when they thought they represented a major national problem. What appears as an emerging theme is resentment toward migrants who are seen as conspicuously different from French citizens or a threat to public order. The narrative is familiar, applauding immigrants who have assimilated and demonizing those who have not for their failure to blend into the society that accepted them.

The Changing Face of French Immigration

Much of the rhetoric of current politics reflects the fears ignited by the horrific events of the past two years in Paris, Brussels, and Nice, and those terrorist incidents epitomize the challenge facing European governments. Immigrants have had a long, mostly peaceful history in France, and even global changes after World War II did not result in major revisions in policy. French concerns about cultural differences and economic burdens became visibly more charged in political campaigns after 1980, but the catalysts of conflict after 2013 have been the surge of refugees and the fear that they would bring dangerous militants into France and radicalize angry minorities. The 2015–16 attacks made immigration a pivotal issue likely to persist in political life for years if not decades.

Three Unresolved Issues

Even as the government works with EU neighbors to deal with unprecedented numbers of refugees, some issues remain basic to any long-term national immigration policy. Although the 2006 Immigration and Integration Law clarified overall policy on planned immigration, three contentious issues remain prominent. Most pressing is the need to deal with immigrants who do not fall naturally into any of the groups included in the 2006 law, which unhappily failed to include provisions for asylum seekers, refugees, and the Roma. The first two have emerged as glaring omissions. In humanitarian terms, the needs of literally millions of displaced persons are compelling, and the proximity of Europe to both Africa and the Middle Eastern ensures an ongoing crisis. More than 170,000 refugees reached European nations in 2014, more than three times as many as reached Italy in 2013. At the end of 2015, the figure exceeded one million; still, more than three million Syrians continued temporary residence beyond Syrian borders and more than 400,000 Africans waited on the northern coast for the chance to cross the Mediterranean. France received over 57,000 applications for asylum in 2011 and accepted 10,647, the largest number since 1991 but still fewer than 19% of those seeking entry. In 2015, the number of applicants rose to 80,000, with fewer than one-third granted asylum. Given the large numbers awaiting decisions and more willing to test borders across the EU, a huge refugee pressure will continue to demand European response, collectively or by individual nations. To date, only Germany has enacted policies beyond token commitments and aversion to mandatory admissions.

That combination of resistance and inaction has also characterized French positions on dealing with the Roma. Local reactions have included restrictive policies and frequent scuffles, and national authority was used to raze settlements of Roma who continue to find France an attractive destination. Frequently lacking documents and regular jobs, they have been a constant source of friction, often escalating into violence. In the first months of 2013, 10,000 Roma were evicted, 11,000 in 2015, and in February 2016 police raided and destroyed a camp in northern Paris known as the "little Paris jungle." Charges of mistreatment by authorities brought rebukes by UN and European commissions, but the shortage of housing exacerbated by increases in refugees made solutions even more difficult.

Similarly problematic are undocumented immigrants. Their numbers are the lowest among all OECD nations and tiny compared to those in the United States; most recent estimates put the number at 350,000. In a system of monitored registration and employment, they are easily identifiable and are subject to relatively swift deportation under the 2006 laws. A law passed in 2011 streamlined deportation, facilitating the expulsion of almost 33,000 irregulars in 2011, twice as many as in 2004.

Still, a robust informal economic sector, which includes trafficking and illegal activity, continues to be a rallying cry for anti-immigrant political forces, pushing governments to create even stricter controls. Policies since the mid-1980s have focused on this issue, cracking down on both immigrants and their employers. The failure to make greater progress in regulating what is estimated at a staggering 17% of the French GDP can be attributed to the efficiency of clandestine activity and widespread eagerness to benefit from low-cost labor and goods, even those linked to criminal activities. Confronting that situation would strain the resources of any government, and the French continue to struggle to establish control in this sector.

French efforts to deal with the second category of unresolved issues—those dealing with socioeconomic problems caused by immigrant marginalization—have been uneven and their results at best mixed. Integration of immigrants has proven an elusive goal. Until 2006, France did not require immigrants to have any familiarity with language and political norms—requirements that had been in place since 1950 in the United States and 2002 in Britain—on the assumption that immigrants would naturally acquire skills and melt into the French culture. Instead, the suburbs of major cities became immigrant centers with mediocre schools, high unemployment, and low income levels. Because the French constitution prohibits classification of residents by race or ethnicity, governments were officially limited in utilizing essential data to target areas for education and training programs. One attempt to focus assistance—the Zones for Educational Priority—received some funding to work with students, but none to aid families and dropouts. By 2010, gaps in education and income remained stark, and unemployment levels were twice as high as those of nationals. Ironically, republican ideals of equality thus bore some of the responsibility for immigrant marginalization. Constitutional obstacles were aptly summarized in a 2011 piece in *The Economist*, which noted the inherent contradiction between French goals of assimilation (which would ideally make immigrants indistinguishable from the larger population) and policies of antidiscrimination (which create programs to safeguard their very separateness). French policies are thus at odds with each other, with disagreements over the essential meaning of republicanism bound to frustrate rational solutions.

Third, what may be the most intractable issue is the primacy of a national identity, which prohibits religion from being the defining element of a French citizen. All salute the flag of French identity, making its culture, language, and commitment to secularism untouchable in a political arena that is increasingly pluralist in composition. That political reality has produced a tenuous opposition to religious attachments and symbols. Unlike Germany (which provides financial support to organized religions), Britain (which funds religiously oriented public schools), and the United States (with firm commitments to religious expression), France has drawn a line that, by prohibiting the public display of religious symbols, encourages marginalization of those whose faith values those symbols. If national identity and religious conviction are seen as incompatible, ensuring a livable environment for Muslims is bound to be fraught with conflict and discontent within that minority.

Finally, there can be little doubt that the Paris and Nice attacks heightened concerns about refugees in general and Muslim immigrants in particular. At least in the short term, public support for accepting new immigrants declined, enthusiasm for the National Front increased, and former president Nicolas Sarkozy—who by any standard should have been dismissed after scandals and loss of public support—announced his candidacy in the upcoming election by calling for a reaffirmation of French identity. Confronting those conditions, the widely unpopular President Hollande pledged that France would remain a "nation of immigration," receptive to Syrian refugees even as national security forces would be increased.

The Two Faces of France in Its Relations with Migrants

The Banlieues. Since 1961, growing numbers of immigrants, most from Africa, have clustered in poor suburbs of major cities where unemployment is twice that of nationals and opportunities scarce. In 1981, "rodeo riots"—where gangs stole and vandalized cars—broke out, angering neighbors and putting area youths on watch lists for police. In 2005 more widespread rioting in Clichy-sous-Bois lasted for two weeks, after two youths hiding from police were electrocuted by unrepaired wires. Within Paris, an encampment of more than 400 homeless migrants was razed, following similar destruction of Roma camps elsewhere in the country.

The post-2013 surge of migrants has created increased tension and confusion about how to handle foreigners and established immigrants. A particularly volatile situation exists in Calais, the French port providing access to the tunnel to Britain, where camps have become centers of frustration and government efforts to relocate residents to other parts of France have failed to quell the unrest there.

Commitment in the aftermath of terrorism. At the same time, French willingness to accept refugees in 2015 was second only to Germany. The period since then has been marked by horrific terrorist attacks, a three-day siege in Paris in January in which gunmen killed 12 people in incidents at the Charlie Hebdo satirical weekly and a local market, a second on November 13 when three teams of terrorists attacked patrons of restaurants, bars, and a sold-out concert, killing 130 and injuring dozens more; and a third in June 2016, when a terrorist drove a truck through crowds in Nice, causing mass carnage.

French president Hollande immediately described the situation as war against ISIS fighters. At the same time, however he reaffirmed his country's commitment to admit and assist 30,000 Syrians, vowing to continue to aid those fleeing violence initiated by the Islamic State. Still, support for anti-immigrant political forces has gained strength, calling into question the ability of governments to implement admissions and integration of those seeking refuge from poverty, war, and ethnic conflict in the Middle East and Africa.

The clash between nationalist sentiments and the presence of increasingly diverse foreigners threatens to overshadow the underlying conflict over what French democracy means. Martin Schain has noted that the last 30 years have been a continuing struggle between competing versions of republican principles (2012, p. 86), and more recently Farhad Khosrokhavar, a sociologist at the Paris School of Advanced Studies in the Social Sciences, argued that refugee and minority dilemmas are the direct product of an inflexible definition of values in the French political system. By insisting that religion can only be followed in private, French practices marginalize minorities—most of them citizens and many of whom suffer from unemployment and poverty in the *banlieues*. Calling for a more pragmatic approach in a nation whose "assimilationist ambitions are increasingly at odds with everyday reality," Khosrokhavar concludes that "the strength—the weight—of France's national identity has become a problem." (*New York Times*, July 21, 2016) Nowhere is that problem more evident than in calls to reinforce historic commitment to that identity by leaders across France's major as well as minor parties.

For Further Reading

Miriam Feldbaum. *Reconstructing Citizenship: The Politics of Nationality Reform and Immigration in Contemporary France*. Albany: State University of New York Press, 1999.

Stephanie Giry. "France and its Muslims." *Foreign Affairs, 85*(5) (2006), 87–104.

Riva Kastoryano. *Negotiating Identities: States and Immigrants in France and Germany*. Princeton: Princeton University Press, 2002.

Martin A.Schain. *The Politics of Immigration in France, Britain, and the United States*, 2nd Ed. London: Palgrave, 2012.

Joan Wallach Scott. *The Politics of the Veil*. Princeton: Princeton University Press, 2007.

6

Comparing Immigration Lessons across Nations

If one truth emerges from examination of immigration in the United States and Europe, it is that this issue has become a permanent challenge to nations everywhere. It is no longer the case that policy can be made quietly by leadership confident that the economy will benefit and home populations will absorb newcomers into their communities. And it certainly is no longer possible to regulate flows easily or recreate the more homogeneous cultures of earlier times. All four nations studied here confront international as well as national forces for change, and how they manage those demands will shape their economic and political futures. Comparing their experiences sheds light on the question regarding what factors will be most influential in defining critical national policies.

It is useful to recall the markedly different contexts of at least the last hundred years. Most prominent is the size and history of the United States, as they define both the nation's capacity and its long record of absorption of immigrants. Even as urban centers have become increasingly diverse and demographic shifts project the emergence of a nonwhite majority nationally, concerns about overcrowding and national identity are still far less volatile than in Europe. Nowhere in Europe has a similar commitment to an ethnically pluralist society emerged, and cautious national approaches to postwar immigration provide little guidance for dealing with the waves of refugees who have sought admission since 2013.

Adaptation would have been difficult under any circumstances. But the extraordinary development of the European Union as a major world power presented new immigration challenges, as over the last twenty years it has eliminated border controls, legislated the free movement of citizens, and mandated common labor standards. Challenged by declining national birthrates the EU has struggled—often awkwardly—to find ways to encourage the admission of skilled immigrants, yet has had no contingency plan for mass migration. Following an acrimonious experience in dealing with the Greek financial breakdown, the refugee crisis has severely strained the EU's capacity to respond to a clear common challenge. The strains are all the worse as terrorist attacks in Germany, France, and Belgium, carried out by radicalized or disgruntled foreigners, have increased popular opposition to accepting refugees from the Middle East and

Africa and one member state (Britain) has decided to withdraw from the EU largely due to widespread resistance to increased numbers of immigrants entering from other EU nations.

Despite significant differences in the tone and intensity of their discourse on the issue, all four nations have seen the ability of centrist parties to craft pragmatic if short-term solutions to immigration issues fall victim to increasingly strident calls to limit or even end foreign admissions. Rightist forces have pushed governing parties in Britain and France to embrace restrictive policies; German leadership, which took bold steps to welcome refugees, found itself facing both popular resistance and opposition from a new, anti-immigrant party; and in the United States, conservatives have stymied attempts to legalize at least some undocumented immigrants and refugees, exacerbating an institutional gridlock more intransigent than any in Europe. With Republicans gaining control of both executive and legislative branches in the 2016 election, the nation of immigrants may, ironically, be set to take steps that significantly limit access to those seeking to enter.

Comparing Basic Components of Immigration

The Disappearance and Reemergence of Geography

The reality of a shrinking globe changed many of the ways in which people, businesses, and governments interact—in instantaneous communication and transactions, common currencies, ease of travel. But recent moves to strengthen borders and assert the primacy of national identities are reminders that while geography may have reduced some barriers, its basic elements still influence policy. Three conclusions emerge from our comparisons. The first is the variable rather than absolute importance of borders, over history and currently. The most dramatic changes appear in Europe, where a history of wars and reconfiguration evolved to create a union without internal borders. Until the recent crisis involving masses of refugees, the migration of laborers did not overwhelm the more prosperous EU members, but generally followed fluctuations in demand. Exceptions included the very small numbers of East European Roma (20,000 in France, fewer elsewhere), prominent mostly for their lifestyle and disinclination to integrate, and British hostility to the influx of East Europeans, a factor that is credited with ensuring the defeat of Labour in the 2010 election. In general, the elimination of border checkpoints was achieved remarkably smoothly, apparently attesting to the power of self-regulation in national markets. Despite the more recent reintroduction of border controls in response to unresolved refugee movement policies, the EU remains committed to the Schengen system of free movement.

The European and American examples converge in their shared concern with external borders. The dominant challenge to EU states has consistently been that of refugees, initially from Eastern Europe and most recently from the Middle East and Africa, and the American parallel is its long southern border, historically porous to

1. external border control (US & EU)

determined crossers from Mexico and Central America. As American political leaders decried the 2013–14 deluge of 57,000 unaccompanied minors and mothers with children, the United Nations High Commission on Refugees reported that applications for asylum in EU nations exceeded 435,000, triple the number reached two years earlier. By mid-2016, there were more than 4.7 million Syrian refugees living in exile, most of them seeking to relocate in Europe. More than 300,000 African refugees in camps in Libya, and 30,000 in Spanish settlements in Morocco, strained local resources while awaiting chances to escape to Europe by sea. The overall figures are staggering. The UN High Commission of Refugees estimated that at the end of 2016, some fifty million people were displaced, fully half of those in the Middle East and Africa. Immigration as traditionally defined in Europe and the United States includes people seeking entry on family or economic grounds, either legally or by evading border agents. The refugee crises differ dramatically, as mass movements of people fleeing violence and arriving without documents, often without resources, and with no intent of slipping through border controls. In other times, they might have been supported as refugees in distress; in the highly charged post-2001 climate they have become the new and potentially dangerous immigrant deluge that justifies secure borders.

Second, geographically defined national capacity—of both space and resources—has become a common theme across nations. The two components are, of course, related. As the smallest in area, Britain suffers from depleted natural reserves and limited land for agriculture or development; larger land areas and more natural resources give Germany and France more industrial and agricultural options; and the American expanse, 27 times larger than Germany, still has immense amounts of land and water suitable for development. The United States dwarfs the others in both residents and habitable area, but still has by far the lowest density of people per square mile at 85 (Table 6.1). Britain has the least land and the fewest people but a population density of 679—almost eight times as many people per square mile as the U.S. Even after unification with the less densely populated East, Germany is closer to Britain in density (591); and larger France enjoys a much lower density figure (306).

Despite variations in resources and population density, and despite the fact that in 2016 Germany, Britain, and France ranked fifth, tenth, and fourteenth among European

Table 6.1. Spatial and Population Characteristics of European Nations and the U.S., 2016

Nation	Land Area in Sq. Miles	2016 Population	Population Density per Sq. Mile
United States	3,796,742	324,118,787	85
Britain	93,788	65,111,143	679
Germany	137,903	80,682,351	591
France	210,026	64,668,129	306

Sources: U.S. Census Population Clock; British Office of National Statistics; Statistische Amt Deutschland, INSEE.

nations in percentage of foreign-born residents, claims that capacity has been reached have been made in all four nations, especially in areas with large concentrations of immigrants. That pattern is almost certainly a function of popular perceptions, which have been part of each nation's geographic self-definition. For Germany and France, histories of foreign invasion reinforced images of occupation, overcrowding, and abuse; even migration from rural areas in periods of industrial growth has created concerns about overpopulation. Such themes almost certainly fueled fears of traditional migrants, guestworkers, and refugees as invaders of precious space. It is hardly surprising that recent, seemingly uncontrolled numbers arriving on European shores and streaming into the American Southwest generated capacity-defined opposition. Even with histories of absorption of huge numbers of refugees—after World War II, in the 1980 boatlift from Mariel, Cuba, the 1980–1990 exodus from Eastern Europe—fears of invasion are common first reactions across all nations. Thus, even as barriers have come down within Europe, secure external borders and the right to limit access remain central values. Immigration discussions in all four nations include strikingly similar commitments to geographic integrity.

The Burden and Perspective of History: Contrasting Themes

Like geography, history, in the larger immigration scheme, is a combination of facts and their interpretation over time. In this context, two major contrasts among our four nations stand out. First, what we might call the overall historical tradition of immigration varies sufficiently to suggest important consequences. The preponderant American theme is openness to immigrants. Despite periods of indifference, wariness, and exclusion, the United States has commonly recognized immigration as an important part of its founding as well as its identity and enacted receptive policies. Initial fears were ultimately diffused by continuous assimilation into an increasingly diverse nation. Also exhibiting openness to immigrants was France, which, over time, welcomed both Europeans persecuted for religious or political views and relatively small numbers of emigrés from colonies in North Africa. Buoyed by the ideals of the French Revolution, the nation's leaders assumed that its political model would be a magnet for migrants eager to assimilate. Although the devastating experience with rebellious Algeria after the war muted expectations that immigrants would always be transformed into French nationals, the longer history boasted generally harmonious settlement and adaptation.

At the other end of the welcome spectrum is Britain, whose long period of colonial rule created a firm if naive belief that culturally and racially different subjects of the Empire would never migrate to Britain. Postcolonial independence and the pressure to accept immigrants found the British unprepared, leading successive governments to flounder in awkward attempts to recast notions of the Commonwealth that would retain fundamentally hostile positions on race and diversity. Traditions of Britain sharing little with its empire's citizens continued long after breakup and, many argue, continue to be central to British national identity.

Yet a different tradition exists in Germany, whose history included only a brief period of colonial rule, insufficient to develop any real relations with other continents. Nineteenth-century European conflicts, on the other hand, included several in which Germany imported foreign labor, often by force, and that practice was repeated in the twentieth century. All such practices ended in 1945, but left behind a history in which foreigners existed primarily as enemies or a conquered workforce. *Germany*

Historical traditions were thus significantly different among the countries under examination. In 1945, however, the three allied victors and the reconstituted Germany confronted a vastly changed world in which all would find themselves having to confront large numbers of immigrants. All four developed policies to deal with people displaced by war and seeking work in more promising labor markets while attempting to forge altogether new lives. Over a half-century, an array of new or modified national traditions were forged, by necessity as much as choice. Prominent among them would be traditions of immigration, essentially new to all but the United States. *postwar adaptations*

Such histories of accepting or resisting foreign entry were central to the second contrast, that of differing rubrics of "national identity." The American commitments to individualism and opportunity, molded by the nation's quest for independence, defined an identity whose emphasis on opportunity necessarily included openness to those seeking it. In the same way, a sense of national superiority appeared in the identities claimed by world power Britain and successful revolutionary France. The former would define foreigners as lacking the culture and achievement of the British and thus presenting themselves as poor candidates for incorporation; the latter would insist that any who migrated accept a makeover in the French Revolution's tradition of republican ideals. Germans, although directed to repudiate their recent history of aggression and repressive policies, nonetheless retained at least some of their wariness of neighbors as well as a pragmatism that would guide them to define immigration in terms of economic necessity. The outcome resulted in four different postwar orientations toward immigration, setting different stages for later attempts to resolve the tensions historical traditions had created.

Common Historical Themes

Given the different histories these nations have experienced, one has to be impressed by the similarities among them that have emerged. The most obvious is the increase in the proportion of immigrants in each country over time. Steady increases in numbers and percentages of the populations represented by immigrants since 1960 appear in all examples (see figures 1.1–1.4). By 2016, the percentage of foreign-born had reached 13.4 in Britain, 14 in the United States, 15.6 in Germany, and 12.3 in France—peak levels for the three European nations and close to peak in the U.S.—despite almost continuous pressure from within all four to reduce immigration levels.

The prime mover for that growth has been labor demand across nations and a willingness to override reservations in order to meet that demand. In 1945, shortages were everywhere, but greatest in a postwar Germany with huge war-related gaps in the workforce, which were initially filled by ethnic Germans and discontented Eastern Europeans, then by hundreds of thousands of workers from southern Europe, Turkey, and North Africa. Britain renewed permits for colonial workers who had served during the war and welcomed more from Eastern Europe. France, distracted by conflicts in Indochina and Algeria, encouraged businesses to recruit foreigners directly. In all three, postwar labor demands trumped antipathy toward immigrants. In the United States, immigration also picked up after 1945, even expanding the Bracero program to bring temporary farmworkers from Mexico. The 1965 immigration reform opened doors to workers at all levels, providing labor throughout receptive industries and agriculture. Persuasive arguments across all four nations were presented on behalf of economic necessity, and governments responded by authorizing short- and long-term entry by nonnatives.

A related theme has been that governments have been reactive rather than proactive on immigration issues. The United States let the marketplace dictate the flow of labor for more than a century before devising rules, and the few laws passed in the next hundred years were largely restrictions on particular groups. After centuries in which immigration was a nonexistent issue, Britain offered an ill-considered invitation to half the world's population before issuing a succession of awkward rules preventing them from ever accepting it. Germany and France aggressively recruited labor for their booming economies, then abruptly changed course to ban new entry, encourage repatriation, and block family reunions. When the EU economy began to grow again, its members rushed to lure skilled immigrants while declaring collective resistance to illegals and asylum seekers. Long-term plans simply have not been part of national dialogues.

It might be argued that government policies are almost always reactive, and the tendency to hope that problems resolve themselves constitutes the norm in democratic systems. But most issue areas do require actual planning: defense programs are calibrated to anticipate threat; education budgets project enrollments and costs; trade policies are based on expectations of current and future demand. The reluctance of governments to plan for immigration has been different, resulting in policies that embrace conservative numbers and integration largely left to the inherent forces of the work and social environments. That pattern reflects another persistent theme, that of varying levels of wariness, and often opposition, toward immigrants, especially during unanticipated surges. In all four nations, past and recent histories have included episodes of widespread resistance, which, in turn, has led to policies of restriction, detention, even deportation, even as most immigrants have settled into host environments.

It is difficult to explain such hostility as reflecting primarily a natural aversion to the unfamiliar, since most immigrant groups have become nonthreatening and productive contributors to their new homelands in relatively short periods of time. In many instances, both public and elite hostility has correlated with preferences for racial and ethnic exclusion. Chinese and other Asians were targeted in nineteenth-century American laws; British leaders insisted that nonwhites could never fit into their society; quotas were placed on Algerian immigrants even when they were considered part of France itself; for years after 1961 Germans routinely referred to foreign workers as *Schwarze* and *Fremdarbeiter* (blacks and alien workers) rather than the official term of *Gastarbeiter* (guestworkers). The United States formalized naturalization rules before 1945, but all three European nations delayed and complicated citizenship for almost fifty years after the onset of postwar immigration. Even in a post–2005 climate with improved access to residence and work in Europe, resistance to accepting refugees from Africa and the Middle East has been notable. In all four nations, political leaders have continued to avoid instituting comprehensive policies, and many still delegate decisions to administrators rather than embrace definitive rules for admission.

On a broader level, all four nations have experienced a common pattern of immigration in which the first waves have consisted mostly of single males, eager to work and making little use of support services. When bans on new admissions were imposed in 1974, all three European nations were unprepared for large increases in secondary, or family, immigration, and all struggled as restrictive policies inconsistent with constitutional guarantees were consistently rejected by national courts or councils. After 1970, all four experienced, for the first time, greater costs than benefits in some areas with high concentrations of the foreign-born. Except in a few cases, second and third generations tended to integrate economically and socially to become part of larger national cultures.

Common Economic Patterns

Although noting major national variations in the geographic and historical components of immigration, we expected that universal rules of economics might well exert a distinct and common force. Two of the economic premises regarding immigration are that it is driven primarily by labor demand and that its benefits outweigh its costs. Across all nations, the pressure to facilitate economic growth has, in fact, consistently been the most powerful driver of immigration. Seventy years after the end of World War II, the need for additional labor persists, guaranteeing that pull as well as push factors will continue to generate population movement and compel nations to construct appropriate policies.

Familiar economic patterns thus characterize national experiences. First, until recently the majority of immigrants came to the host lands with skill levels below those of native workers and took jobs rejected by them. They filled openings among lower-level occupations and at the same time created new jobs and services, expanding local economies. As had been the case in earlier periods in the United States, the first postwar waves of migrants in Europe were mostly single males from poor regions; businesses were the key recruiters and, in the case of France, actually served as agents. All hosts initially enjoyed outsized benefits from labor forces contributing labor and taxes but requiring little in the way of public services.

A natural corollary to this flow emerged when dependents joined established immigrants. Faced with new costs to accommodate the integration of permanent families, all three European nations took steps to discourage or prohibit relatives from entering, by stiffening fraud laws, instituting difficult language requirements, requiring documents often not available in home countries. In all three countries, governments claimed well into the 1990s that residence could be denied if economic conditions changed. In the United States, family reunion was by then an established criterion for admission, but the unanticipated surge of mothers and children seeking to join relatives in 2013–14 cultivated a level of native resistance similar to that shown in Europe thirty years earlier. Opposition to the provision of services to dependents is a constant across nations.

A second group of similarities are associated with the economic impact of immigrants. Foreign workers have propped up labor-intensive industries and agriculture, maintaining supplies and steadying prices for a wide array of products. Immigrants often became the first workers in new enterprises, some based on ethnic products and even more in expanding fields such as health care, tourism, and personal services. Many sectors in which lower-level jobs are shunned by nationals have been and continue to be dependent on immigrant labor.

In the broader labor equation, the most controversial impact has been on employment. Critics have claimed that even as they take jobs unfilled by locals, migrants increase unemployment rates. Data from all four nations, however, indicate no consistent correlation between immigration flows and current unemployment rates, and unemployment rate differences between the foreign-born and nationals exist only in France. There, higher school dropout rates among immigrant teens have been cited in characterizing foreigners as lacking skills and demonstrating aversion to work despite government efforts to assist employment. Interestingly, school dropout rates in Britain are higher among nationals than immigrants, indicating that factors other than nationality affect employment patterns, at least in that nation.

Similarly, concerns that immigrants depress the wages of native workers are evident across nations but largely unsubstantiated. Immigrants have, for the most part, not competed with native workers for jobs. Lower wages among immigrants are common in all four nations, as they achieve parity with other immigrants but expect their children and grandchildren to narrow the gap between themselves and the natives. Lower wages for the newly arrived are consistently correlated with poor language skills and the educational and skill deficits they bring to the marketplace, deficits that typically decrease or disappear by the second generation.

A final common concern about economic impact involves the costs of supporting immigrants relative to the contributions they make to local and national economies. Here, data are mixed and comparisons complicated by differing measures and the absence of reliable data on undocumented immigrants. A major OECD report estimated that costs were higher than contributions in France and Germany, but attributed that pattern to unusual demographic distributions created when both curtailed immigration between 1974 and 1990. That move resulted in smaller numbers entering the labor force (and contributing to pension funds to support retirees). In Britain, figures are skewed by the fact that a large percentage of all residents receive more in benefits than they contribute in labor, consumption, and taxes. In spite of those patterns, contributions of migrants to Britain from other EU states have created an overall positive ratio of contributions to costs. The American models differ by region and are particularly confounded by lack of data on the undocumented, but still conclude that over their lifetimes immigrants contribute at least as much as they take from the system. The chief beneficiary is the federal treasury, as it collects taxes and retirement contributions; major costs are borne by localities, which provide services without reimbursement from federal funds.

The most compelling case for positive economic impact across nations is the evidence that economic growth, or at least sustainability, requires a stable or growing population. Immigrant flows into the United States have increased the national birthrate needed to provide a replacement workforce and support for retirees. In Europe, persistently low national birthrates continue to underscore the need for additional immigrants; in all three of our three cases governments project worker shortages as early as 2015 with no relief for decades after that. Across the continent labor is needed in both primary and tertiary sectors and seasonal work opportunities consistently outnumber the workers available to fill them, indicating that demand is not being met. Prior to the refugee surges, the estimated 600,000 undocumented workers in Germany and 200–400,000 in France were almost certainly indicators of labor shortage, not an uncontrolled deluge of unemployable migrants.

The economic impact of unskilled labor may have been unusual in Britain. Although the need for additional labor was pronounced during and after World War II, conditions most receptive to immigrant labor may have been muted by features of Britain's class system. That entrenched culture has discouraged individual mobility, motivating nationals to continue to work in industries that in other nations had become magnets for immigrant labor. In the wartime and postwar periods, the labor shortage caused by war casualties was alleviated by admitting a half-million colonials, but after reconstruction leveled off, Britain opted to curtail immigration for almost thirty years before new shortages appeared after 1990. By that time, European states had already begun to revise their systems to favor skilled immigrants and Britain became a late entrant in competition for talent in a society confronting high numbers of retirees and inadequate numbers of workers to replenish insurance funds. Such imbalances are likely to persist for years without measures to increase labor supplies.

Despite historical and geographic differences, all four nations have shifted to similar approaches to immigration standards. All facilitate the admission of applicants with high-level skills but also admit foreigners to sectors with labor shortages, especially agriculture and service industries. Although only the United States gives priority to applicants with family in residence, others accept the likelihood that family will follow if not accompany skilled immigrants. All understand that native birth rates cannot guarantee economic health, and all have at least identified education as essential in combating unemployment in areas with large concentrations of immigrants. If political leaders and their institutions respond to these concerns, questions about immigration will not ask whether it will happen, but who and how many will be admitted and how their adaptation will be supported.

Political Actors in Immigration Policy

political
factor [handwritten margin note]

In a 2006 *New York Times* piece on immigration in the United States, Roger Lowenstein argued that although economists strongly supporting an admission system based on skills were baffled that Congress paid little attention to their research, "immigration policy has never been based on economics" (July 9). That conclusion is only partly true, since such research has consistently documented the strong relationships between economic conditions and migration, which ultimately drove policy. But it does point to the reality that immigration debates and much policy have always been framed—and often battered—in political arenas. And those arenas have most frequently produced policies reflecting popular sentiment as much as economic logic.

Contrasting Experiences

Since the end of World War II, policies have rarely been developed comprehensively to meet long-term needs. When immigration occurred relatively infrequently and unpredictably, it was understandable that policies were developed as responses rather than in anticipation of unknown events, and that they were shaped by public opinion. What is remarkable in the current context is the persistence of that pattern. After more than two centuries of American immigration and almost seventy years in European states, immigration has not been a standard item on political agendas but one that has, typically, presented as a crisis or new problem defying resolution. Comparing national responses has illustrated that political forces, however lax in their approaches, are still critical factors.

Because context has been consistently crucial in understanding immigration politics, it is important to recall some basic philosophical orientations to immigration, established before the postwar era began. Of two contrasting general worldviews, the American version linked immigration to a destiny of territorial expansion and population growth, based from early times on the concept of *E Pluribus Unum* (from the many, one) in an increasingly multicultural society. The most similar European case is France, whose revolutionary break with its past established a republicanism firmly committed to citizen equality. It differs from the American model in that its notion of identity—created by the French rather than immigrants—precluded or at least limited any role for non-French cultures. The equally fundamental concept of *laïcité* added a political loyalty consciously separate from and superior to others, including religion. In such a system, assimilation would be the only logical course for those who might choose to live there.

A contrasting philosophy defined British and German orientations. For the British, the legacy of world dominance fostered a sense of cultural difference that distinguished them from colonial and most other national populations. When wars and global change exposed the unsustainability of the Empire, the British assumed a position of conscious separation from former colonies, and later from other nations, relying on natural borders and restrictive laws to keep foreigners from entering (and altering) the home culture. In that context the 2016 Brexit vote, rooted largely in public opposition to the EU mandate of free movement of people among member states, is eminently understandable. By contrast, the origins of German wariness of foreigners (in nineteenth and twentieth-century conflicts) were sufficiently different (and the postwar labor needs sufficiently greater) to allow postwar governments to pursue pragmatic programs to recruit foreign labor, which they defined in terms of temporary rather than permanent and as constituting diverse additions to its society. While all four nations promised tolerance and basic protections for foreigners, only the United States and France anticipated integration and assimilation.

The corollaries of those philosophical differences have been evident in critical political arenas. Most obvious have been different policies toward the future of immigrants in the host society. Before the 1989 seismic changes and later in refugee crises arising in 2013, Germany and Britain recruited foreign labor under rules that made permanent residency difficult and periodically encouraged foreigners to leave. Although Germany was required to accept ethnic Germans and offered receptive procedures to asylum seekers for more than 40 years, reforms in 1992 brought its policies closer to the restrictive laws of its EU neighbors. The French experience in Algeria led to the end of lax immigration processes and created quotas for North Africans. Only the United States actually expanded opportunities for immigrants from Latin America, Asia, and Africa. The new American policy, despite expectations that overall immigration patterns would not significantly change, invited diversity, just as European policies sought to limit it. Policies also reflected contrasting attitudes toward family reunion, with the United States raising the priority of family and European nations erecting barriers, many of which would be voided by judicial decisions. One important consequence of those variations was that the birthrate in the U.S. increased as that in Europe fell in the years since 1965.

Immigration has always been unequally distributed, as new entrants gravitate to areas where others have settled. Those areas have been major urban centers and their immediate suburbs in all nations, and more recently American border states. In the United States, that has moved states to enact restrictions that conflict with federal law. Unlike Europe, where the primacy of national government has been clear in defining policy, localized conflicts pose far greater challenges in an American system with substantial real and presumed state powers. By 2014, federal district and appeals courts had become arbiters of immigration policy, in often lengthy processes of judicial consideration and decision. By 2016, it was clear that those courts would not uniformly strike down state and local restrictions on immigrants, and that Supreme Court decisions would ultimately have to determine the shape of much immigration law.

Finally, anti-immigrant sentiments have varied greatly, and the views of national leaders have not always agreed with those of the public. In Germany, negative views have been relatively understated and their voices limited by a strong tendency to avoid sentiments that implied any link to the nation's Nazi past. Until recently, even in periods of high unemployment or refugee pressure, strident opposition has been confined to marginal groups. In Britain and France, however, parties defined by opposition to immigrants have proven surprisingly durable. The French National Front has continued to influence elections for more than thirty years, achieving support from as much as 28% of the electorate in 2016 polls; the UK Independence Party has emerged as a serious challenge to both major British parties as they flounder in the face of opposition to both the EU and new immigration. Both of the nativist parties have broadened their agendas, still emphasizing immigrant threats to the economy, national security, and cultural identity but targeting the EU as the authority that is diminishing national policy options, and pressuring governing and opposition parties to adopt restrictive positions. Although the staying power of the Alternative for Germany Party has yet to be demonstrated, its surprising strength in 2016 state elections suggests a more active role than such parties have had over 60 years there. Similar resistance to immigration has emerged in the American Tea Party movement's influence in the Republican Party. Unlike the FN and UKI, Tea Party identifiers have avoided breaking off into a third party—historically a losing strategy in winner-take-all electoral systems—but have elected supporters to state and national offices. Its success has been uneven in the short period of its existence but has clearly exerted an influence disproportionate to its numerical strength. Most notably, party fringe groups and factions of the Right have succeeded in moving traditional party positions to the right.

Common Trends

Despite major contrasts between the four countries, national political similarities may be more significant. Although it has not always been evident, a central common element has been the direction and shape of public opinion. Across all four, the salience of immigration has most often been low, rising in times of crisis but falling when other issues command center stage—which until recently has been most of the time. As noted in earlier chapters, there are apparent differences in general opinion. Britain, at first blush, stands out consistently for mostly negative opinion; respondents in Germany and France are the least negative, and those in the United States hover around the 50% level of hostility. Those figures, however, exist within a broader evidence base, which displays a host of contradictions in data collected at different times and with differently stated options. In the areas summarized in chapter 5, for example, the most negative responses were recorded by Germany. Perhaps more significantly, despite negative opinions chosen when people are surveyed, the public across all four nations prior to 2013 have generally shown little resistance to policies that facilitated immigrants' admission and residency within their communities. Responses during times of migration surge have been consistently more negative, but have tended to moderate as crises—even those as serious as those after World War II, and several in the United States since then—abated.

Second, overall acceptance of immigrants increases over time, but events and political activists can provoke abrupt shifts in opinion. Americans expressed alarm with the arrival of Cubans in Miami in 1980; Europeans have had similar responses to surges in 1989–91 and the rush of refugees entering since 2013. When France was suffering from high unemployment (2008–13), net increases in negative opinion, which would not have been predicted earlier, arose, but decreases were observed in the United States and Germany and only minor increases in Britain during the same period.

Given the chronically low salience of immigration issues before 2013, negative opinion might be seen as grumbling without intensity of focus or action, discontent not rising to a level where it might permanently affect policy. More specifically, negative opinion has almost always been linked to the perception that immigrants threaten jobs or weaken the economy, that their cultural differences defy national identity, that they are lawbreakers or, most recently, that they may be especially susceptible to terrorist appeals. Since most of those are the same complaints that have characterized American views of new immigrants over a span of 250 years, it is at least conceivable that hostility will soften if and when the disruptions of 2013 and beyond are resolved. The key term is *recent*. Fears of new arrivals have consistently faded as they have become longer-term residents, but there is no precedent for situations in which recent comes to mean constant, challenging all patterns and solutions in modern history.

Third, generally negative but not intense opinion has encouraged political leadership to avoid taking strong positions and to avoid openly embracing immigration. Despite a generally more enlightened political environment, immigration issues have been handled in ways mirroring earlier periods. Governments have combined vacillation and non-action with hopes that immigration issues would, like the ideal market, be self-correcting. In much of the discourse, political leaders support reductions in the number of immigrants even as businesses report needs for additional labor. American presidents have stood out for their praise of immigrant contributions, but reform of the system has either been treated as a low priority or stalled in Congress. Most recently, executive actions taken by President Obama to limit deportations to those having committed serious crimes were opposed by opponents in Congress and challenged by several states in federal courts, then reversed by executive orders in the first months of the Trump administration. Whether those new initiatives will be upheld by the courts or modified by Congress is likely to be determined by a combination of labor needs and new definitions of priorities for immigration decisions. A more pronounced paralysis has been evident in Europe, where the EU has been unable to agree on any common policy and members have reverted to the old bromides of closed borders.

Fourth, majority and opposition parties have consistently found themselves internally conflicted around immigration choices. Conservative parties affiliated with business interests have supported keeping labor costs low but objected to the admission of culturally different foreigners who make that possible; parties of the Left have had to rationalize favorable immigration laws to their working-class base. Not surprisingly, all have downplayed immigration issues whenever possible, proposing only limited laws while in power, then opposing similar legislation when they are the out party. As a consequence, political institutions charged with making national policy have been, at best, reactive, delaying decisions whenever possible and responding minimally when crises arise. Evidence of contradictory policies is abundant: British calls for universal access by former colonial subjects followed by years of restrictions; Germany's thirty-year definition of foreign workers as temporary; French resistance to multicultural identities among immigrants in a free society; America's welcoming mantra distorted by resistance to refugees and those seeking asylum. Cross-cutting ideological cleavages, regional variations, and volatile public opinion have combined to obstruct rational planning in increasingly gridlocked political systems. In the midst of ongoing avoidance of immigration issues by mainstream parties, groups and their leaders, who would ordinarily have been marginalized, have found platforms. Despite consistent public support in the United States for addressing the status of refugees and the undocumented, supporters of deportation and closed borders have generated enough opposition to create stalemates, effectively jettisoning legislation.

Interestingly, with political leadership and legislatures stymied or reverting to inaction, two institutions have assumed more important roles in guiding immigration policy in these nations. One, with a history of influence below the surface of political conflict is national administration. Cabinet-level departments overseeing immigration have increasingly exercised discretion unusual in major policy areas; delegation of authority has left midlevel agents to interpret national mandates, taking the heat off elected officials but also allowing varied and inconsistent rulings. In the same vein, downloading the resolution of difficult issues—the headscarf issue in France, accommodation of asylum seekers in American states, education for noncitizens in Germany and Britain—has inevitably produced selective enforcement, local biases, and an overall lack of uniformity in implementing national law. In none of the nations studied have national leaders consciously shifted responsibility for immigration policies to other levels of government, and cases that challenged lower-level decisions have tended to bring about the reversal of discriminatory or inconsistent applications of the law. Nonetheless, the pattern is disturbing, as it has allowed national figures to avoid key problems.

The second institution to emerge as critical has been the judiciary and other appellate bodies, including human rights commissions. Guided by constitutions uniformly protective of individual rights, groups as varied as subnational American courts, the National Council in France, and national asylum panels have issued decisions generally favorable to immigrants. However limited immigration programs might have been intended to be, extended consequences and sheer numbers of cases have made appellate courts crucial. Like the experiences of subnational agencies attempting to implement ambiguous policies, court cases highlight the need for strong central authority to define critical immigration laws.

Finally, it is important to note that the most predictable recurring theme of immigration politics in all nations is the primacy of economic needs. In all contexts, the demand by the business sector for labor has outweighed ostensible barriers to immigration, including quotas, promises to limit foreign labor, fears of the pressure such workers may put on local services. Business's and economists' claims that crops will go unharvested, factories closed, or services curtailed consistently trump efforts—and policies—to restrict recruitment of labor that is almost certain to become permanent. That pattern, coupled with equally consistent failure to construct comprehensive immigration policies, strongly suggests that whatever the political climate, economic forces will be the prime movers behind whatever actual policies evolve.

The Challenge of Immigration to the European Union

It is no exaggeration to suggest that the refugee crisis that emerged in 2013 has created the most serious challenge to face the European community in its almost-60-year history. Summarizing a United Nations Population Division report in September 2015, *New York Times* analyst Eduardo Porter described the crisis as an "unstoppable force of demography," in which twin factors of global drought and unending strife in failed states have combined to drive millions of desperate Africans, Syrians, Iraqis, Afghanis, and others fleeing violence and geographic disaster to seek new lives in Europe. Accelerated crossings into Greece and Bulgaria show no hint that the flow will lessen, even after European and other nations have pledged billions to support refugees in neighboring states in the region.

A critical question is whether the EU has the political will and resources to provide a unified response. At least two opposing paths present themselves. The first is to follow the lead of several members: resistance and restrictive policies that reintroduce border controls and limit opportunities for admission. Attempts to reinforce external border security and assign quotas for member acceptance of refugees have been minimal or ended in failure; nations bordering Greece have closed borders; Eastern and Central European members have rejected any mandatory quotas; others have created new restrictions on benefits. After terrorist attacks in Berlin, Paris, Brussels, and Nice and local incidents of violence in Germany, public hostility to refugees has increased and a renewed concern about security risks has overshadowed efforts to facilitate refugee resettlement. In this scenario, the reluctance of mainstream parties to support policies of acceptance and integration may lead to an EU with internal variations among its members and the revoking of at least some of the Schengen Agreement's open borders rules. With no end to war and instability in the Middle East and Africa, that option seems more likely than not.

The second path would see at least a majority of EU members supporting the leadership of its most powerful nations to combine acceptance of large numbers of immigrants with stricter rules—of admission vetting, of asylum requirements, of deportation mandates, of waiting periods for family unification, even of charges to immigrants to support their residence. Some moves in this direction have been made by Angela Merkel's government, even as it has been undermined by political opposition. For Merkel and the EU, finding a balance between internal security and both the humanitarian and economic cases for accepting refugees is compelling. A Europe whose natural population is slated to decline even with the addition of several million immigrants will, at least in the foreseeable future, need to craft rational economic policies that can be supported by a wary public.

Refugees as the New Normal in Immigration

Both Europe and the United States have struggled to control borders in the face of massive, unplanned surges in immigration. The United States initiated one response with the 1985 act linking amnesty for undocumented immigrants to reinforced borders and stiff penalties for employers who continue to hire those without papers. Having managed massive population movement from Russia and Eastern Europe after 1989, the European Union initiated common policies by tightening external borders at the same time that it removed internal controls (1995). At the same time, Britain, Germany, and France began to rationalize immigration policies by consciously calibrating qualifications to meet national needs. By 2005, all four had succeeded in accommodating both refugees and increasing numbers of highly skilled immigrants, demonstrating impressive adaption to changing circumstances.

Still, neither the United States nor Europe was prepared for the surge in refugees or the prospect of continuing pressures after 2010. The numbers have been staggering. In addition to 4.7 million refugees and six million internally displaced Syrians, two million Iraqis and another million Afghanis filled camps and facilities abroad; 25% of Afghanis and 40% of Nigerians claim to want to emigrate; millions more have left or are likely to leave their homelands in Africa. Asylum procedures have proven inadequate to handle applicants. And efforts by destination nations to encourage migrants to return or not make the journey could hardly have persuaded them in times when successful migrants were sending more than $33 billion in remittances to their homelands by 2015. The United States continues to be a destination worthy of increasingly dangerous journeys made by similar migrants—those fleeing violence and poverty in nations unable to control gang rule and corrupt institutions of governance and law enforcement—but could not summon the resolve to enact comprehensive legislation defining legitimate procedures for asylum or measures that would assist security and reform programs in Central America.

EU guidelines make it clear that refugees recovered from European waters are entitled to enter Europe, but they have not been adapted to confront the realities of unmanageable numbers arriving by sea from Turkey. A March 2016 agreement for the EU to provide Turkey with 3 billion Euros to support refugees either seeking to enter Europe or having been denied opportunities to apply for asylum was fraying months later, after a foiled coup attempt in Turkey brought severe government reactions, subsequently denounced by EU leaders. Member states have resorted to invoking the 2003 Dublin Resolution, which stipulates that asylum applications must be processed in the nation first entered. As noted earlier, all three European nations studied here have been unable to win support for refugees in the face of the growing strength of right-wing parties who insist that "being on an overloaded boat is not an admission ticket to the EU" (*Der Spiegel*, April 15, 2014).

[handwritten margin note: post 2013]

There is ample evidence in the refugee surges since 2013 to indicate that this form of unsolicited and frequently uncontrolled immigration will continue to outpace mechanisms for dealing with it. As the EU attempted but failed to reach agreement on either admission procedures or how to incorporate refugees as immigrants in member societies, many states moved to adopt restrictive national laws. Hungary defied international rules to detain asylum seekers; Macedonia shut down charitable relief groups; Greece refused to address inhumane conditions in overcrowded refugee camps; France continued to raze Roma settlements and deny Roma children admission to local schools; Poland, Austria, and others tightened borders with EU nations; Belgium authorized deportation of legal resident immigrants for suspicion of engagement in terrorist activity or seen as posing a risk to security, without criminal conviction or even involvement of a judge. Even in the Netherlands, long known for welcoming minority groups, popular support for the extreme nationalist candidate Geert Wilders created major fears that the 2017 election would follow British and American patterns legitimizing conservative stands on immigration. Wilders' party gained only five parliamentary seats and control of 13% of the body, precluding it from any role in a governing coalition, even as its supporters claimed growing support for their positions in other parties. French and German elections later in the year would provide additional clarity as to whether anti-immigrant parties have peaked or pose a continuing challenge to European governments' ability to govern. In this context it is remarkable that neither the EU nor any of its member nations have articulated policies which directly address refugees as a continuing component of immigration law.

U.S. immigration laws have been more specific, authorizing 70,000 refugees to be admitted annually, but that number is distributed among all regions and officially only allows a few thousand from any one country. In the first nine months of the 2014 fiscal year, more than 150,000 arrived from Central America alone. An anti-trafficking law passed in 2008 guaranteed full immigration hearings for unaccompanied minors from nations other than Mexico, but INS offices were unable to meet that obligation. Even after committing to accepting 10,000 Syrians in 2015, U.S. agencies managed to place fewer than 1,800, and the total by the fall of 2016 was still only 10,000. The Obama administration pledged to increase that number to 110,000 in 2017, amid growing resistance in Congress to accept that goal. In fact, one of the Trump administration's first executive orders was to suspend admission of immigrants or refugees from seven (later reduced to six) African and Middle Eastern nations enmeshed in civil strife and to halt admission of all refugees to allow review of existing guidelines and vetting procedures. Although the president also called for a new immigration policy based on skills and employability, he avoided any mention of refugees, the overwhelming source of applicants for admission internationally. *[handwritten note: avoidance to acknowledge refugee crisis by Trump]*

The patterns of crisis avoidance are uncomfortably clear. EU governing bodies have had refugee issues on the agenda since 1997 but have been unable to gain support for a common or even an emergency policy. Conventions on treatment of asylum seekers have been on the books for years with little funding for anything beyond enforcement of border laws. In the United States, a Congress historically inclined to avoid long-term planning was quick to condemn both the administration's failure to deter refugees and its executive actions to protect hearing rights, but tabled all bills responding to the crisis. The highest international authority, the UN High Commission on Refugees, has issued alarming annual reports but received scant response from either national governments or the UN as a whole. Just as governments have historically shown little resolve in dealing with immigration directly, they have avoided the reality of refugee migration as a new normal. As the American president noted in the summer of 2014, border security is not the real issue. Although illegal entry without detection continues to plague efforts to control immigration, the larger, epic problem is people appearing at borders and asking for help. Until governments address that issue, resolution cannot follow.

Constructing Immigration Policies: Lessons Learned for Facing New Realities

Immigration Lessons

Immigration has rarely been an issue confined to one location, one time, and one solution, and this analysis suggests that nations are increasingly responding to similar immigration experiences. Four stand out in in defining contemporary challenges.

The first rule of major migrations is that they follow disruption. In the nineteenth and twentieth centuries, industrial revolutions and wars led to massive relocation; famine and regional strife created smaller but still significant movement. By the end of the twentieth century, new waves of internal violence, popular uprisings, and even instances of genocide, combined with climate and other natural threats to traditional homelands, raised the specter of widespread and continuous migration. Ethnic and religious conflicts have emerged as prime movers in creating failed states, leading to massive displacements in Africa, the Middle East, and Asia. As long as instability exists, it will trigger population movement.

Second, the conflicts leading to emigration continue to be regional but have expanded the reach of their impact, causing maximum stress to neighboring nations and frequently spreading their concerns and their refugees to distant continents. What has given the crises of the twenty-first century a more foreboding dimension has been their frequency and increased impact. In the twentieth century, two decades passed between two major wars in Europe, and postwar recovery has taken more decades, creating relatively long periods of calm. Since 2000, the pace of unrest and technology-aided mobility has accelerated, increasing both regional conflagrations and the numbers of people fleeing them. Many refugees are likely to belong to repressed minorities, poor and dissimilar from both the societies they are fleeing and those they seek to enter. Not surprisingly, an important corollary of the changed pace and increasing numbers of distressed areas has been the difficulty of distinguishing between those fleeing ethnic conflict and those using refugee channels to launch violence abroad. A formerly limited phenomenon has become a major concern for receiving nations. At its extreme, it has spawned efforts by American state governors as well as national leaders to refuse settlement of refugees. Echoing in louder volume earlier fears of Catholics or Asians, the twenty-first-century tragedy of refugees has added huge barriers to accommodation of the displaced in the United States.

That said, a third reality is that despite enormous increases in displaced populations, emigration and immigration are still relatively selective processes. Historically their numbers have never amounted to large percentages of sending or receiving nations (less than 15% in the U.S. and Europe), they have represented myriads of different groups over large expanses of territory, and none has approached either the critical mass or the level of activism necessary to become nationally influential. Three of the four nations studied here (France, Germany, the U.S.) saw below-average changes in the foreign-born population between 2001 and 2011, even as all claimed increasing immigration pressures. Overall, immigrants have managed—with government support in most nations—to maintain some cultural identity while settling into productive economic roles. It still remains mostly true that successor generations improve their economic status within or outside the ethnic enclaves of their parents.

A corollary of this reality is that surges as well as normal admissions of immigrants have rather closely reflected labor market needs. Unemployment percentages may be higher for some new entrants, but in the larger picture are either similar to those of national workers or lower. Immigrants continue to accept jobs that nationals reject, or jobs that the national labor supply cannot fill, a pattern that is a result of both low national birth rates and dynamic economies. Ultimately, the need for labor will force immigration policies to recruit rather than restrict workers, and rationalize their decisions in terms acceptable to the societies which employ them.

The refugee surges of 2013 and after, of course, have been far larger than earlier immigration waves, making it more understandable that governments have been struggling to create effective responses. It is also easy to see why those governments have tended to follow historic patterns, suggesting that official policies will almost certainly continue to be ad hoc and inconsistent. Over time, market demands have led to large flows of labor; pressure for family unification has been entirely predictable; and governments have consistently treated each situation as an unanticipated crisis. Although the most recent surges have exceeded almost all historical examples, continuation of the plight that engulfs large regions of the world makes it foolish to hope for a gradual return to normalcy. What will almost certainly be required is the political will to confront problems with realistic programs designed to ease absorption, rather than the futile hope that any nation can isolate itself from the issue. In the 2017 political climate that prospect appears unlikely, at least in initial reactions. In each of the four nations studied here, existing party structures have been threatened by anti-immigrant movements whose leaders have been emboldened to create new parties focusing almost exclusively on immigrants as threats to security, the economy, and national identity. Despite lacking comprehensive policy programs, they have thus far succeeded in drawing support from existing parties without offering credible capabilities to govern.

It has to be noted that while public wariness and hostility have abetted anti-immigrant parties' success in blocking comprehensive immigration programs in Europe, dysfunction in the United States cannot be attributed wholly, if at all, to public opinion. In 2015, almost three-quarters of the public supported legalization of the nation's 11 million undocumented immigrants, but Congress failed to take up the bill passed in the Senate, or offer an alternative. Failure to address pressing issues exists across a wide array of policy areas, suggesting that immigration will continue to suffer from inattention caused more by structural breakdowns than ideological or public fervor. The end result of unaddressed policy issues, however, is the same as in polarized Europe.

Fourth, it is empirically clear that public opinion is highly susceptible to both first impressions and provocative claims made by prominent leaders and groups. Both have been observed over long periods of history in the United States and during the 70-year period in Europe since 1945. The Pew Research Center reported disapproval by the majority of Americans of the admission of Hungarian refugees in 1958, Indochinese in 1979, and Cubans in 1980. Cross-nationally, two interesting patterns emerge. The first is that initial hostility is often correlated with inaccurate information about immigrants, especially that they take jobs, live off welfare, and raise crime rates, but also that they are overrunning the host nation. *Transatlantic Trends* surveys in 2014, for example, revealed that in all four nations, respondents who were not told the actual percentage of immigrants in the country were more likely to believe there were too many (by a large margin in Britain and the U.S., smaller in France and Germany). The second is that, over time, residents in all four nations have come to live with, work with, and generally accept most immigrants. The Gallup Poll revealed that the percentage of Americans favoring pathways to citizenship for undocumented immigrants had risen from 59% in 2007 to 65% in 2015; Brookings Institution surveys in 2015 reported that over half (51%) supported the U.S. decision to accept additional refugees. Still, opposition can spike when leading political figures dramatize the issue. A lingering reason for wariness is almost certainly the perception that immigration is out of control. In all, small but vocal numbers have joined parties of the Right in attributing bad economic conditions and loss of national identity to foreigners, contributing to current stalemates across Europe and the United States. As Gallya Lahav observed in 2013, the "value of mass attitudes is in their capability of being politicized by elites who can then convert issues such as immigration or security and translate them onto the political agenda" (244). In all four nations, the result has been a level of dysfunction harmful to any resolution of the issue.

Finally, it should be noted that for all four nations, the disconnect between anti-immigrant claims that immigrants displace native workers and burden public services and evidence to the contrary is significant. Virtually all economic analyses conclude that over time immigrants not only contribute more in productivity and consumption than they receive in benefits, but are critical to each nation's future economic health. Without continued or even increased immigration, each faces labor shortages and an imbalance between workforce contributions to retirement accounts and income for retirees benefiting from them. Business and industry leadership, influential forces in all, are likely to press whatever government is in power to recognize that issue and respond with policies they may well have rejected in campaigns. How governments reconcile previous hostility with current economic realities will test both their political adaptability and the strength of their systems to adjust to the changing global environment described extensively in this volume.

Constructing a Future of Positive Immigration

One important but often overlooked variable in the immigration equation is what appears to be a dearth of prominent immigration advocates. The histories of the nations studied here are replete with examples of resistance and discrimination but relatively sparse in evidence of support from highly visible leaders. Historic aversion among political leaders, combined with more general public wariness or indifference, delayed eventual acceptance with few dramatic battles but multiple scars borne by immigrants. Across nations, the successes that immigrants have achieved have most commonly been on their own.

To be sure, those who actually favor policies to increase immigration have provided consistent support and funding for progressive policies. The 2016 report by the National Academies of Science, Engineering, and Medicine stated unequivocally that immigrants were responsible for a net benefit of over 50 billion dollars annually in the 1990–2010 period. The American National Chamber of Commerce, coalitions of employer organizations, a large number of small but dedicated national and local organizations assisting immigrants, and respected foundations have produced extensive research and lobbied for positive immigration policies, and their influence has to be seen as significant. At the same time, more visible public campaigns by protest groups and anti-immigration political figures often overshadow those efforts with campaigns based on fear and public resentment of foreigners. Although the numbers in any given location are rarely large, it is important to remember that scale and intensity matter. Small numbers may indicate small levels of support, but can easily generate attention disproportionate to their actual role in the overall population. It is ironic that anti-immigrant groups with few solid supporters and even fewer members have been able to influence majority parties, while the foreign-born who constitute larger proportions have not yet created a competing force. That situation reflects the reticence of ethnic groups to call attention to themselves in environments still filled with suspicion. Two future courses have to be seen as likely. The first is that ethnic groups, especially those with large numbers of citizens, will emerge as potent political forces. Some such change has already begun to appear in the United States—in the increasing numbers of Hispanic candidates in elections and the increasing numbers of voters, in demonstrations supporting legalization of the undocumented, in pressure by African and Middle Eastern associations to expand the admission of refugees, in civil suits brought by Muslims against alleged discrimination by government and businesses. Respected organizations such as the American Civil

Liberties Union, the UN High Commission on Refugees, and Amnesty International have increased their advocacy of immigrant causes, raising the profile of human rights issues and bringing the weight of their reputations to increase awareness of immigrants' plight. Demographic shifts raising the profile of immigrant groups will occur later in a Europe with smaller entrenched generations, but are inevitable given population movement and higher birthrates among ethnic minorities. Hispanics will soon constitute critical voting blocs in the United States, North Africans in France, South Asians in Britain, and Middle Easterners in Germany—all increasing the likelihood of greater ethnic political involvement.

The second likely change is a natural corollary of the first. Political parties, recognizing the decisive electoral force immigrants represent, will move to gain their support, and immigrant candidates will increase their representation. Small but significant change has already appeared in the United States as the Hispanic caucus has gained political stature and increasing numbers of minorities are finding employment at all levels of government. European governments solicit input from immigrant leaders, and national as well as EU commissions oversee programs and problems specific to those minorities. Even if the motives for such change are rooted in basic electoral math, they portend futures in which the interests of new nationals will be raised and heard in American and European governments.

In a world where change will become the norm and rejection of change the exception, defining new ways to adapt will be essential to effective nations and international unions. Homogeneous populations may be the goal of regimes attempting to construct monolithic states, but the experience of the West suggests how unrealistic such an objective is. Speaking of the American immigration challenge in 1996, David Kennedy concluded that the present might echo, but could not replicate, the past. Recalling that previous generations had scorned newcomers but assumed the patriotism of their children, Kennedy posited a future in which the path to an integrated society would have to be "more clever than our ancestors were but also less confrontational, more generous, and more welcoming than our current anxieties sometimes incline us to be" (1996). That challenge could well be the rallying theme for all nations striving to become productively diverse societies.

References

Abali, O. (2009). *German public opinion on immigration and integration.* Allensbach: Institute fur Demoskopie.

Addy, S. (2012). A cost-benefit analysis of the new Alabama immigration law. Center for Business and Economic Research, University of Alabama.

American Immigration Policy Center. (2013, March). Comprehensive immigration reform.

Baker, M., & Benjamin, D. (1997). The role of immigrants' labor market activity on evaluation of alternative explanations. *American Economic Review, 87,* 705–27.

Blau, H., et al. (2003). The role of the family in immigrants' labor market activity: An evaluation of alternative explanations: comment. *American Economic Review, 93,* 429–27.

Blitz, R. C. (1976). A benefit-cost analysis of foreign workers in West Germany, 1957–1973. Unpublished manuscript, Vanderbilt University, Nashville, TN.

Bolick, C., & Bush, J. (2013). *Immigrant wars: Forging the American solution.* New York, NY: Simon & Schuster.

Borjas, G. J. (1985). Assimilation, changes in cohort quality, and the earnings from immigrants. *The Journal of Labor Economics, 3,* 463–89.

Borjas, G. J. (1986). The self-employment and experience of immigrants. *Journal of Human Resources, 21,* 485–506.

Borjas, G. J. (1994). The economics of immigration. *Journal of Economic Literature, 32,* 1667–1717.

Borjas, G. J. (1999). *Heaven's door: Immigration policy and the American economy.* Princeton, NJ: Princeton University Press.

Borjas, G. J. (2016). *Immigration economics.* Cambridge, MA: Harvard University Press.

Brettell, C. B., & Hollifield, J. F. (Eds.). 1994. *Migration theory: Talking across disciplines.* New York, NY: Routledge.

Brubaker, R. (1992). *Citizenship and nationhood in France and Germany.* Cambridge, MA: Harvard University Press.

Bundesrepublik Deutschland Department of Interior. (1986). *Record.*

Bush, J., & Bolick, C. (2013). *Immigrant Wars.* New York, NY: Threshold Editions.

Camarato, S., and Ziegler, K. (2009). Jobs Americans won't do? A detailed look at immigrants' employment by occupation. Center for Immigration Studies.

Card, D. (1990). The impact of the Mariel boatlift on the Miami labor market. *Industrial and Labor Relations Review, 43* (2), 245–60.

Castles, S., & Kosack, G. (1985). *Immigrant workers and class structure in Western Europe.* (2nd ed.). Oxford, UK: Oxford University Press.

Castles, S., & Miller, M. J. (2009). *The age of migration: International population movements in the modern world.* (4th ed.). New York, NY: The Guilford Press.

Chokshi, N. (2013). Left and right agree: Immigrants don't take American jobs. *National Journal* (March 22); online version available at Yahoo.com/news.

Chiswick, B. (1978). The effect of Americanization on the earnings of foreign-born males. *Journal of Political Economy, 86*, 581–605.

Cornelius, W. A., & Rosenblum, M. R. (2005). Immigration and politics. *Annual Review of Political Science 8*, 99–119.

Cornelius, W. A., Martin, P. L., & Hollifield, J. E. (1994). *Controlling immigration: A global perspective.* Stanford, CA: Stanford University Press.

Dahrendorf, R. (1967). *Society and democracy in Germany.* New York, NY, Doubleday.

Der Spiegel Online. June 7, 2013; April 14, 2014; May 4, 2014.

Deutsche Welt. (2013). May 20; May 26.

Die Welt. (2013). December 12.

Dustman, C., & Frattini, T. 2014. The fiscal effects of immigration to the UK. *The Economic Journal, 124*, 1–51.

The Economist. (2006). May 4.

Ederveen, S., et al. (2004). *Destination Europe: Immigration and integration in the European Union.* New Brunswick, NJ, Transaction Press.

Esser, H., Korte, H., & Hammer, T. (eds.). (1985). *European immigration policy: A comparative perspective.* Cambridge, UK: Cambridge University Press.

Federal Office for Migration and Refugees. (2005). The impact of immigration on German society. German contribution to the European Commission Pilot Study.

Fetzer, J., & Soper, C. (2005). *Muslims and the state in Britain, France, and Germany.* New York, NY: Cambridge University Press.

Financial Times/Harris Poll. (2010).

Finnegan, W. (2006). New in town. *The New Yorker* (December 11).

Freeman, G. P., Hansen, R., & Leal, D. L. (eds.). (2015). *Immigration and public opinion in liberal democracies.* New York: Routledge.

Fromentin, V. (2013). The relationship between immigration and unemployment: The case of France. *Economic Analysis & Policy, 43* (1), 41–66.

Geddes, A. (2003). *The politics of migration and immigration in Europe.* London, UK: Sage.

Gerber, D. A. (2011). *American immigration: A very short introduction.* New York, NY: Oxford University Press.

German National Contact point, European Migration Network. (1995). The impact of immigration on German society. Federal Office for Migration and Refugees, Nuremberg.

Giersch, H., Paque, K. H., & Schmieding, H. (1992). *The Fading Miracle: Four Decades of Market Economy in Germany.* New York: Cambridge University Press.

Giesek, A. et al. (1995). The economic implications of migration in the Federal Republic of Germany 1988–1992. *International Migration Review 29*, 693–709.

Giry, S. (2006). France and its Muslims. *Foreign Affairs, 85* (5), 87–104.

Gordon, J. (2013). Subcontractor servitude. *New York Times*, September 12.

Gougard, A., Petrongolo, B., & Van Reenen, J. V. (2011). The labour market for young people. In Gregg, P., and Wasdsworth, J. (Eds.), *The labour market in winter*. Oxford, UK: Oxford University Press.

Gourevitch, J.-P. (2009). Immigration and its impacts in France. In Grubel, H. (Ed.). *The effects of mass immigration on Canadian living standards and society*. Vancouver: The Fraser Institute.

The Guardian. January 25, 2001; November 27, 2013.

Havar, G. (2013). Threat and immigration attitudes in liberal democracies: The role of framing in structuring public opinion. In Freeman et al. *Immigration and public opinion in liberal democracies*. New York, NY: Routledge.

Hingham, J. (1955). *Strangers in the land: Patterns of American nativism*. New Brunswick, NJ: Rutgers University Press.

Hochschild, J., Chattopadhhyay, J., Gay, C., & Jones-Correa, M. 2013. *Outsiders no more? Models of immigrant political incorporation*. New York, NY: Oxford University Press.

Hoskin, M. (1984). Integration or non-integration of foreign workers: Four theories. *Political Psychology, 5*, 661–86.

Hoskin, M. (1985). Public opinion and the foreign worker: Traditional and nontraditional bases of opinion. *Comparative Politics, 18*. 193–210.

Hoskin, M. (1989). Socialization and anti-socialization: The case of immigrants. In Sigel, R. H. (Ed.). *Political learning in adulthood: A sourcebook for theory and research*. Chicago, IL: University of Chicago Press.

Hoskin, M. (1991). *New immigrants and democratic society*. New York, NY: Praeger.

Hoskin, M. (1991). Public acceptance of racial and ethnic minorities: A comparative study. In Messina, A. et al. (Eds.). *Ethnic and racial minorities in advanced industrial democracies*. Westport, CT: Greenwood Press.

Hoskin, M. (1991). Socialization to citizenship: The successes, failures, and challenges to government. In Sigel, R. S., & Hoskin, M. (Eds.). *Education for democratic citizenship*. Hillsdale, NJ: Lawrence Erlbaum.

Hoskin, M., & Mishler, W. (1983). Public opinion toward new migrants A comparative analysis. *International Migration, 21*, 440–61.

Hoskin, M., & Fitzgerald, R. C. (1989). German immigration policy and politics. In LeMay, M. C. (Ed.). (1989). *The gatekeepers: Comparative immigration policy*. New York: Praeger.

Hull, E. (1983). The rights of aliens: National and international issues. In Papademetriou, D. G., & Miller, M. J. (Eds.). *The unavoidable issue: U.S. immigration policy in the 1980s*. Philadelphia: Institute for the Study of Human Issues.

Huntington, S. J. (2004). *Who are we? The challenges to America's national identity*. New York, NY: Simon & Schuster.

Jones, R. P. et al. (2014). *What Americans want from immigration reform in 2014*. Washington, DC: Institute for Public Religion Research/ Brookings Institution.

Joppke, C. (1999). *Immigration and the nation-state: The United States, Germany, and Great Britain*. New York, NY: Oxford University Press.

Kennedy, D. (1996). Can we still afford to be a nation of immigrants? *Atlantic Monthly* Digital Edition.

Lahav, G. (2004). *Immigration and politics in the new Europe*. New York, NY: Cambridge University Press.

Lemos, S., & Portes, J. (2008). New labour? The impact of migration from Central and Eastern European countries on the UK labour market. IZA Discussion Paper No. 3756, Institute for the Study of Labor, Bonn.

Loeffelholz, H.-D. (1994). *Auslaendische Selbststaendige in der Bundesrepublik*. Essen: Wirtschaftsforschung.

Loeffelholz, H.-D.,von Buch, H., & Giesecke, A. (1991). *Auslaendische Selbstaendige in der Bundesrepublik unter besonderer Berucksichtigung von Entwicklungsperspektiven in den Neuen Bundeslaendern*. Berlin: Duncker & Humbolt.

Loeffelholz, H.-D., & Kopp, G. (1998). *Ökonomische Auswirkungen der Zuwanderen nach Deutschland*. Berlin: Duncker & Humbolt.

Lowenstein, R. (2006). The immigration equation. *New York Times*, July 9.

Maddison, A. (1971). *Class structure and economic growth in India: India and Pakistan since the Moghuls*. London, UK: George Allen & Unwinn.

Manacorda, M., Manning, A., & Wadsworth, J. (2007). The impact of immigration on occupational wages: Evidence from Britain. CEP Discussion Paper No. 754.

Marcus, J. (1995*). The National Front and French politics: The resistible rise of Jean-Marie Le Pen*. New York, NY: New York University Press.

Massey, D. S. et al. (1994). An evaluation of international migration theory: The North American case. *Population and Development Review, 20*, 699–751.

McCormick, A. (2012). Migration myths: Migration and unemployment. Migration Policy Center Policy Brief.

Messina, A. M. (2007). *The logic and politics of post-WWII migration to Western Europe*. New York, NY: Cambridge University Press.

Meyers, E. (2007). *International immigration policy: A theoretical and comparative analysis*. New York, NY: Palgrave Macmillan.

Moulier, Y., & Tapinos, G. (1979). France. In Kubat, D. (Ed.). *The politics of migration policies*. New York, NY: Center for Migration Studies.

National Academies of Sciences, Engineering, and Medicine. 2016. *The integration of immigrants into American society*. Washington, DC: National Academies Press.

National Advisory Commission on Human Rights. (2013). Racism, anti-Semitism, and xenophobia in France. Annual Report, Paris.

New York Times. 1995–2016.

Oberman, K. (2015). Poverty and immigration policy. *American Political Science Review, 109* (2), 239–51.

Organization for Economic and Community Development. (2013). Immigrants contribute more than they cost. Special Report, June.

Peri, G. (2010). The effect of immigrants on U.S. employment and productivity. *Economic Letter*. Federal Reserve Bank of San Francisco.

Pew Research Center. (2013). *Second generation: A portrait of the adult children of immigrants*. Washington, DC.

Portes, A., & Bach, R. L. (1985). *Latin journey: Cuban and Mexican immigrants in the United States*. Berkeley, CA: University of California Press.

Reimann, H. & H. (1979). Federal Republic of Germany. In Krane, R. E. (Ed.), *International labor migration in Europe*. New York, NY: Praeger.

Rist, R. C. (1978). *Guestworkers in Germany*. New York, NY: Praeger.

Sarrazin, T. (2010). *Deutschland Schafft sich Ab*. DVA: Random House.

Schain, M. A. (2012). *The politics of immigration in France, Britain, and the United States*. New York, NY: Palgrave Macmillan.

Schildkraut, D. J. (2011). *Americanism in the twenty-first century: Public opinion in the age of immigration*. New York, NY: Cambridge University Press.

Simon, R. J., & Lynch, J. P. (1999). A comparative assessment of public opinion toward immigrants and immigration policies. *International Migration Review, 32* (2), 455–67.

Smith, D. (1977). *Racial disadvantage in Britain*. Harmondsworth, UK: Penguin Labor Assimilation Studies.

Soysal, Y. N. (2012). Citizenship, immigration, and the European social project: Rights and obligations of individuality. *British Journal of Sociology, 63* (1) (March), 1–21.

Stovall, T. (1997). The resurgence of racial hate in France. *The Journal of Blacks in Higher Education, 15.*

Wadsworth, J. (2015). Immigration and the UK labour market. Center for Economic Performance, London School of Economics and Political Science, Paper EA019.

Whitol de Wenden, C., & Costa-Lascox, J. (1984). Immigration reform in France and the United States: Reflections and documentation. *International Migration Review, 18* (3), 199–214.

Zimmerman, K. F., & Bauer, T. (2002). *The economics of migration.* Cheltenham, UK: Edwin Elgar.

Zimmerman, K. (Ed.). (2005). *European immigration: What do we know?* Oxford, UK: Oxford University Press.

Index

Made in the USA
Middletown, DE
23 May 2018